THE MAKING OF LITERATURE

THE MAKING OF LITERATURE

SOME PRINCIPLES OF CRITICISM EXAMINED IN THE LIGHT OF ANCIENT AND MODERN THEORY

BY

R. A. SCOTT-JAMES

KENNIKAT PRESS
Port Washington, N. Y./London

THE MAKING OF LITERATURE

First published in 1928, 1930
Reissued in 1970 by Kennikat Press
Library of Congress Catalog Card No: 72-105832
ISBN 0-8046-0977-2

Manufactured by Taylor Publishing Company Dallas, Texas

Note to the New Edition

THE author of a book about criticism takes his life in his hand, for the reviewers are lined up in position, ready to strike if they think themselves challenged. I have no reason to complain of rough treatment. I even have to admit that there were moments when my sympathies were with them rather than with the author, and I was ready to revile myself for having chosen " principles of criticism " for my subject. When one writer objected that " the author tends to seek for confirmation from the great critics rather than illustrations in the great artists " I felt the deadly force of the blow. I had removed myself from actual contact with the Pierian waters, the " endless fountain of immortal drink," and was only now and again able to turn back to it for refreshment.

It was the fault of my subject, or, rather, my fault for electing to write on a theme which many may think parched and barren. But there it was. I was writing, not about so-called creative literature, but about ideas about creative literature—ideas held by the writers concerning their own art, ideas which critical readers have held about literature from age to age, and the growth and recurrence of such ideas; and it was my hope that in the accumulated opinions of men " experienced in the arts " we might find enough consensus of evidence on which to base some conclusions.

I have been blamed for quoting with (qualified) approval Ben Jonson's saying: " to judge of poets is only the faculty of poets "—" poets," in this context, indicating writers proficient in any creative art. Mr Herbert Read has gone so far as to say: " The truth is rather that poetry and criticism are entirely different faculties; they are established on different grounds and have a different point of view. We might even venture the observation that the excellent poet is almost always an indifferent or at any rate an amateur critic."

In regard to the last sentence, the pages of this book

furnish evidence to the contrary. In regard to the first, is not Mr Read, by the emphasis of his assertion, reintroducing an old confusion, one which, indeed, I had been sanguine enough to believe was disposed of? Well, of course, the poet writes poetry, and the critic writes criticism, and those are two different things. But criticism (of poetry) which lives, moves and has its being in a different world from that of poetry—and how much there has been of it!—is a miserable anæmic thing born of pedantry or impertinence. When I say that "what the artist has been able to construct, the critic must be able to reconstruct," I do not mean, as Mr Read seems to think, that the latter is trying to find out "how the dish was cooked," or even merely the way in which the work of art "is created and presented." I mean that no critic can appreciate a work of art till he has reconstructed in his own mind the mental vision constructed by the artist.

A perfect appreciation of a poem is only possible to a reader who has adjusted his perception of life to the poet's perception. The objective work of art should call up as far as possible the same impressions which were in the artist's mind when he created it. The stuff of life itself which the poet's imagination played upon, and which was shaped by him into a poem—that poem being his "construction" of some of the elements of life—must reappear in the appreciative critic's mind, charged with the same, or nearly the same impressions, enlivened by the same, or nearly the same imaginative perception. "If we reason," said Shelley, "we would be understood. If we imagine we would that the airy children of our brain were born anew within another." That bearing anew, that reconstruction, that act of understanding and appreciation, is not, it is true, the whole business of a critic. But it comes first. It is indispensable. Any would-be critic who is not able or willing to perform that elementary act of justice to his author has not—as a critic of art—the slightest claim on our attention. Indeed he is one of the natural enemies of the arts, dangerous in proportion as he has the ear of the unstudious public, and the opportunity, therefore, of sowing the tares of ignorance or prejudice. The more we encourage the old superstition that the critic of literature belongs to a completely different order of beings from those who create it, the more we encourage tainted propaganda. That ancient misconception in the eighteenth century assisted the rule of convention and pedagogy. To-day it is more likely to help the crank, on the one side, the ignorant and the fatuous, on the other.

But I do not think it is gaining new ground among us. The ablest living critics constantly venture into other fields of literature, and on all sides novelists, poets and playwrights may be seen rushing into the fray with the critics. To take an example which has forced itself on my attention, I found, among the critics of this book of mine, Mr Arnold Bennett, a novelist, Mr Edmund Blunden, a poet, Miss Rebecca West, a novelist, and three or four others who have written novels; and none of them, in their criticism, appeared to me less competent than the professional reviewers. (Mr Read himself, it should be mentioned, is a poet.) The fact is, the world of imaginative literature is not many worlds, but one, though it may be divided into many parts. No one can take a place in it with the highest distinction—whether he be artist or critic—unless he has read widely, has the faculty of understanding and imagining, and has studied the means by which literature becomes communicative.

If we must have sacerdotalism, let us confine it to religion and leave it out of the arts. In this domain the clerical cloth is a hindrance. If we must have literary professionals, let all men of letters specialize in the art of literature, whether they be novelists, or critics, or novelist critics. Better still, that all the novelists and all the readers should have some clear idea of what they are aiming at when they write, or what they are looking for when they read. If that should come to pass, every writer would realize his tremendous responsibility as a writer, and every reader would realize his share of responsibility as an audience.

I am not, of course, suggesting that every moderately competent artist is a moderately competent critic; for if the range of his excellence is narrow he will betray his limitations when he tries to pass beyond them. If we do not habitually look for the shrewdest criticism from poets or novelists, that is because their sympathies are often confined or their knowledge slight. But given the catholicity of a Dante, a Jonson, a Dryden, a Goethe, or a Coleridge, then we shall find no criticism more penetrating than the poets'. Even those who have more limited interests—like Emerson, or Swinburne, or Francis Thompson—are capable of admirable criticism within the range of those interests. And do we not find in such a one as Voltaire, bound as he was to the strict academicism of his period, the most urbane and enlightening presentation of the case for that academicism? Nor could we ever be certain of getting the critical landmarks established without the zealotry of a Blake, a Wordsworth, a Shelley, trumpeting their self-justifications and their half-truths.

I am not advancing a case for interesting or sensational half-truths. The point rather is that the element in them which is true is true for poet and critic alike, and the element which is false is as damaging to the one as it is discrediting to the other. It is not by virtue of a special calling—that of the Bayle whom Sainte-Beuve so ironically exposed—that the ideal critic receives grace. That critic, if we can imagine his existence, will have studied arduously to equip himself; he will be perceptive to life and letters; he will be contemplative; he will have a sense of humour; he will be serious, imaginative, zealous, honest, and not without humility. Nor does this by any means exhaust the list of his virtues. But all of them are virtues for the possession of which the poet, too, would be a better poet, the novelist a better novelist.

February, 1930.

Preface

FOR several reasons a preface is necessary to this book. Especially, because I wish to express my indebtedness to two persons, and also to a group of persons, but for whom I should not have set myself to this exacting though agreeable task.

The two first are not here to accept my thanks—it is a hard fact that I should have to describe both of them, Sir Sidney Lee and Thomas Seccombe, as "the late." They have gone, and can neither praise nor condemn my effort. The others are widely scattered, and have probably forgotten most of what I had to say in my lectures on "The Principles of Criticism of Literature and Art," which I delivered to them when they were students of London University between 1919 and 1924. By their friendly appreciation they encouraged me to undertake the present work.

Those lectures, twenty in all, were given at King's College in connexion with the Diploma in Journalism. They were the basis on which this book has been built.

When Sir Sidney Lee assumed direction of that new course of University study he invited my friend Seccombe and myself to collaborate in the "Criticism" section. The subject attracted both of us, and we divided the work to suit our respective tastes—though it happened, owing to the fullness of Seccombe's time-table, that the larger number of lectures fell to me.

We at once became aware that the task presented difficulties, both for ourselves and the students, arising from the lack of text-books. Much has been written on the philosophy of æsthetic—but that was not quite our subject. A good deal has been written on the psychology—or pathology—of the æsthetic experience (a later example being Mr I. A. Richards' *Principles of Literary Criticism*, published in 1925). But that was far less relevant. There are many books, also, dealing with critics and the history of criticism—outstanding amongst them the comprehensive and indispensable *History* of Professor Saintsbury. But that again was not our subject, for we were to be concerned with critical principles, not examples of criticism. So there was nothing for it but to direct our pupils to many books, and many passages in books, where the greater critics have given an account of themselves, and enunciated the principles by which they were guided.

In a rather rough-and-ready manner we divided between us this vast field of inquiry, extending over the Sublime and the Beautiful, the grave and the comic, the pleasant and the instructive. And then, each appropriating his share of the ground, Seccombe went his way and I went mine. We both intended to hear each other's lectures. It happened that we never did. After two years Seccombe left England to become Professor of English Literature at Queen's University, Ontario, and I took over his territory, administering it, unaided, as best I could. And so, alas, I cannot invoke his high authority in favour of anything in this book, or impute to him any share of the blame where it is at fault.

In arranging my material for publication I have entirely reshaped it, and also added to it. The book is concerned, as I have said, with critical principles, not examples of criticism, and deals with the evolution of certain general ideas about literature, considered as a fine art. I have found that the pertinent question generally assumes the form "What is the artist?" rather than "What is the critic?" For it is only when we understand the problems of the artist that those of the critic come into being. The answer to the first question almost gives us the answer to the second, though there remain, outside this principal issue, certain subsidiary questions. What, for example, is the relation of the critic, not directly to the artist, but to the society in which he lives?

All such questions, except perhaps the last, may and have been treated strictly on philosophic methods. But I have not so treated them. I have not attempted, as some have done, to deduce the practical principles of art and criticism from the higher principles of philosophy; nor have I, except in one or two special cases, included in my inquiry the works of philosophers who exclusively pursue that method. I have been content to work upon a lower plane of truth, and to discuss the genesis or progress of certain ideas as expounded by individual writers at crucial periods—the central problems of the art of literature as they have presented themselves to men experienced in the arts. In turning for light to older writers I have constantly had in mind the demands, the standards, the critical questions of the twentieth century. And such comparisons are natural, for the main problems recur with amazing persistence. We shall not, of course, forget that the recurrence of ideas is no guarantee of truth, for there are recurrent errors as well as recurrent truths, against which it behoves us to be on our guard as against witchcraft and idolatry. Nevertheless, in so far as the most discerning creative minds at widely separated periods are found to have arrived at the same or similar conclusions—wrested from experience, not from *a priori* reasoning—may not these be worth as much to us as the results arrived at by the logician?

Not that I have been able to avoid altogether the philosophic theories of art. For sometimes they have directly influenced the artists and critics. Thus the language of Signor Benedetto Croce has entered into the daily jargon of living critics, and Pirandello has written plays which are said to be governed by his principles. And again, I could not discuss the literary principles of Coleridge without some reference to his speculative philosophy, and even that of Kant and Schelling. On the other hand, though I owe much to Bernard Bosanquet's *History of Æsthetic*, I felt that his and similar work lay outside the scope of this inquiry.

I hope it will be quite evident that this book makes no claim whatever to be exhaustive, or nearly so. I have been able to select for discussion only the works of some representative writers, conspicuous in the line of a continuous tradition, which leads from Homer to Hardy, from Aristotle to the modern critics.

In regard to quotations from foreign languages, I decided to present them, in most cases, in an English rendering. Wherever a standard translation is easily accessible I have generally thought it best to use this—as I had no reason to suppose I should improve on it. But in this respect I have not been very consistent. For example, I have used my own rendering of Longinus, Plotinus, Boileau and Sainte-Beuve, and also of Aristotle, except where I have made special acknowledgment. For Aristophanes, I could not hope to equal Dr Gilbert Murray's translation, for the use of which I am grateful. In Plato, I find that I have used both Jowett and Davies and Vaughan, and in some cases my own rendering. I have quoted passages from Mr Douglas Ainslie's translation of Croce's *Æsthetic*. For the difficult expressions used in Dante's *De Vulgari Eloquio* I have borrowed, so far as it was available (in *Loci Critici*), Professor Saintsbury's forceful English.

R. A. S.-J.

Contents

CONTENTS

Chapter One

THE LIGHT FROM HEAVEN

TO the criticism of the arts, and especially literature, custom has given an independent place. In this respect it differs from all other kinds of criticism. When we want a judgment upon the soundness of Waterloo Bridge we call in an engineer or a practical architect—a man whose business is the making of bridges. But when we want a judgment upon the soundness of a poem, often it is not a maker of poems whom we consult, but a "critic." Whilst we should distrust a book upon gardening by one who was not himself a gardener, we are willing to respect a "criticism" of a play or a novel by one who is neither playwright nor novelist.

It would be difficult to say just when this separate title to exist was accorded to critics. That their letters patent to-day are in good order we all know—there is an accredited tribe of penmen whose function it is to praise or denounce works of art, and make or modify literary reputations; and the excellence with which these critics fulfil their functions is held to be a quite different excellence from that of the creative artists whom they judge. Like poets, novelists and painters, they may have attained their reputations by talent and study, or by luck; but they need not themselves be poets, novelists or painters—they are just critics. It is not necessary that they should have been successful practitioners in any art, except the art of criticism. Nor unsuccessful practitioners, for we may pass over the rude suggestion that they are those who have tried elsewhere and failed.

Such, then, is the view of criticism still in vogue. Whether it be regarded as a noble profession, like that of law-givers, or an ignoble one, like that of lawyers, in either case it is held to be independent, and in a class by itself. And this view of their separate status is not affected by the high or low esteem in which they may be held. It is the same whether they be regarded as members of a sacred guild, with noble mysteries all their own, or low-caste creatures addicted to disagreeable habits. Mr Orlo Williams only limits his reverence by making them a little less than divine. "The wise critic," he says, "observing himself and his fellow-practitioners, will not presume that he or they can attain the undistorted view of eternity." Mr Osbert Sitwell, on the other hand, is contemptuous in his irony. "The critic is popularly supposed to have a more logical mind, to wield a more consistent pen than the poet's." (Note the severity of that "popularly.") But both Mr Williams and Mr Sitwell seem to agree that the critic belongs to a class of his own—that there is a separate order of beings whose professed function is to criticize.

And we find the same view generally held if we look back to periods before our own. Keats pours out his bitterness upon the whole class of "dank-haired critics." Johnson, more respectfully, recognizes the distinctiveness of his own craft when he speaks of those whom "nature and learning had qualified for judges." Pope still earlier had written of the critics as if theirs was a kind of literature not less specific than that of the poets :

> Both must alike from Heaven derive their light,
> These born to judge, as well as those to write.

In Dryden's time it is obvious enough that the critics were in a class by themselves—but he was speaking only of "ill writers" when he remarked that "the corruption of a poet is the generation of a critic."

Whence the origin of this notion that criticism, implying the exercise of taste and judgment, is a branch of literature practised by others than the "creative" writers? When did the world first begin to put the poet in one category and the critic of poetry in another, giving to the latter a status and *raison d'être* comparable to that of the former, but distinguishing him as we do not distinguish the critic of engineering from the engineer, or the critic of seamanship or soldiering from the seaman or the soldier? It may seem idle to pursue the notion back into antiquity, for wherever we turn in the field of self-conscious literature we seem to stumble upon the critic and the criticaster. "Some will say critics are a kind of tinkers," said Ben Jonson, "that make more faults than they mend ordinarily"; and he reminds us that the critical busybody existed also in antiquity:

> Cato Grammaticus, Latina Siren,
> Qui solus legit, et facit poetas.

What if we turn to the times of Quintilian, of Horace, of Aristotle, of Aristophanes? Even in the age of Aristophanes there were greater and lesser lights who claimed to be among the pundits, and the sophists played their part in fixing the terminology applied to poetic drama. What clamour of critical controversy went to the shaping of that public opinion which appraised the best poets of Athens! Aristotle, however, though he came to be regarded as the law-giver in matters poetic, did not so regard himself. He was not the lawgiver, but the codifier. The rules he laid down were the rules he found provided for him in the example of the greater poets. It was their example which afforded the basis for his precept.

That the equipment of the poet is one thing, the equipment of the critic is another—such at least has been the general view handed on to us. Are we right in adopting it, without qualification? Is it not disturbing to those who hold it to study the roll of the world's most remarkable critics, including as it does Aristophanes, Horace, Dante, Ben Jonson, Dryden, Goethe, Coleridge, Matthew Arnold—a company in which none would dare to "chatter" criticism or criticasty? And if we turn to the words of the greatest of Elizabethan critics, who had soaked himself in the literature of the ancients and of his own time, we find him declaring that "to judge of poets is only the faculty of poets; and not of all poets, but the best." Jonson, who wrote these words, was surely a qualified witness.

Perhaps then, after all, we ought not to accept unreservedly the current pedagogic notion of the peculiar and separate function of criticism. For convenience, and for orderly classification, we are doubtless compelled to place in one group that mass of literature, in many languages and from many ages, devoted to what is called literary or art criticism. But it may be profitable to admit the possibility that the prevailing conception of this class of literature is not quite just. It may be worth while to consider it more from the artist's point of view; to consider it in so far as it is the authentic voice of the artist himself—in so far as it is literature become self-conscious about itself, about its own processes, its technique, its aim. "Not every critic of art is a genius," said Lessing; "but every genius is born a critic of art. He has within himself the evidence of all rules." It may be a gain to attend to the writers of this critical literature precisely in so far as they are not standing aloof, like magistrates who were never guilty of crime, pronouncing dispassionately upon the blamelessness or the misdemeanour of artists; but rather to attend to them, in so far as they are either the artists themselves concerned for the time being with one aspect of their work—poets giving an account of themselves—or the friends of the poets, who know them through and through, having the same interests at heart, and the sympathetic knowledge which qualifies them to speak on their behalf. Such men, when they engage in criticism, have more than a professional claim to discourse on the subject-matter which concerns the "creative" writer, the language and forms he employs, the ideas he wishes to communicate, and the pleasure, satisfaction, thrill that he may have endeavoured, by this or that technical means, to stir in others.

Chapter Two

THE FIRST CRITIC

THERE is a kind of criticism which exists before art itself, and is presupposed in all art, just as there is a kind of criticism which follows art, taking art as its subject-matter. The distinction is that between the criticism of life, which comes first, and the criticism of the criticism, which comes second in order of thought, though perhaps almost simultaneously in order of time.

You cannot criticize a work of art until the work of art exists. But it needs very little reflection to see that there is no work of art which is not preceded by criticism.

Consider what the artist is doing when he creates something. In the simplest sense of the term he is, I take it, primarily a *maker*. That is what the word *poet* means. But what is he a maker of? Let us, for simplicity, take some very rudimentary type of man who sets himself to the making of something. Suppose we take for the purpose of the argument an imaginary caveman—subject all the time to appropriate correction from the anthropologists, with whose science this work has nothing to do.

At what moment could we say that a caveman, in making something, was performing any function which would entitle his making to be described as artistic creation? Suppose, having been constantly in the habit of sitting down on a log of wood, he took it into his head one day to knock away the rough bark and the projecting knobs, and thus made himself a more comfortable seat. He might be said to have "made" a chair. But even if he had made the most perfect chair possible he would only have shown himself a perfect carpenter—a perfect craftsman if you like—but not an artist in the fine sense of the term.

But supposing the same caveman chips out on the surface of the wood, or on the side of his cave, the roughest imaginable figure which is meant to represent a man, or a reindeer, or a mammoth, or any other object in life. What has he done? He may not have made anything nearly so useful as the chair. He may not show nearly as much skill in draughtsmanship as he showed skill in the craft of carpentry. But he has done something of a different order. When he made a chair he made something that was definitely a chair; when he carved a man he made something that was definitely not a man, and was never intended to be a man. It was a carving intended to express as well as he could his idea of a man.

For what would an actual man be to him? We cannot tell. A lump of flesh and blood, I suppose—a quarrelsome and probably amorous creature—a hard-fisted, quick-tempered monster—hairy, warm, bulky—a thing that casts a shadow if it gets in the way of the daylight that comes through the cave entrance—all these things, and much more. But he has drawn none of this. The carving has no flesh and blood, no warmth, no gluttony, no amorousness. It is destitute of almost all the qualities that make an actual man mannish. Everything has been abstracted, and only a few lines remain. Why do we call this "creation"?

Because, though he has made something obviously less than a man, he has also made something more. Those lines which stand for legs indicate not legs alone; they are a recognition of the two-leggedness of a man. That image of a head rudely poised above the body indicates a relation between head and body which the artist has observed in his human friends. Head, arms, trunk, legs—there are only lines which hint at them, but these lines stand for a relation between the parts of the body which are here fixed in this declared relationship. Out of a material which is not human at all—namely, out of stone or chalk—he has made a form which stands not merely for a man, but for what he takes to be his essential characteristics. He has put down his observations about man, his critical conception of him.

He has criticized human nature. He has separated some essentials from the whole—those qualities which to him at least seem essentials, the two-leggedness, the head-above-body-ness, etc., and has set these down to the exclusion of a thousand other qualities which, if he had been a different sort of caveman, might have impressed him as more essential to the idea of a human being. This separating of part from part, aspect from aspect, was an observant, critical act. He has defined a man. He has defined him in his own way, according to his own bent, his own interest—in accordance with what we call his imagination, or image-making faculty.

I take this illustration of a primitive drawing by a primitive man merely for the sake of simplicity. The palæolithic savage, for aught I know, may have splashed colour about on his body and on the skins he wore long before he drew, taking pleasure in the decorative effect. It may be that in fact the earliest picture was the work of an unconscious draughtsman idly scratching on a rock or a bone, and that he neither intended to represent anything, nor was conscious of representing anything ; and that the first imaginatively inspired person was not he who thus drew, but he who first detected in the careless drawing a resemblance to life (in which case, it would seem, the first conscious critic of art might, after all, have appeared before the first artist). But it does not matter. At some time or another a creative artist drew the first outline—it may have been with his finger in the dust—with intent to indicate life. "The animal I killed was like this," he may have meant, as he consciously defined a bear or a reindeer in a few crude lines. "This is what I judge reality to have been when I try to pass on my conception of it to another," he might have said, if he could have analysed his purpose. That is also what Rembrandt might have said when he was painting his own portrait. There is a difference in the mentality and in the technique, but the purpose is the same.

But it is more than likely, it may be objected, that the earliest drawing was really a kind of writing, its object being merely to give information, not to please. That may be, but it does not affect the point that whoever could call up an image of reality through a rendering of it in a medium different from the reality itself was guided by the creative impulse which we call that of the artist. He did not exhibit an actual reindeer, and say : "This is the animal I killed." He drew some lines in the dust, and said : "This is it."

There you have imagination, with a vengeance. It was dust. But for him it was a reindeer.

Having thus expressed his amazing vision in lines drawn in dust, or on wood, or stone, it would be natural for him to say or think : "I like this. It amuses me. What do you think of it? Is it not beautiful?" But : "Do you see what I mean?"—that is a question he is bound to ask. For man is a social animal. "That is the reindeer I killed," he will say, demanding appreciative comment. And if we suppose that he was imaginatively far in advance of most of his fellow-cavemen we can believe that they would stand round scratching their heads and asking: "What are those silly marks? Don't waste our time. We haven't got anything for dinner yet."

Less gifted men would be certain to miss the significance of his drawing. If you show a dog a photograph of his master he will not recognize it. He will not betray the least excitement if you put before him a picture of the dog next door. He might be interested in a mechanical toy bear, and bark at it; but his interest would be in the fluffy concrete thing that was before him, not in that thing as a representation of something else—namely, the bear at the Zoo, which all children would think of at once. The dog has formed none of those critical judgments about reality which enable him to distinguish the simplified essentials of the idea of bear from the bear itself. The master he knows must have flesh and blood. A master that exists only on paper is not his master—it is only a bit of paper.

And so with the less developed caveman. He would be merely puzzled, or not even interested. But perhaps one of them, having the same order of intelligence as the draughtsman, will look at the drawing, examine it, think it out, and then—in a flash—*see*. He will see it in exactly the same way as the other saw it. "A reindeer," he will say. "Don't you see? Those lines spread out like horns. And that—the long straight back. And this—and this. . . ." Can we not see this discerning savage excitedly talking, for the first time, that talk which was to evolve one day into the very jargon of modern criticism?

It is evident that the most primitive critic must have the imagination of the artist. His sight, too, must be keen. It may be, even, that having in his own mind's eye some form clearer and harder than that he sees before him he may complain that the drawing falls short in this, exceeds in that—measuring the created thing before him against the half-created form fashioned in his own mind. He, too, must have the artist's vision; for the artist is stimulated by reality into the discernment of a form; the critic, in the act of appreciation, reverses the process, discerning, behind form, not merely the reality which stimulated the artist, but that reality as something already implying and necessitating form. For artist and critic alike, fact is nothing till, as the occasion of enlightened perception, it has been transmuted into the *object* of perception. The artist must have the imagination to initiate the process, the critic, from beginning to end, to repeat it.

But here I am anticipating. I will content myself with saying that, while I do not suggest that the business of criticizing is just a matter of sympathetic vision, or intuition, and no more, I do suggest that for all criticism worth the name this is the first essential. On other characteristics, which distinguish the critic from the artist, I will not now dwell; obviously there are many calls upon the energy of the man engaged in "creative" work—he may have little time to give himself to criticism. But there are also many calls upon the critic.

For his task, too, if well done, is exacting. How, for example, could you ever form a true opinion of a caveman's drawing if you did not know that it was by a caveman—if you did not already know the sort of life he lived and the tools he used? If you were ignorant of the fact that this was palæolithic work what mistakes you might make! "This cave was evidently visited by Mr Epstein." "A very interesting example of Mr Wyndham Lewis's earlier work," someone might say; and, straining eagerly to see it through Vorticist eyes, might discern something suggestive and fascinating indeed, but never that aspect of the reindeer as the caveman saw it.

Chapter Three

THE LITERATURE OF POWER

IT is a paradox of criticism that before we can begin to explain what we mean by art we must suppose that its meaning is already in some degree understood. It is with literature as an art that I am concerned in this book, and at the outset it should be clearly distinguished from the literature which sets out to impart knowledge or produce moral conviction. Obvious as the difference may seem to us, it was not always obvious, and the border-line is blurred even to-day. It is the distinction which may be made between two drawings of a house, one being a "picture," the other an architect's plan. The first has an æsthetic character. The second is a piece of information—its purpose is didactic.

How do we draw the line? Which are the books that are books—in Lamb's sense—and the books that are not books? At one extreme we may have a poem, whose excellence lies in its beauty, at the other a dictionary, which is merely accurate, or inaccurate. Between these extremes lie many varieties of writing which may be judged partly on their merits as registers of fact or argument, partly on their merits as works of art.

The main distinction is that laid down by De Quincey between the "literature of knowledge" and the "literature of power," the function of the first being to *teach*, the function of the second to *move*:

> All that is literature seeks to communicate power; all that is not literature, to communicate knowledge.

And again:

> In that great social organ, which, collectively, we call literature, there may be distinguished two separate offices

> that may blend and often *do* so, but capable, severally, of a severe insulation, and naturally fitted for reciprocal repulsion. There is, first, the literature of *knowledge*; and, secondly, the literature of *power*. The function of the first is—to *teach*; the function of the second is—to *move*: the first is a rudder; the second, an oar or a sail. The first speaks to the *mere* discursive understanding; the second speaks ultimately, it may happen, to the higher understanding or reason, but always *through* affections of pleasure and sympathy.

De Quincey's antithesis is "literature (that is, Literæ Humaniores) and anti-literature (that is, Literæ didacticæ—παιδεία)." It is a fundamental distinction, by which all that has been written is divided into literature which serves a *didactic* purpose, and literature which has no end beyond itself, and can be judged only on *æsthetic* grounds. Under the first come all works whose object is to inform, prove or persuade. Bacon's *Novum Organum* primarily exists to set forth a theory of Induction; Newton's *Principia* to explain his conclusions concerning the law of gravity. To this class belong all books of philosophy, religion, science, economics, history, biography, travel, politics or morals which exist to state an argument, adduce proof, record fact or convert us to an opinion. The criticism applicable to them is not "literary criticism," but scientific or philosophic criticism, and is concerned only with the accuracy of the statements and the validity or relevance of the arguments.

It is literature of the second class which is to be regarded as the proper object of literary criticism. It belongs to the domain of the Fine Arts. Poetry, drama and fiction, when treated artistically, cannot, like didactic literature, be *proved* right or wrong. They cannot be shaken by logic. They are subject to their own laws, which are apprehended in the last resort not by the discursive reason but by intuition, imagination, æsthetic sense. Both kinds of literature may be concerned with truth, but they arrive at it in different ways—the first by a judgment about it, the second by intuition.

Few writers of the former class are content—or indeed able—to confine themselves strictly to their didactic or scientific tasks. The eager scientist is constantly trembling with the excitement and imagination of the artist. The historian is compelled to lift his story above bare fact, to recreate and dramatize incident, reclothe his persons and shape the setting in which he places them. In a later chapter we shall see why both are bound to go beyond the limited objective, which is to inform, and enter the precincts of literature proper, offering themselves for criticism not only on scientific or historic but also on "literary" grounds.

The critic, then, whose interest is in literature as a fine art, is also concerned with didactic literature so far as it goes beyond its special didactic purpose and assumes an artistic form. In his *History of Rome* Mommsen marshals the events of an empire in such a way that everything is felt to be leading to the triumphant achievement and tragic death of Julius Cæsar. It is a work of art as well as a history and, as such, it is a proper subject for the literary critic. It is not, however, the latter, but the student of history, who must decide whether, for example, Mommsen's attenuated account of Marcus Tullius Cicero is or is not an adequate record of fact.

In like manner the historian of literature must be distinguished from the critic of literature. The task of research among the remains of a literary period is distinct from the task of estimating those remains for what they may be intrinsically worth. A literary historian who may do invaluable work in compiling, sifting, annotating, editing, is often a very poor critic. And, vice versa, the most discriminating literary critic, having neither the inclination nor the industry to master masses of third-rate work, is seldom also a first-rate literary historian.

It is through overlooking this simple difference that many brilliant and painstaking scholars, who have done important work in the field of literary science, are sometimes wrongly appraised. The authority which they rightly exercise as experts in research they are also invited to exercise in the quite different field of literary taste. It is wrongly assumed that a man who has devoted his life to studying the texts of Shakespeare and his contemporaries must be a good judge of Hamlet's character, or that the compiler of a glossary to *Othello* best knows the secrets of a husband's jealousy. But to scholars—who may have done much thankless work in the interests of culture—this popular error is often gratifying, and it can do little harm. For if such a man has the power to "get over" to the public, to make it listen, to enlighten it, he has already passed the narrower limits of scholarship, and has proved his wider claim. If he has not, his power to mislead is slight.

Chapter Four

BEFORE PLATO

BEFORE the golden age of Greek literature had come to an end the main problem of criticism had already been stated :

> Pray, tell me on what particular ground a poet should claim admiration ?[1]

It is the poet Aristophanes who puts the words into the mouth of the poet Æschylus, in his controversy with Euripides in the *Frogs*.

To us this may seem to belong to a very early period of the world's literature. But to the Greeks of the latter part of the fifth century B.C. the world already seemed old and sophisticated. Literally sophisticated. This question in the *Frogs* was evidently just one of the many too familiar questions with which all accepted things were challenged. To Euripides, Aristophanes, Gorgias, Protagoras, and all the intellectuals, the Greek race must already have seemed to have gone through all possible phases of valid human experience. The wars of the gods and the heroes lay for them far back among the myths and mists of antiquity. It must have seemed that almost everything had happened since the deeds of their divine ancestors had been first sung for the delight and religious admiration of a simple race. The kings had gone. The tyrants had gone. Aristocracies and democracies had risen and fallen. The simple festivals of Dionysus had grown and blossomed into the final perfection of Attic drama. The world conflict between East and West, begun, according to the tradition, in remote antiquity at Troy, seemed to have been settled once and for all at

[1] *Frogs*. Translated by Professor Gilbert Murray.

Marathon and Salamis. Politics had passed through every phase which the ingenuity of a citizen of the City-State could conceive. Athens had emerged pre-eminent among all the cities of the world by her triumph in democracy, in seamanship, in architecture, in sculpture, in forensic and political oratory, in drama, music, and perhaps painting, and held her own among the first in philosophy, rhetoric, geometry, grammar, and in her schools of sophistry. For conventional religion, far removed from its primitive origins, the inspired poems of Homer and Hesiod still provided a Bible. It was the glory of Greek religion and morality that it was inseparable from the sweetening influences of Greek poetry. And conversely poetry in its turn acquired the authority of religion.

But that was not all. For the active Greek, experience did not stop there. In the latter part of the fifth century he was far advanced in the activity of disbelief. No doubt the majority of men, like the majority always, accepted the conventional maxims of religion, morality and art just as old Cephalus accepted them, simply and unquestioningly. But the very existence of such complacent persons was no doubt a constant spur to those who, like the Ibsens, the Nietzsches, the Butlers, the Shaws, in the nineteenth century, were always eager to challenge accepted ideas and conventional maxims. Xenophanes had long before complained that the gods in Homer were fashioned too much like men. Heraclitus had chilled the blood of easy-going optimists by his doctrine of the perpetual flux ("all things flow, and nothing abides"). Protagoras, classifying the parts of an Oration in one set of lectures, in another taught that Knowledge is relative, that Being is Seeming, and that man is the measure of all things. Nor was the sanctity of the arts more respected than the sanctity of the religion with which they were associated. Aristophanes makes Æschylus say that the poet should choose a great subject and great sentiments which lend themselves to magnificence of language. The language of poetry, according to the traditional view, was not the language of daily life. But Euripides was an innovator. He criticized the conventional morality and religion, and the conventional view of women. He made his characters think in the "modern" way, and use the realistic language of common speech. Aristophanes holds him up to ridicule by making him say :

> I put things on the stage that come from daily life and business ;

and

> I mingled reasoning with my art
> And shrewdness, till I fired their heart
> To brood, to think things through and through ;
> And rule their houses better, too ;

and

> Oh, let us at least use the language of men.

And he justifies the choice of plot in the *Hippolytus* not on the ground that it is a great subject, but that it was true.

Here was the old idealism challenged by realism, authority by reason, formalism by humanism. All that was established, in art as well as in religion, seemed to be wilting before the chilly touch of the sophist and the Higher Critic—men like those described in a later age :

> Light half-believers of our casual creeds,
> Who never deeply felt, nor clearly will'd ;

or others, more earnest, more perturbed, who looked round for some other way :

> Ere quite the being of man, ere quite the world
> Be disarray'd of their divinity.

No wonder Cephalus was disturbed before such tumult of talk, and withdrew himself to his sacrifices.

But we should mark, amid the turmoil, the emergence of that question, clearly stated, and pertinent to this inquiry :

> Pray, tell me on what particular ground a poet should claim admiration ?

Had any such question as this been put before the days of the sophists ? Are there any traces of such curiosity as to the meaning or purpose of poetry and song among the earlier Greeks, in remote periods described by Homer ? Shall we dare draw out of all the pages of the *Iliad* and the *Odyssey* one rare, strange passage, referring, not indeed to poetry, but to the art of the cunning artificer in gold, and discover, there, an example of penetrating insight into the significance of illusion in art ?

It is Professor Bernard Bosanquet who has endeavoured to extract the utmost value for critical theory out of two lines in the eighteenth book of the *Iliad*. They occur in the description of the fine workmanship of the shield which Hephæstus, at the request of Thetis, made for her son Achilles. It was beautifully and dexterously ornamented with representations of all manner of things—the earth, the heavens, the sea and the sun—and scenes in two fair cities, including a marriage procession, a trial in the place of assembly, and two armies in battle array—and a scene of peaceful rustic activity, in which ploughmen are busy at their work. In describing the field which Hephæstus wrought on the shield in gold, the poet says:

> ἡ δὲ μελαίνετ' ὄπισθεν, ἀρηρομένῃ δὲ ἐῴκει,
> χρυσείη περ ἐοῦσα' τὸ δὴ περὶ θαῦμα τέτυκτο.

which Messrs Lang, Leaf and Myers translate:

> And the field grew black behind and seemed as it were a-ploughing, albeit of gold, for this was the great marvel of the work.

The significant words are thrown out even more prominently in Professor Bosanquet's rendering:

> And behind the plough the earth went black, and looked like ploughed ground, though it was made of gold; that was a very miracle of his craft.

The Greek poet observes that though the artist was working in gold, nevertheless the effect he attained was that of blackness. We see the artist setting himself to refashion matter according to his heart's desire, using the raw material as a vehicle for his thought. He put into gold something that was more than gold. "The real underlying interest," says Professor Bosanquet, "is in the conquest of the difference of the medium."

The thought in Homer is not elaborated. It can hardly be said to be fully explicit. It is a brilliant suggestion, a happy flash of critical inspiration, induced by wonder and appreciation, and we hear no more of it. Had it been followed up and developed it would have cut the ground from under Plato's feet when he complained that a work of art, as a mere imitation of reality, is only a copy of a copy.

It is not perhaps altogether surprising that there should have been more self-consciousness in regard to the art of the goldsmith than in regard to the art of the poet, at this early stage of Greek civilization. For if we may judge from the evidence of the archæologists there must surely have been a much higher development in the plastic arts and in the arts of the metal-worker than in that of literature, which still used as its medium only the word spoken or sung. Greek civilization in the Homeric periods was very young; but Asiatic civilization was old. In the decorative and applied arts the Greeks undoubtedly drew largely upon the Asiatic store of experience and technique. But in the matter of language and literature they depended on their own resources. Like the French of to-day, they were little disposed to learn barbarous foreign tongues. Thus their conscious technique in decorative art may have been far in advance of their conscious technique in poetry. And perfection in technique implies study of the rules, precepts, principles of an art, and evokes theory.

Apart from this single passage, I believe that we can find no other glimmerings in Homer of any theory of fine art. But none the less we learn much from the Homeric poems about the character of minstrelsy and song, the esteem in which the minstrels were held, and the emotions which they stirred; and especially in the eighth book of the *Odyssey*, which describes a social period generally supposed to be somewhat later than that described in the *Iliad*, or even elsewhere in the *Odyssey*. The minstrel was held in honour above all men. He was blind, but he was loved dearly by the muse, who gave him in recompense the gift of sweet song. As he sang he was stirred by the god. It was his power to make men glad; and he could so touch the chords of reminiscence that tears of sorrow were mingled with their pleasure.

Thus Demodocus, who sings among the assembled

Phæacians, is "divine," and dowered by the god with the gift of making men glad:

> "Bid hither [says Alcinous] the divine minstrel, Demodocus, for the god hath given minstrelsy to him as to none other, to make men glad in what way soever his spirit stirs him to sing."[1]

He is loved by the muse, and dear, or companionable (ἐρίηρον), to men:

> Then the henchman drew near, leading with him the beloved minstrel, whom the muse loved dearly, and she gave him both good and evil; of his sight she reft him, but granted him sweet song.[2]

And the minstrel is described as being "stirred by the god" (ὁρμηθεὶς θεοῦ[3]) as he begins his song. And the lyre, "the mate of the rich banquet,"[4] completes the satisfaction of the good feast. Odysseus himself is moved to tears by the memories evoked by the song; and in paying compliment to Demodocus says:

> For minstrels from all men on earth get their meed of honour and worship; inasmuch as the muse teacheth them the paths of song, and loveth the tribe of minstrels.[5]

But we may note also that the minstrel is expected to recite stories that are true, for Odysseus hints that the truth of his story will be the test of his divine inspiration:

> "If thou wilt indeed rehearse me this aright, so will I be thy witness among all men, how the god [illegible] his grace hath given thee the gift of wondrous song."[6]

---

[1] *Odyssey*, viii. 43-45 (translation—Butcher and Lang).
[2] *Ibid.*, viii. 62-64.
[3] *Ibid.*, viii. 499.
[4] *Ibid.*, viii. 99.
[5] *Ibid.*, viii. 479-481.
[6] *Ibid.*, viii. 496-498.

There is nothing, then, at this stage, to suggest that the poets of their day — namely, the minstrels — were "teachers." That was to be a later idea. Their function was to cause pleasure, to make more complete the satisfaction of a banquet. But so wonderful, so unaccountable, was their gift of making men glad or sorrowful that a god was brought in to account for it—they were "inspired." And, because inspired, what they sang was also true.

That was all. This simple theory of the function and character of poetry served; and no doubt it was encouraged by the professors of the art, who thus enjoyed the protection of the gods as well as the favour of men—a privilege not always accorded to the poets of later ages.

It is a far cry from the mixed civilization of the *Odyssey* to that of the time of Aristophanes. In that later and already elderly age all the arts seemed to have reached the stage of their complete and final development. Like the Greek city-state, of whose social life they formed a part, they had grown and become mature, and were now coming under the scrutiny of the philosopher and the philosophical critic. Owing to the social conditions of ancient Greece the spoken word still held its own as against the written. The epic poems had been handed on from one reciter to another, and even in the fifth century the ordinary Athenian seldom read them, but heard them interpreted orally, by rhapsodes. It was the same with Hesiod, and with the fervent religious hymns which were ascribed to Orpheus or Musaeus. And so, too, at the Dionysiac festivals, the assembled citizens heard and saw the plays of the great dramatists. They seldom read them. Poetry was the poetry of the spoken word.

It was the same also with prose. Prose was speech. It was the language of an ordered oration delivered at the Assembly or in the law courts. It was addressed to the body of Athenian citizens, whose ears were cultivated to appreciate the manner and arrangement of a speech, the choice of words, the cadence, and the unfolding of an argument designed to "persuade." The sophists lectured or argued in public, and the form of demonstration by debate is preserved by Plato in his *Dialogues*.

That, then, was one governing factor in most Greek "literature" up to and during the fifth century—it was oral.

There was a second governing factor which affected poetry in particular. Up to at least the middle of the fifth century it tended, in its more important forms, to become not more secular, but less. The minstrel, as we have seen, was at an early stage regarded as inspired by the god. But he sang to give pleasure, not instruction. Gradually, however, poetry came to be adopted, if we may use the expression, by both Church and State. Homer and Hesiod came to be not merely inspired singers; they were inspired teachers. The religious fervour which made men familiar with the Orphic hymns found satisfaction also in the inspired religious "teaching" of Homer and Hesiod. The ancient epics have been described as the Bible of the Greeks, enshrining the truths of religion and of morality. That poet only was thought worthy to succeed them who followed in their footsteps as teachers.

The Attic drama, then, developed under this dual authority—if I may repeat the expression—of Church and State. The Dionysiac festival was essentially a religious festival; but it came to be also a civic, or patriotic, festival. The tragedians who submitted their plays to the judgment of the people of Athens handled with religious reverence the well-known themes of gods and heroes, or presented, as in the *Persæ* of Æschylus, a serious treatment of a great subject designed to appeal to the moral or patriotic sense of the people. In the popularly accepted view of poetry, even at the end of the fifth century, the older poets were the scripture of the Greeks, the newer poets were the teachers. It is impossible to be fair to Plato's austere, didactic view of the arts unless we have this fact in mind.

Now the sophists, like the evolutionists, the Higher Critics, the Modernists and social philosophers of the half-century or so preceding the Great War, had not hesitated to question the current conventional views of religion, art, society. They asked searching questions : What is Being? What is Good? What is Knowledge? What is Virtue? and again : What is a Speech? What is style? What are the character, functions and purpose of poetry? Euripides himself had been to school with the sophists. He became a Modernist among poets. He thought that poetry should deal with the burning problems of contemporary life. He was the feminist of his time, believing in the emancipation of women. Like Wordsworth—himself reacting against the classicist conventions of the eighteenth century—he was ready to apply in practice, as in theory, the view that poetry should use the language of common speech.

But even so, he does not seem to think of departing from the accepted Greek view that the function of the poet is to teach, to make men better, to produce more patriotic citizens. Aristophanes wishes to represent Euripides in the worst possible light. He accuses him of demeaning the language of poetry, of dealing with unworthy subjects, of indulging in the sentimentalism of the gutter. But he never accuses him of denying the principle that the aim of the poet is a moral aim.

When he asks his leading question : On what ground should a poet claim admiration? Euripides is made to reply glibly, with the rest of them:

> If his art is true, and his counsel sound ; and if he brings
> help to the nation,
> By making men better in some respect.

There we are on ground that was common to all of them —to Æschylus, Euripides, Aristophanes and Plato. If they differed, it was not so much in regard to art, as in regard to morality. They were all patriots. They were all aiming at good citizens. They were all under the obsession of the "ideal State." The Aristophanic Æschylus agrees with the Aristophanic Euripides that it is the duty of the poet "to teach." He differs from him in what he should teach and the manner of the teaching: the one has the moral ideals of a Die-hard Tory, the other of a sentimental Radical with Bolshevik sympathies. Whilst the latter is ridiculed as a demagogue, a sentimentalist, a sophist, whose art was demoralizing to the people, the former advocated a return to the old-fashioned virtues of the swashbuckling hero. But whatever the civic ideal of the one or the other, it is common ground that his claim to admiration must depend on the character of that civic, or moral, ideal, and the degree in which his poetry subserves it.

That being the view of poetry held by the poets themselves, it is much to ask of a moral philosopher that he should be more of an advocate of poetry for poetry's sake than any poet had been, and less concerned about morality and philosophy. In this respect Plato did not prove himself a better poet than the poets, or a better literary critic than the literary critics.

Chapter Five

"IMITATION"

TO some it has been profoundly disappointing that the philosopher who, of all philosophers, was the most richly endowed with poetic sensibility, who had absorbed the works of the great poets and unhesitatingly adorned his prose with lines and phrases culled from them, should have produced a theory which not only did not justify, but disparaged them. It was as if Plato had cast off his most intimate and congenial friends. In his impassioned defence of truth at the expense of æsthetic beauty he seems to immolate a cherished part of himself on the altar of philosophy.

He admits his affection. He confesses it as one might confess a sin. "I confess I am checked by a kind of affectionate respect for Homer, of which I have been conscious since I was a child. For of all those beautiful tragic poets he seems to have been the original master and guide. But it would be wrong to honour a man at the expense of Truth, and therefore I must . . . speak out."[1]

The earliest poets or minstrels had claimed, as we have seen, that they were inspired by a god; and for a later age the proof of this inspiration lay in the truth and excellence of their teachings. Plato, in the *Ion*, ironically explains the traditional view accepted by the rhapsodes:

> The Muse first of all inspires men herself . . . For all good poets, epic as well as lyric, compose their beautiful poems not by art, but because they are inspired and possessed. And as the Corybantian revellers when they dance are not in their right mind, so the lyric poets are not in their right mind when they are composing their beautiful strains . . .

---

[1] *Republic*, x.

> For the poet is a light and winged and holy thing, and there is no invention in him until he has been inspired and is out of his senses, and the mind is no longer in him ; when he has not attained to this state, he is powerless and is unable to utter his oracles.[1]

But Plato was not to be seduced into any such doctrine, however attractive. Had he pursued this line of inquiry, purging it of its absurdities, it might have led him to the doctrine of æsthetic " transport," or ecstasy, which it was reserved for Longinus to express in its most satisfying form. But the only transport which Plato sanctioned was that of the reason, in its purity, divorced from the errors of sense ; any other was for him based in delusion. The " inspired " view of poetry did not accord with his philosophy, nor the teachings of the poets with his account of moral value.

He was content to criticize that valuation of the poets which his own time accorded to them. It was claimed that they were teachers. If they were good poets, they were good teachers. Homer was the greatest of all poets, therefore he was the greatest of all teachers. The virtuous Athenian of the fifth or fourth century acted in accordance with the moral laws of the Epics.

And so Plato does not ask, as we should like him to have done, " Is this a right conception of the Epics ? " but, " Is this a right conception of virtue ? " Which is, after all, the question we should expect him to ask; for in the *Republic*, the book in which we have the fullest discussion of this subject, he is concerned to construct, firstly, an ideal State, and secondly, the ideal man who is the individual counterpart of that State. He is examining " justice " writ large in the State, and tracking it to its source in the individual. He is primarily interested therefore in discovering " justice "

[1] *Ion.*

or " goodness " in these two aspects—from the social point of view, we find him making everything, including art, subservient to *morality*, or civic virtue; and from the individual point of view, everything subservient to the *philosophic* ideal, or the pursuit and realization of truth.

Looking at the matter, then, from the first, the social, point of view, Plato is interested in literature, or art, only in so far as its influence is beneficial in moulding the life of the good citizen. None other is to be allowed to contaminate his State. It shall be no argument that a poem or poet is charming, admirable, or even sacred [1]—vain arguments of æsthetes—if the teaching is not such as the Guardians prescribe. He establishes an unrelenting censorship,[2] and the principles upon which it will operate are clearly laid down in Books II. and III.

And so he launches his attack on Homer and Hesiod and the other poets who have followed their example. Can the Guardians of the State allow the poets to misrepresent the gods, and show them as revengeful, or lustful, or cruel, or as waging war among themselves? Can they allow God, who is good, to be described as the author of evil? Can they permit the gods to be shown as assuming fictitious shapes, or telling paltry lies, or in any way demeaning themselves? It is intolerable that falsehoods should be told about the next world, and that it should be reviled in pitiful accounts of death and suffering. Nor is it right that the poets should describe honoured heroes like Achilles or Priam as indulging in weak lamentations, or using insolent language, or as being gluttonous, vengeful or choleric. Nor can the Guardians allow citizens to " imitate " the words

[1] *προσκυνοίμεν ἂν ἀυτὸν ὡς ἱερὸν κὰι θαυμαστὸν κὰι ἡδύν, εἴποιμεν δᾶν ὅτι* . . .—*Republic*, iii. 398.

[2] *Δεῖ δή, ὡς ἔοικεν, ἡμᾶς ἐπιστατεῖν* . . . *τοῖς ἐπιχειροῦσι λέγειν, κὰι δεῖσθαι* . . .—*Republic*, iii. 386.

or actions of inferior men. For the good man will be unwilling to imitate any but the noblest characters.

Homer and Hesiod, then, are convicted of immoral teachings, and the tragedians and comedians are condemned because they imitate unworthy objects. In the ideal State there is no place for them. Let them be crowned with fillets—let perfumed oil be poured on their heads—but they must be sent on to another city. Plato has taken up his stand on the side of the most ascetic of the Puritans. The more lovely and fascinating the arts may seem, the more deadly they may be in luring us to false views of life or the emasculating influence of emotion.

But he is not content to leave the argument there. As a moralist he has disapproved of poetry because it is immoral. As a philosopher he disapproves of it because it is based in falsehood. His ideal man as a citizen pursues the moral ideal; as an individual, he is intent upon the pursuit of truth. But the arts deal in illusion.

The artist, he finds, is concerned with appearance only, or rather the appearance of appearance. He deals with the world which we apprehend with our eyes and ears, the world of seeming in which each object as perceived comes and goes, now seeming large, now small, now hot relatively to this, cold relatively to that, sweet at one moment, sour at another—always changing, many, illusory, whereas the real is Unchanging and One. There are many appearances which we call red things, but only one Redness, the idea behind it; and there are many appearances which we call beautiful things, but only one Absolute Beauty, the reality apprehended by the mind. It is the appearances which the artist imitates, not the Reality.

The bed or the chair which the carpenter makes is an appearance only, not a reality. There cannot be more than one real, or ideal bed, for if there were more, each would presuppose as the form or idea, which made it what it was, an absolute bed behind itself. The carpenter can make no more than an imitation of the reality, and the bed he makes is once removed from the truth. But the painter's bed is twice removed. For he does not imitate the reality, made by God, but the imitation, made by the carpenter. His work therefore is no more than an imitation of an imitation.

And in like manner the poet, using not paint, but verbs and nouns and rhythms—appealing to the ear, where the other appealed to the eye—can re-create no more than a weak imitation of phantoms, appearances, unsubstantial images. He too creates only a copy of a copy. His subject and his method are false. He appeals not to the reason, but to the emotions. He excites, feeds and strengthens the most worthless part of the soul, appealing to those unrestrained sentiments and disordered impulses which in ordinary life we should be ashamed to indulge.

Homer and Hesiod, then, must be banished. Tragedy and comedy must go. If we permit poetry at all, it must be confined to hymns to the gods, and verses in praise of noble men.

It is easy enough, in our day, to state Plato's errors. He is right when he says that the poet or the artist produces something which is less than the reality it purports to represent. As we saw when we were speaking of our imaginary caveman, that primitive draughtsman cannot reproduce the actual qualities of the object he attempts to portray. But though he creates something less than that reality, he also creates something more. He puts an idea into it. He puts his perception into it. He gives us his intuition of certain distinctive and essential qualities. He is not further from the ideal, but has attempted to impress upon the material he uses the clearer impress of a Form, or Idea, and in so doing has given to some little bit of the world—which, in Plato's language, is changing, manifold, and disordered—a permanence, a unity, an order, introduced into it by that faculty of the mind which we call Imagination.

He has stated the antithesis, debated through the ages, of Art and Morality. We know to-day—or should—that there is no such fundamental opposition. Morality teaches. Art does not attempt to teach. It merely asserts—it is thus or thus that life is perceived to be. That is my bit of reality, says the artist. Take it or leave it—draw any lessons you like from it—that is my account of things as they are—if it has any value to you as evidence or teaching, use it, but that is not my business. I have given you my rendering, my account, my vision, my dream, my illusion—call it what you will. If there is any lesson in it, it is yours to draw, not mine to preach.

I hope it is clear that when we speak thus of "art" we mean "fine art." If I speak of literature in this connexion, I do not include "didactic" literature. I do not necessarily include, for instance, all the plays of Mr Bernard Shaw, in some of which, in whole or in part, he is concerned to promote certain views, and to that extent is propagandist, or rhetorician, not artist. A poem or a play or a novel may have a moral purpose, or an immoral motive, but it can only be actuated by the one or the other in so far as it departs from the aim which is distinctively that of the artist, so far as he is an artist.

We have seen some of the conditions which predisposed Plato to take an attitude antagonistic to poetry. We have seen that the Greeks of his time were not content to regard the poets as the Greeks of the Homeric age had regarded them, as sweet singers who ministered to pleasure through their gift of divine song, but insisted on regarding them also as teachers. It was just because they were accepted as teachers, and because their teaching tended to stereotype the inferior virtues of a semi-barbarous age, that an enlightened moralist was bound to condemn their morality, just as any enlightened person of to-day might condemn the harshness and cruelty of the Hebrew prophets.

But supposing the Hebrew doctrine had not been that of a jealous and vindictive God—supposing it had not contained the forbidding maxim of an eye for an eye and a tooth for a tooth—but rather had been winning and humane, pleasant rather than repellent, easy-going rather than hard and restrictive ; and supposing it had been couched in language charming and seductive ; supposing moreover this doctrine and these rules of action had not merely the sanction of the priesthood, but were associated with all the influence which the Attic theatre could wield, with its actors, its stage, its swaying chorus, its music, and the vast concourse of people wrought up to a high pitch of emotion ; and supposing you have associated with it also the sensuous pleasures of the arts, and the approval of the highly cultured, and all this in a society peculiarly responsive to emotional appeals, of a highly nervous sensibility, clever, yet dangerously excitable and volatile —should we not, in such a case, see conditions which would make the "immoral" doctrines of the prophets a thousand times more dangerous ? Yet these were the conditions which favoured the cult of the poets in ancient Athens. Surely they were such as to predispose the philosopher and the stern ascetic to take the hardest view of poetry and the arts.

And even we, in our own time, and in our own not

too impressionable and sensitive Anglo-Saxon society, are not unaware of the fact that the "artistic temperament" may have its dangers and its anti-social temptations. For Plato is right to this extent—each and all of the arts must always work through a material medium, which we apprehend with sharpened senses, in terms of the sights and sounds and tastes of the things of "this world." And those sights and sounds and tastes, as Plato realized, are sweet and seductive things. They may even be perilous things for a sensitive and unstable character, deficient on the intellectual or rational side. The priests of the muses have a more terrific responsibility than others in that the very medium through which they work exposes them at all times to the attractions of the world of sense. For them it may seem that all material things are pure because they are the vehicle for the spiritual, and that there is no impurity unless it be in the absence of the spiritual. Hence it is that the extreme Puritan, terrified of life, fleeing always from temptation, shrinks from the high responsibility and the possible perils of art.

The way that Plato sought was the mystic way. His task as an educator was to "turn the whole soul round to see the light of the sun . . . by studies which tend to draw the mind from the sensible to the real, the visible to the invisible." Often the word "mystic" has been wrongly applied to the artist. Your true mystic is never content till he can leave the body behind him and contemplate the spirit in its absolute essence. The true artist, on the contrary, is never content till he can make manifest the spiritual through and in terms of the body. Plato was a mystic in the proper sense of the term; and he followed the true mystic's inclination when he condemned the arts.

Not that the way of the mystic is not fraught with the

very same perils which beset the artist. The records of the saints testify that they were subjected to torturing fear lest visions of the Holy Passion might be counterfeit—lest apparitions sent by the Evil One might tempt and deceive.

We can easily detect the error that Plato falls into in his theory of art. We are unable to accept his conclusions. None the less he has helped to clear the ground. He has made some valid distinctions. He has given us some important starting-points.

To him we owe the first statement of the mimetic, or imitative, character of art. The painter or the poet is not one who simply makes "something beautiful." He imitates or represents what we call reality, what Plato calls phenomena—objects which are at least real to our five senses—in a word, life.

And the artist represents in such a way as to give pleasure—it is the sweetness, or pleasurableness, of his fictions that makes them, in his view, so dangerous.

He makes use, moreover, of various media, the painter using paint, the sculptor stone, the poet, words.

And when in the use of this medium he copies a real object he must be content to give just that aspect of reality which can be represented through that medium. A real bed has many properties and many parts which cannot be shown in a picture. Therefore the painter can produce no more than an aspect of the bed. His picture is something less than the original, and to that extent inferior. Plato did not inquire in what way it may also be something *more*.

Having got thus far, we observe that he has discovered a real community between all the fine arts. A poet who makes a poem and a painter who paints a picture are engaged in the same sort of activity. They do not use the same medium, but otherwise they are engaged on the same task, even though Plato thinks of this merely as the task of copying, in the same delusive way, things that are not worth copying; pleasing men by giving them the same sort of perilous pleasure; seducing them by appealing in like manner to their emotions.

Having recognized the form (εἶδος) that is implicit in a bed or a chair, we might have hoped that he would examine the form that makes a poem or a picture what it is. Having seen that the artist's medium was different from the original, we might have hoped that he would have exclaimed with Homer: "And this was a very miracle of his craft!" But his preoccupation with other activities of the soul—the purely intellectual—and with other problems of life—the purely ethical—stood in the way. Was it that he lived in the only State in the world in which, among the higher activities, the arts exercised more than their due share of influence, and that the spectacle of many disasters of unbalanced temperament filled him with disgust? We only know that his sympathy was withdrawn, his imagination and his thought were not turned with their full illuminating force on to just this, the distinctive problem of the arts; and his example leads us to reflect that often, perhaps, philosophy is not so much a logical avenue to truth as a logical justification of those constructions of experience which belong to intuition, and are liable to be twisted by prejudice.

Chapter Six

THE "POETICS"

I

IT is not easy to disentangle Aristotle from the commentaries, arguments, and legend that have grown out of him through the ages. One epoch after another has fallen under his pervasive influence. He was the acknowledged master during the centuries of Greek and Roman culture; he imposed rules of reasoning on the schoolmen of the Middle Ages; and after the Renaissance, as if he had not already enslaved the world enough, he conquered a new Empire and became lawgiver and absolute monarch to the poets and critics. It is only in our own undeferential age that the glamour of divine right has fallen from him.

Yet there is still tonic quality in his cool, passionless good sense. How refreshing it would be if we could actually think away the tangle of commentary, and catch a glimpse of him in his contemporary setting, a clear-headed scholar of Macedonian origin, discoursing to Athenian students on learned Athenian topics! Refreshing also, if we could manage to approach him as if he were a new author, for what we could find in him of intrinsic worth for our own or any other time, without thought of historic values. Shakespeare, in a lesser degree, presents some of the same difficulties—he, too, has been encrusted in the views of his interpreters. But in his case we have a remedy. Shakespeare can be acted. He may come at any time under the hands of a company of actors and a producer, with a living, listening audience before them, so that he stands or falls for what he is worth to a modern playgoer.

Well, Aristotle is not a dramatist, and we cannot "produce" him. None the less, I see no harm in an attempt, here and there, to "modernize" him: to take his principles, which were applied only to Greek art, and consider how they stand when applied, as he himself might have applied them, to the broader conditions of modern art. For if, and in proportion as, he is right for Greek literature, we may expect that the principles he applies will be right, in a broader interpretation, for all literature.

That he should be so right, even for Greek art, is strange. What did this logician, we may ask, know about poetry? Can we discover in him any of that rare intuition, which Plato certainly had, that finer sensibility which should confer on a critic some special right to lay down the law about tragedy? He himself says that the art of poetry demands a man of born talent (εὐφυής), *or*, one inclined to madness (μανικός). The one is εὔπλαστος—by sympathy or understanding he can take the mould of his subject. The other is ἐκστατικός—he is easily lifted out of himself into a state of transport. If, then, the good poet, as Aristotle says, must be able to put himself into the emotional frame of mind of his characters, to sympathize with them, we may assume that the critic, in his turn, must be able to sympathize with his proper subject, the poet. Aristotle would evidently have preferred to range himself with the ἐυφυής, the man of all-round natural understanding; and would have been inclined to put his master and rival, Plato, amongst the μανικόι, the ἐκστατικόι—amongst just those, in fact, who had the quality which to Plato seemed distinctive of the poet, that divine madness which made poetry something to be dreaded and shunned.

Aristotle was in no such danger. His common sense was proof against enchantments. His learning was many-sided, and with the limited range of knowledge of the fourth century B.C. it was possible to be fully versed in many branches of inquiry without the narrowness of the mere specialist. But he knew his limitations. He confined himself to the "theoretic life." He wrote of politics, but he was not a politician. He discoursed on rhetoric, but he was not an orator. He theorized on poetry, but he was neither poet nor rhapsode. If we mean by "Aristotle" all the work of his school that is left to us in his name, we might conclude that he knew everything that could be known to an ancient Greek, and participated in nothing. His subject was the Greek world as he found it. His method was to analyse it reasonably, without passion and without prejudice. He had a genius for distinction and classification. He is perfectly detached. He is without any philosophical axe of his own to grind. He arrives at just generalizations by sheer clear-headedness and a humane good sense.

And so, when he comes to poetry, he examines it simply as poetry. When he deals with drama he examines drama as it is, and for what it is. Not more, not less. Simply by the process of isolating a subject, and analysing its essential parts, he gives us a theory of poetry. By separating the art of poetry from that of politics and ethics, his logical method at one lucky stroke gives fine art an independent place in the scheme of human activity—it has released it from the tyranny of the philosopher, the politician and the moralist. In turning to the *Poetics*, after reading Plato or any earlier writer, we find ourselves transported suddenly tc a familiar world—it might be that of our own time. The poet in the *Frogs*, who agreed as a matter of course that the poet aims at "making men better in some respects," seems to belong to the Dark Ages. Plato's view of art as an imitation of an imitation, twice removed from the truth, seems sheer obscurantism. Aristotle hardly deigns to contradict these primitive views, though they were certainly tenable not long before, and perhaps at the time when he lectured and wrote. Without the demonic genius of Plato, without his poetic gift, he avoids his inspired errors. Confining his attention to what is before him he adheres coolly to his logical method—he examines poetry in itself—he distinguishes its kinds—he observes the essential quality or power (δύναμις) of each, and how the poems which in fact we find good have been put together—and under his careful hands the parts of the truth disentangle themselves like those of a complicated machine which only needed to be assembled and fitted together. The result is that he is the first man in history to expose certain principles, purely æsthetic, to which the artist, in fact, conforms. Plato confused the study of art with the study of morals. Aristotle, removing this confusion, created the study of æsthetics.

We find, then, that Aristotle in the *Poetics* takes it for granted that a work of art, whether it be a picture or a poem, is a thing of beauty [1]; and that it affords pleasure appropriate to its own kind.[2]

It is not within the scope of his inquiry to ask what beauty means, or in what way the conscious mind apprehends it. That is a metaphysical question. He assumes that to be beautiful is part of the essence of a work of art. When we have said that a poem is a good poem we have said that it is beautiful, and when we have found the conditions which make a poem excellent we have found the conditions of its peculiar kind of beauty. When he says that a poem or a picture must have order, pro-

[1] *Poetics*, vii. 1450b, 38-1451a, 12 (Butcher's text).

[2] *Ibid.*, xiv. 1453b, 11-14.

portion and organic unity, he has named qualities which cannot be separated from his conception of the beautiful.

And so, again, when he takes it for granted that a Tragedy affords pleasure, he is content with the fact that it does do so. He may discuss the particular kind of pleasure which the Tragedian aims at giving—when a dramatist presents, for example, the terrible, but rejects the monstrous. But the ethical problem which disturbed Plato, that of the goodness or badness of all pleasure, is not so much as mentioned in the *Poetics*. And if he does at one moment digress into pathology (in his account of the *Katharsis*—the purging or purifying effect of tragedy) he probably only does so in order to brush aside Plato's challenging attack on the poet's right to exist.

The critics of the seventeenth century forgot that Aristotle was not writing about all poetry, but about the only poetry which existed for him—that of Greece. Dryden had the good sense to pull them up sharply. "It is not enough that Aristotle has said so," he wrote, "for Aristotle drew his models of tragedy from Sophocles and Euripides: AND, IF HE HAD SEEN OURS, MIGHT HAVE CHANGED HIS MIND."

For Aristotle there was only one literature, that of the Greeks. He could not compare Greek poetry with any other, for there was none other that he knew. He had before him primitive literature of various periods expressed in various dialects, and also the perfected examples of the fifth century. Just as in the *Politics* he regards the State as a living organism passing through all the stages of childhood, till it reaches its proper adult form, so with poetry. It began, he held, with modest improvisations; passed through a succession of changes; and finally, having reached its proper, its natural form, stopped. For each kind of literature, then, there was, in his view, a perfect form which could be regarded as the highest development of that art beyond which it could not go—the Epic of the Homeric age, the tragic drama of Æschylus, Sophocles and Euripides. It was with these, the classic examples, that he was alone concerned. His theory of poetry is based, not upon some unrealized ideal, but upon the models he had before him. These he analyses as a chemist might analyse a compound substance. He tells us what he finds there.

In one passage he does hint at possibilities outside his ken—of developments of art unknown to him. It occurs in the sentence in the fourth chapter, when he raises a question which he refuses to enlarge upon, whether tragedy has yet adapted itself to its true forms, and whether it is to be judged absolutely (αὐτό καθ' αὐτό) or in relation to an audience. It would be easy to write a treatise on that sentence; but, as Aristotle says, it is "another question"; and, like him, we must pass on, observing that the only poetic excellence with which in fact he concerns himself is the excellence of the limited body of literature available to him.

It included Epic poetry, lyrical poetry, Tragedy and Comedy—these were the principal forms of literature known to Greece in his day belonging to the order of Fine Art, as opposed to that of didactic literature. How much was excluded from so limited a survey—the pastoral of Theocritus and Virgil: the satire of Horace or of Pope: the prose fiction which is the modern substitute for the older verse narrative! He had never seen a Grand Opera, or a Light Opera, or a realistic drama. If he had seen these, might he "have changed his mind"?

Not that we need understand by Dryden's sentence

that Aristotle might have changed his mind about Greek poetry—only that he might have said something different about all poetry. Aristotle must be taken to have said his last word about Attic drama in relation to an Athenian audience. (I have just alluded to his interesting reservation which hints at other audiences and other poetic forms.) His principles for Greek literature are clearly given. That is what matters, and it would be idle to guess what he would have said about Shakespeare or Shaw if he had been differently brought up. But it does interest us very much to know what there is in his wise analysis of Greek poetry which touches the principles of all literature, and is therefore not irrelevant even for the student of Shakespeare or Shaw.

Nor is there the least reason why the prose drama of Shaw should be excluded from such an inquiry, nor, for that matter, the prose narrative of the modern novel. Aristotle said perfectly clearly that it is not writing in verse that makes a poet. Empedocles wrote in verse, but he should be called a physicist rather than a poet. The mimes of Sophron and Xenarchus, and the Socratic dialogues, are written in prose, but, like the poetry which is in metre, they are "imitations," and it is the *imitation*, in Aristotle's view, that makes the difference. *Imitation* distinguishes what we call creative literature from literature which is didactic. The term is the equivalent, almost, of our word *representation*, except that the latter, in modern parlance, has come more and more to mean the exact imitation of objects seen by the eye or distinguished by the ear. *Imitation*, for the *Poetics*, is the objective representation of life in literature—what in our language we might call the imaginative reconstruction of life. If he did not distinguish between representational art and impressionist, or expressionist, or symbolical, or abstract art, that is because he knew nothing about such art, and because these interesting novelties had not come his way—the tendency of the Greeks, in striving to give expression to their visions in poetry or sculpture, was to seek distinction by selection and concentration rather than by novel devices for showing the "originality" of the artist.

There is, however, no reason to suppose that Aristotle would have dropped the word *mimesis* even had he been confronted with an extremely difficult example of modern art. Whatever can be objectively expressed in line or language is still an imitation of something, if it is only an idea in the head of the artist.

II

Mimesis, then, or imitation is, in Aristotle's view, the essential in a fine art. It is that which distinguishes creative or fine art from all other products of the human mind.

He begins by narrowing his inquiry to certain kinds of imitation—Epic poetry, Tragedy, Comedy and Dithyrambic poetry, along with the music of the flute and the lyre which accompanied them.

Being imitative, these arts imply (1) certain objects which they imitate, (2) a certain medium in which they represent those objects, and (3) the various modes of treatment which may be adopted within that medium. In the case of the arts with which Aristotle is concerned, the media chosen are language, rhythm and "harmony" or melody—"harmony" and rhythm in instrumental music, rhythm in dancing, language in literature (whether it be the language of prose or verse). In the case of painting, the media used are colour and form.

Aristotle, then, distinguishes what we call the subject treated (which he calls the object imitated), the medium in which it is treated, and the manner of treatment.

The objects of imitation are beings in action (not necessarily human beings—they might be gods—I see no reason why they should not be the animals of *Alice in Wonderland* or of the *Jungle Book* or *The Call of the Wild*). Upon the serious or the frivolous character of these beings depends the tragic or comic character of the poem. They will be of a higher type, says Aristotle, in the one case, or a lower in the other. Men may be represented as better than they are in ordinary life, or as worse, or, realistically, as they actually are. The first method is that of the serious writer of Epic or Tragedy; the second is that of the writer of Comedy.

It is argued, and probably rightly, that Aristotle here introduces a moral consideration, and that it is this which affects his distinction between Tragedy and Comedy. The word πράττω with him implies conduct—or action which is determined by moral character. The man in action whom the poet represents is a man revealing in every word or movement the character which actuates him. But when he says that the serious poets like Homer or Sophocles imitate men of higher moral character we need not suppose him to mean men necessarily endowed with conventional moral excellences. The word σπουδαῖος which he uses means "serious" rather than "good"—a man who has a character which serious people can take seriously. Prometheus was a fit subject for Attic tragedy, though his conduct was that of a rebel against Zeus. Even Ajax was a tragic hero, though he was insolent, cruel and self-centred. The main thing is that the character should be important, and should be held up as something worth our consideration; and when he is thus treated, the poet is writing in the "serious" manner of Sophocles or Homer.

In choice of character, then, and in characterization lies the difference between the tragic manner and the comic. This should be remembered in connexion with his later statement, that in Tragedy "the plot is the first thing." The serious poet (σέμνος) idealizes his characters. The meaner poet (εὐτελέστερος) reveals human nature in all the nakedness of its defects, or with the defects exaggerated. But the defect or ugliness which the comic poet reveals is such as to cause laughter and not pain. Aristotle knew nothing of the "realistic" or "fleshly" school of fiction—the school of Zola or of Gissing—whose subject might be human beings enduring petty hardships, cruel passions and undeserved pain. He had never seen an "intellectual" play like *Man and Superman* or *Justice*—though perhaps Euripides came nearest to the type. He knew nothing of the agreeable social sentiments which befit the characters of a Somerset Maugham. A Noel Coward never came within the limits of his experience. He knew only the Greek tragedies, and the Greek satiric and comic drama. There, as Mr Gordon Craig has said, "to perform in plays which dealt sentimentally with divine things, or which dealt suggestively with vicious things, or which pampered domestic self-content, or 'groused' or howled about domestic trivialities, would have been an impossibility."

But even when we admit that the models before him were limited in kind, it may seem surprising that he should not have treated the subject of Comedy more fully. He has not been at pains to analyse it, to examine its component parts, to discuss its characteristic merits and defects. At first reading we might suppose that he has passed over it so lightly, with just a little of the superiority of the "highbrow," as undeserving of further attention.

But his neglect of lyrical poetry is more remarkable still. It is due to no lack of worthy models, with Sappho and Pindar available to him, and the magnificent lyrical poetry which was composed for the Chorus in the Drama.

Nor can this neglect be explained by saying that his subject is really limited to Tragedy. His subject is ostensibly poetry, and he treats the Epic at some length, only excusing the comparative brevity of the treatment on the ground that the principal elements of the Epic are to be found also in Tragedy. Yet he dismisses the whole subject of lyrical poetry as if it were no more than a subordinate element in Tragedy, a sort of external decoration, or, at best, a part of the action, which it falls to the Chorus to play.

Having in practice limited his subject as he has done, we might be tempted to wish that he had limited it even more, giving us simply an account of tragic drama, but giving us that in its completeness—confining himself, I mean, to Tragedy, but extending his treatment to include not only the drama as composed by the poet, but also as rendered by actors, chorus and musicians at the Panathenaic Festival. As it is, having taken the whole field of poetry as his ostensible subject, he has examined Tragedy mainly from the literary man's point of view—rather as dramatic poetry than as poetic drama. What would we not have given even for the coldest Aristotelian analysis of the specific effect aimed at by the producer of a Greek play for a Greek audience? What if he had taken for his subject the art of the theatre as the Greeks knew it—not the inner action of the play alone, but all that went to the making of an event so stirring and memorable as the performance of a trilogy in the theatre at Athens—the tragic theme—the actors moving in the appropriate setting of the theatre—the scenery—the song —the music of instruments—the patterned rhythm of the dance—the colour—the co-ordination of speech, song, spectacle and recurrent movements !

If Aristotle had taken this complete thing for his subject he would have given us what neither he nor any other supreme critic has given, an account of the composite art of the drama, as composed, produced and presented. The real unity of the drama, with all of the elements which together, and inseparably, impress the minds of an audience, would have been acknowledged once and for all. Incidentally, had he attempted a complete analysis of the real Greek drama as the Athenians knew it, and so vividly lived it, he could never have been so absurdly misinterpreted as he was in the seventeenth and eighteenth centuries, or have exercised so ridiculous an influence upon neo-classicist poets, for it would have been obvious that the " rules " of Aristotle presupposed unique conditions of the theatre which the world will never know again, in just that—the Attic—form.

Aristotle, who for two thousand years has accustomed the world to think along his lines of thought, might as easily have persuaded it to think of drama as a composite art composed of many elements, like Grand Opera. It would have learnt that even appropriate scenery—be it simple, or elaborate—matters in the production of a great play. It would have learnt that the dance may be a serious art, having its own precise technique, appropriately subordinated to theme and correlated to music, and only to be learnt by hard discipline. It would not have been astonished at the miracle of the Russian ballet, which just before the War came as a revelation to our hitherto unopened eyes of the possibilities of movement, colour, pattern and music united into a single design, though, perhaps, owing to the disintegrating effect of the tradition, it was still defective on the intellectual and "dramatic" side.

In treating the tragic drama mainly as poetry, in separating the intellectual work of the dramatist from the rest of the work which goes to the creation of a play as the audience sees it, Aristotle taught the intellectual world to think of drama as an almost exclusively literary thing. The thinkers and so-called "serious" people of all the world have been profoundly and unduly influenced by his thought and his advice. It is due in great measure to this one-sidedness of the *Poetics* that cultured people, everywhere and always, have tended too much to think of "serious" drama in terms of that part of drama which belongs to literature. And naturally the converse has come to be true, that those whose practical business is with the stage—with production, with acting, with stage-effects, with all that hits the public—tend to be separated from intellectual influences, and to behave as if that part of drama which Aristotle did not discuss is the only important thing for men whose business is to fill a theatre.

However, Aristotle chose his own limited task, and we can hardly blame him for the intellectual slavishness of subsequent generations. It is scarcely his fault if, because he isolated one aspect of a subject from the rest, they proceeded for all time to treat the part as if it were the whole. He, having briefly mentioned scenery, song and diction as three subordinate elements in Tragedy, turns to concentrate his full attention on the three inner elements—Plot, Character, Thought.

It is idle to regret that Aristotle did not do something which he never intended to do. The fact is that he was on the track of other quarry. He had set himself a task just as difficult and as important—a task which needed performing, perhaps, before the other could have been attempted. The wider discussion which I have indicated would have meant loss to his own chosen inquiry. It was a prior necessity to fix attention on the essentials of a work of literary art ; and that was the task which he performed. He refrained from enlarging upon all of the many elements which the art of the tragic poet may include, and dwelt on those which it must include. He has simplified, and in so doing has universalized. In showing us the thought elements which belong by inner necessity to Greek drama he has concentrated on the essentials of all literary art, if not of art itself.

Remembering, then, that we are speaking of the most systematic and deliberate of philosophers, we may conclude that it is not through carelessness that he has nearly neglected lyrical poetry and dealt so cursorily with Comedy. He reveals his intention when he says that whoever knows what is good and bad in Tragedy knows also about Epic poetry ; and, again, when he says that Tragedy is superior in that it functions better as an art (τῷ τῆς τέχνης ἔργῳ). Is it not clear that he is so interested in Tragedy because he takes it to be the most representative of the arts ; or rather, that one which, when examined, will most reveal the qualities essential in art in so far as it is art. Again and again he compares poetry with painting ; and when he is speaking of plot and character he unhesitatingly names their counterparts in the painter's treatment of line and colour. He is emphatic also in saying that what makes a poet a poet is not the use of rhymes ; he is a poet because he imitates or represents life. Aristotle gives his main attention to Tragedy because it is for him the grand type of all the arts. In giving us this theory of Tragedy he has given us something very like a theory of Fine Art.

And surely this is exactly what we should have expected from our encyclopædic philosopher. Having set out to treat of man in his knowing capacity (metaphysics), man in his reasoning capacity (logic), man in his willing and choosing capacity, whether as an individual or a member of the State (ethics and politics), we should expect him to give an account of man in his perceptive-intuitive-imaginative capacity. These last words are not his, but *mimesis* implies no less. Though he did not produce a complete theory of Fine Art, he did the next best thing when he prepared his theory of Tragedy—that is to say, his analysis of what goes on in the best Tragedy known to him.

Imitation, or representation, then, is of the essence of the matter. It will be beautiful—that is presupposed. It will give pleasure—its appropriate pleasure. It must be persuasive—what we call "convincing." Though a representation, it will be an idealized treatment of life. Though it deals with the individual, it aims at universal truth. Its appeal is through the emotions.

III

Let us here recall his familiar definition of Tragedy (using Professor Butcher's rendering):

> *Tragedy, then, is an imitation of an action that is serious, complete, and of a certain magnitude; in language embellished with each kind of artistic ornament, the several kinds being found in separate parts of the play; in the form of action, not of narrative; through pity and fear effecting the proper purgation of these emotions.*

Imitation being the first significant term in this defini tion, the second is *action*. Tragedy is concerned with an action, and for Aristotle that word means the action of rational human beings who think and will. It follows that it is concerned also with character and thought, for by these action is determined.

Plot, character, thought — here we have the hard-worked trio which were destined to play so big a part in the language of criticism. Which comes first, asks Aristotle, in order of importance? He plumps outright for *plot*. The structure of the incidents, the arrangement of the things done—that, exactly, is what he means by plot; and twice he makes this bald and rather depressing statement. Yet we cannot be content with a perfectly plain, mechanical interpretation of the words; for he himself gives them a more interesting significance by adding that the *plot* is the underlying principle of a tragedy and, as it were, the very soul of it.

We need not attach undue importance to his almost parenthetic remark that there can be a tragedy without character, but not without action. He illustrates this from the example of unsatisfactory "modern" tragedies in which the characterization was poor, rather than absent. Indeed, he has already said that action, according to his own definition, presupposes character; therefore an action acting without character would be a contradiction in terms. We are justified therefore in saying that even from Aristotle's point of view you cannot have an important plot without character. Plot presupposes both character and thought. None of these elements can be lacking. Therefore he is drawing a distinction between plot and character, and character and thought, which is valuable as a distinction only so long as we remember that it differentiates between aspects of a thing which in fact is one and indivisible.

But is he right in stressing so much that aspect of a tragedy (or an epic, or a novel) which is called plot? Is not a great part of our own English literature a direct denial of this view? Are not Shakespeare's plots loosely woven, and is it not the character of a Hamlet, a Lear, a Lady Macbeth, an Othello or Iago, which gives the play such substance and compelling quality as it has? Have not Fielding and Sterne been content to string episode and episode together, and to win their effect by the persuasiveness of their persons and through a series of incidents most slenderly related? What are we to say of Jane Austen, Dickens, Thackeray, Wells, and modern novelists by the score? Is it not character, character all the time, with the plot left to take care of itself?

Well, that is partly true. But the Greek point of view implies, not the failure of these authors—it would be absurd to suggest failure—but a measure of failure, the measure by which they have fallen short of something they might have done. The "well-made play"! What fun has been poured upon it! What watery stuff has been palmed off upon academic critics—in France, more than in England, where we have few academic critics—in the form of the well-made play! Nevertheless, if Dickens's novels had been "well-made"—would it not have made a difference? Would he not have held a more indisputable place in the world's regard? Thin stuff will be thin stuff always, and no "making" will render it good. But if we ask for a good plot, we do not mean a good plot made of poor material. Aristotle said that the plot was the "soul" of a Tragedy, and we are not straining his meaning far if we say that plot is the whole situation, and that a good plot is a significant situation, so arranged that its significance is wrung out of it to the uttermost. When we demand a plot in any important sense of the term we are asking for a situation in which characters, themselves alive and interesting, shall be caught, tried, perplexed or harassed, and so put to the test by circumstance that what is humanly essential in them is exposed to our view. This is the sort of plot which Æschylus and Sophocles chose. In like manner our own George Eliot, Thomas Hardy, Meredith, Henry James, made their characters subservient to a pattern of life, or at least an interesting fragment of a pattern, into which the characters fit. Prosper Mérimée, Flaubert, De Maupassant, Turgenev, Tchekhov, on a large scale or a small, present us again and again with a single motive to which each incident, each spoken word, is subordinate. Even for the prodigal, extravagant Shakespeare, whose plots are so often the object of blame, character is an instrument for creating a significant situation. And I do not think that effectual use can be made of Shakespeare as an argument against Aristotle. The great characters of the tragedies may live in our minds as characters. But those characters have been thrown up stark against the human skyline under the urge of circumstances in which the drama has trapped them.

If, then, we interpret Aristotle's words in this broader sense, his conclusion is valid for the critic of modern literature no less than of ancient. By selecting a piece of life which shall stand in some sort of interesting relation to life as a whole, the artist appeals to the imagination and satisfies the intellect. Any writer with some power of observation and a good memory can give us an *imitation* of life as it actually is, of character casually expressed in daily speech and action. That is what too many modern novelists are content to do. But though all art for Aristotle is " imitation," it only becomes art when the object of imitation is chosen, when the plot is constructed, or the elements of a picture composed. " If you string together a set of speeches expressive of character, and well finished in point of diction and thought, you will not produce the essential tragic effect nearly so well as with a play which, however deficient in those respects, yet has a plot and (artistically) constructed incidents."

So the elements of an Aristotelian plot have to be chosen and put together as the elements of a picture are composed. If we carry his thought one stage further than Aristotle actually went, we may add that this act of composition must be preceded and accompanied by an act of the constructive imagination which pounces upon something significant and interesting in life, and perceives it as an harmonious and satisfying whole. Though this truth is not explicit in his words, it is fully consistent with them. For though he does not discuss the thought-processes of the artist—his vision, intuition, inspiration, imagination—he does state the objective results of these thought-processes. He does affirm the necessity of unity of plot. "Tragedy is an imitation of an action that is complete, and whole, and of a certain magnitude." It is that which has a beginning, a middle, and an end—the end being that which succeeds all that went before as its necessary and inevitable conclusion. The end is already present in the beginning, and from the moment the action starts the author who accepts Aristotle's principle will introduce no event, situation or piece of dialogue that is not there as an element essential to the dominant motive, playing its part in the process which leads to the tragic ending. Nothing will be thrown in irrelevantly. All must be shown, as in perspective, so that the mind can grasp the whole and see it as one.

Aristotle explains the meaning of "poetic Unity" through an example. It is not enough that the tragic or epic poet, or the novelist, should confine himself to the life of a single hero. Homer's *Odyssey* is not a casual collection of incidents in the life of Odysseus. It turns upon a single action in which Odysseus is the leading figure—the motive is that of the fated wanderings of Odysseus, his home-coming and revenge. It is not *anything* about Odysseus which makes an *Odyssey*. In like manner we may say that it is not *anything* about Tom Jones which makes a novel. It is not anything about a boy at school, or an adolescent at Oxford, or a young adult seeking adventures over Europe which will turn the realism of a Mr Compton Mackenzie into a work of art. The unity of the heroine in Miss Dorothy Richardson's subjective analyses of an egotistic spinster does not give the unity of action which art demands. On the other hand, even if we should have a novel as long as *Jean Christophe* or *A la Recherche du Temps Perdu*, we should not deny it unity if those hundreds of thousands of words could group themselves in the mind's eye, and unfold the author's conception of an individual reacting to certain social forces of his time. I do not say that Rolland or even Proust succeeded in this difficult task. But the task was not an impossible one.

Mere realism, when it is just the presentation of the accidents of life—the things that happen to have happened—does not meet Aristotle's demand. The poet is concerned with truth—but not the truth of the annalist, the historian, or the photographically realistic novelist. I have stressed in an earlier chapter the distinction between didactic literature—which informs or instructs—and literature which depends upon æsthetic perception. The one expounds; the other reveals. For Aristotle this distinction is implicit in all that he writes about the art of poetry. It becomes explicit when he says that the poet's business is not to write of events that have happened, but of what may happen, of things that are possible in the light of probability or necessity. For this reason poetry is a "more philosophical," a "more serious" thing than history. For whilst history deals with the particular only—this event, or that event—poetry deals with the universal.

Here, then, we have Aristotle's reply to Plato. Art is not a slavish imitation of reality, twice removed from the truth. Presenting as it must do individual men or women in the trappings and circumstance of life, it does not leave them there, but pierces to what is significant in action and character, expressing through their words and actions what is true for all human nature—the poet's truth, the universal. If, then, the poet, as we have seen, must necessarily give us something less than reality—he cannot in his verses give us the physical warmth of flesh and blood—he gives us in compensation something more, evoking so much of spirit and heightened feeling as life itself can only yield to the choicest minds in their happier moments.

So the mere "human document" of which we hear so often, the presentation of "slices out of life," accurate pathological records of happenings in the lives of sons and lovers, or young men artists, or "creatures that once were men," would none of them have satisfied Aristotle. The matter presented in such works may be of great interest to science, in so far as it is recorded fact. Such things may have interest, too, for curious, exploring minds. But however informative, interesting, or even thrilling they may be, the author of the *Poetics* would conclude that they have nothing to do with poetry, that they do not touch the province of fine art. For the artist, concerned with poetic truth, it is of no great importance that a thing actually did happen. The point for him is, Ought it to have happened? Is its happening in this way an accident among the episodes of life, or is it representative of life, and expressive of what the artist feels to be true? The suggestion that every man or woman has in his own life the material for a novel, would have had no interest for Aristotle. Surely he would say that for an artist it is not enough to have lived. The chapter of accidents which make a life is not a theme. The whole life of Odysseus is not an *Odyssey*. In such a case the part is greater than the whole, and the artist will select according to the principles of poetic unity and poetic truth. He will seek to draw out what is relevant and representative, and to present it harmoniously, in a self-contained situation. The truth with which he deals is not that which the anatomist may lay bare on his dissecting-table, but that which a poet divines and translates.

The capacity to discern what is of universal interest is presupposed in the poet. But it is his job not only to see truth poetically, but to communicate it to an audience. He must therefore study the means of communicating it. He works in a world of illusion which he must not destroy, and he will be at pains to handle his delicate material so that he may not shock us into incredulity. There are some things, Aristotle points out, which can be done in the narrative form but could not be done before our eyes on the stage. It is for this reason, he says, that Epic enjoys one advantage not possessed by Tragedy; it affords wider scope not merely for the *marvellous*, but even the *irrational*. Hector pursued by Achilles round the walls of Troy whilst the Greeks stand still and look on, would be ludicrous if realistically presented on the stage. But the absurdity is not noticed in Homer, who, says Aristotle—a little disrespectfully to Plato—has taught other poets how to tell artistic lies. A thing is true for the poet if it is true for the *milieu* in which his characters are placed. Even a fairy tale has truths and falsities of its own. There are things which it would have been impossible for Alice in Wonderland to have seen and heard. Mole and Rat in *The Wind in the Willows* have no adventures but those which are possible for them in the world in which they move and have their being.

And so the plot of an Epic Poem may rest upon events some of which may be superhuman and irrational. Odysseus can be miraculously transported across the sea and left upon the shore of Ithaca. But he must not be represented as committing actions inconsistent with his character—that would be a poetic falsity. This is what Aristotle means when he says that the poet will prefer *probable impossibilities* to *improbable possibilities*. The error he will study most to avoid will be that which strikes at the root of his art. To be ignorant that a hind has no horns is a lesser error than to paint it badly.

IV

It is not within the scope of this inquiry to enter into a discussion of the meaning of *Katharsis*—"Through pity and fear tragedy effects the purgation of these emotions." In turning for a moment to this pathological question of the manner in which Tragedy affects the emotional organism of the spectator, Aristotle intends to destroy in a sentence Plato's argument that poetry, appealing not to the reason, but to the emotions, excites, feeds and strengthens the most worthless part of the soul. Whether *Katharsis* means the purging away of the emotions (which I think improbable) or purifying them by purging away the dross, providing an outlet for emotions which are a part of man's nature, which, though they might wreck him if called forth in the experience of actual life, may pass through him with a harmless shudder in the experience of poetry—these interesting questions I leave to those concerned with the pathology of art. Enough, for the moment, that the author of the *Poetics* lays it down that tragedy at all times makes its appeal through the emotions—through pity and fear—that it can succeed only when it arouses the pity and fear proper to it.

It is the spectacle of life, of men in action, which calls them forth—men acting, thinking, expressing their personality in a natural way under tragic circumstances. Not all circumstances, and not all men—according to Aristotle and the Greek tragedians—will serve the purpose of the poet. For tragedy, with them, is not just the spectacle of pain, it is not " horror on horror's head." It will not be tragedy, as they mean it, if it just shocks us, as when we have the brutal spectacle of a virtuous man brought through no fault of his own from prosperity to adversity. They would have shrunk from the grim story of *Jude the Obscure*, in which blameless men and women, sinned against by a cruel " Universe," are tortured for no reason.

And again, says Aristotle, there is obviously no tragic quality in the situation of a bad man who passes from adversity to prosperity. There is nothing in such a case to call forth terror or to excite our sympathy. Nor will tragedy exhibit the downfall of the very wicked, for we cannot sympathize with a mere villain or be aghast at his punishment. I doubt if any example of this case can be adduced to show Aristotle wrong. Shylock in *The Merchant of Venice* calls forth our pity precisely in proportion as we recognize a certain nobility in his character. Satan has often been described not as the villain, but as the hero of *Paradise Lost*. A good example of the utter villain meeting with the appropriate end is provided in Fielding's *Jonathan Wild*; but this is satire; we are not required to shed tears on the hero's sufferings, and we had no pang of regret when he was "hanged by the neck till he was dead."

The conditions of tragedy are only satisfied, says Aristotle, when the hero is one who is not surpassingly just and good, and when he comes to disaster, not because of vice or depravity, but through some fault of his own (ἁμαρτία)—some error or frailty. But though not pre-eminent in virtue, the character should be good, Aristotle tells us in a later chapter; and he accepts the practice of the Greek tragedians when he says that the hero should be one who is highly renowned and prosperous.

The fault which brings a man to disaster must be his own. The possibilities of tragedy lie within human nature itself. The man who pursues his course with undeviating rightness may suffer affliction; but, precisely because it is not he who has failed, there will be no element of tragedy, which lies in the storm and stress set up between character and circumstances too strong for it. There is no tragedy in the life and death of Christ, for he never erred and never failed; but there may be tragedy in the situation of Peter, who heard the cock crow when he had denied his Master thrice.

There are some who have carried the argument further

and maintained that tragedy lies wholly in character; that there is a type of character which makes its own disaster inevitably—a distinctive "tragic type." This view has been stated in its most extreme and uncompromising form in Mr Albert Beaumont's ingenious work, *The Hero*. Mr Beaumont suggests that "there is a definite element, which, if present in any character, will react to circumstances to produce that behaviour which we know as tragic, and that character without this element will never express itself in tragic behaviour under any circumstances." Influenced too much, perhaps, by the examples of Hamlet and Hedda Gabler he concludes that the fault (ἁμαρτία) lies in a sort of self-mistrust due to real "inferiority," mingled with a sort of arrogance by which the hero seeks to assure himself of "superiority." Hamlet suffers from a sense of "insecurity"; he has a feeling of being "inferior and effeminate," from which he tries to escape; he becomes self-assertive and arrogant in order to "prove himself a man"; yet the king, "in spite of Hamlet's detractions . . . is apperceived by Hamlet as in many respects superior, more capable, and more masculine than himself." Thus the hero is only to be distinguished from the villain by his pitiable weakness and failure, and the absence in him of obvious moral ugliness.

This interesting over-statement of a case helps us to see what Aristotle, at least, did not mean. It is true that there is always some fatal trait of weakness which gives us the sense of "the pity of it." But there is no pity, only contempt, if it is all weakness. (Tchekhov's *Ivanoff* comes perilously near to this defect.) But it is not weakness by itself that is affecting. It is the weakness of a strong character. When, or if, we assert that Hamlet is inferior to Claudius we mean that he is inferior only in respect of the practical efficiency of the commonplace man; Hamlet is infinitely his superior in intellect, imagination, humour, fineness of perception and magnanimity. There is no tragedy in the petty mistakes of a petty person, except when those mistakes may contribute to the tragic circumstance of another. It is not weakness which is tragic, but the weakness of those who should know better.

Aristotle certainly would never have subscribed to the view that there is one clearly definable " tragic type " whose existence is not only necessary to, but inevitably results in, " tragedy." Any such idea is clearly negatived by his judgment that " the plot is the first thing." A tragic situation is the essential of a " tragedy." It is true we can never have such a situation unless the persons acting within it are fit to play their tragic parts. But their mere existence is not enough. Tragedy demands, for Aristotle, a " reversal of fortune," and for us, too, at least some fateful hinge of fact and circumstance on which the action moves. This must provide the moment that calls for a decision, the crisis before which we are held in suspense, till character determines the fatal plunge and leads the hero to disaster.

Man in action—that is the subject of the Aristotelian tragedy—man in conflict with circumstances which are too strong for him—man, idealized a little, but like ourselves, in whom we can recognize our common humanity, battered and puzzled by the immeasurable forces of the Universe, and brought to disaster when he defies its strength or neglects its laws.

Chapter Seven

CENTURIES OF RHETORIC

> So, with the throttling hands of Death at strife,
> Ground he at grammar ;
> Still, thro' the rattle, parts of speech were rife.
> While he could stammer
> He settled *Hoti's* business—let it be !—
> Properly based *Oun*—
> Gave us the doctrine of the enclitic *De*,
> Dead from the waist down.

PERHAPS it may seem that I have tried to make Aristotle too wise and prescient. But it is not so much Aristotle whom I have praised, as the wisdom of the Greek poets whom he chose as his models. Their practice is based upon experience so deep-rooted in human life that it cannot fail to repeat itself from age to age ; and they revealed it in its simplest and grandest proportions.

But I must add a word of qualification. We moderns are in no danger of being mesmerized by the example of the Greeks. It is all profit to us to turn to them for refreshment ; and the student who with so sure a hand has stated the principles of their poetry is, for us, not a writer of guide-books, but a helpful native who knows the land through which we would travel. But for the ancient Greeks who came after him his influence may not have been so helpful. For as a critic Aristotle had one supreme fault. His gaze was concentrated on the past. He looked only backwards. There was no welcoming glance to the poets who might be growing up around him, to the new things that might be done. No stimulus, in his work, to the growth of fresh ideas, or the adaptation of poetic forms to ever-changing experience. He discoursed of a perfect art. But the art was dead. He explained the magnificence of men who had lived and created. But it was no part of his task to prepare the way for others as great. Rather, in so far as he did prepare a way, it was for men like himself—students, analysts, dissectors, who zealously wrought at their task of embalming the poets, treating the mummies with unguents of rhetoric and grammar.

I cannot attempt to discuss the causes of the decay of Greek art and the absence of a vital criticism in the learned Greek world which became scattered over the Mediterranean lands. The rhetoricians whose works have been handed down to us in such profusion were learned University gentlemen, scholars content, in the main, to carry on a parasitical existence. Men of culture, all the world over, no doubt picked up the jargon which they talked.

Aristotle's own book on *Rhetoric* is to a great extent concerned, like the work of the rhetoricians who succeeded him, with what I may call the grammar of style and composition. The prose with which he deals, we must remember, is still, formally, that of the spoken word. The rhetoricians of his time were professional instructors in the art of speech, and the art of the speaker was to "persuade." So Aristotle defines rhetoric as the "faculty of discerning the available means of persuasion."

But many of the problems he raises are problems of prose (whether spoken or written)—the question, for instance, of the distinction between poetry and prose, which must be dignified, but not far-fetched, employing rhythm, but not metre—the problems of style, whose first excellences are *clearness*, and the *concealment of art*—and of diction, which must be appropriate. "The rule of good taste is, that your style be lowered or raised according to your subject." "Appear not to speak in a studied manner, but naturally."

The student of the principles of criticism will not find much to detain him in Aristotle's account of the figures of speech. Still less will he find it necessary to search the pages of the *Rhetores Græci* or the Thesaurus of Roman Rhetoricians. Of course, pedantry serves its own purpose. The grammarians of Alexandria played their part in the history of learning. The Scholiasts, with their close textual criticism, are still of value to classical scholars. How can we fail to admire those schools of persistent students who could apply themselves so laboriously to the philological study of the ancients, spending lives of toil upon grammatical peculiarities, the niceties of metre, and the exact meaning of words? Under their skilled hands grammar was explored, the figures of speech were tabulated, and prosody became a science. They were doing spade-work which somebody had to do. They were giving us the grammar of composition, the A B C of a literary education.

In the centuries of ancient Greek decadence there is little that can be called criticism, and still less that belongs to the theory of criticism. There are flashes in Dionysius of Halicarnassus, a pregnant allusion to "Imagination" in Philostratus (which has been regarded as the earliest use of the term in the modern sense), and brilliant good sense in passages of Lucian. And finally, like some unexpected, unexplained phenomenon in the sky, there is Longinus, belonging to no age, to no school, to no tradition, uttering his amazing wisdom from the wilderness.

But before him there were the Latin writers. To the student of criticism they are disappointing. Most of them labour under precisely the same disadvantages as the neo-classical writers of the seventeenth century—they were overawed by their sense of the superiority of the Greeks, and by centuries of authoritative pedantry. Cicero's influence in this matter must have been wholly bad. His taste in literature, correct to a fault, is that of the first-class scholar who takes to politics, and decorates his learned leisure with the arts. He was intellectually solid as well as agile. He was fastidious. He was always conventional. He played for safety in matters of taste, as in politics. Thus in the elegant Latin prose of the *De Oratore* he gives little more than a transcript of the views of Aristotle and the rhetoricians.

With Horace it is different. He is by nature a Conservative. His essential preference, like that of all born Classicists, is for the thing that has stood the test—the branded wine that is mellowed, choice companionship, the poetry that has been with us in youth and in solitude. What therefore can he do but praise the models and the methods of greatest Greece? Follow the Greeks, he says, as so many were to say after him. "Let the Greek models be never out of your hands." Keep to the metres that have been established as proper to each form of poetry. Observe proportion and order. Adhere to the type. Be consistent. Of good writing the *fons et origo* is right thinking. And he gives us the maxim that was to be a proverb of criticism throughout the ages—the aim of poetry is "to instruct, or to delight," or both. A little here from Aristophanes and Plato, a little from Aristotle.

"To instruct and to delight." We shall not forget the maxim. For many whose joy is in literature—and perhaps in vellum bindings, in rare editions, and in old Falernian—that is enough. We shall ask no more, it may be, from the delectable verses of Horace himself. They will serve to pass away the hours without weariness, and with the most exquisite, delicate sense of well-being and refinement. But Virgil? He too may instruct and delight, but to account for our feeling for him we must go further —we must go as far as Longinus.

Of all the Roman critics Quintilian is the most competent, the most urbane, and the most catholic. He, too, concentrates his attention on form, and has little to say about matter. He tells us what the critic should look for in a prose composition. He will consider its arrangement, its clearness, its conciseness, its design, and the extent to which artifice is concealed. (Always *ars est celare artem.*) He will study also its persuasiveness—the force of the argument, the excitement aroused, the humour—the devices, in fact, which are used in appealing to heart and head. (The model considered seems always to be an advocate appealing to the judges.) He will give special care, of course, to style and diction, where the variation of rhythm and the study of the sound of words—to which the Latin ear is so attentive—will count for much.

There are three points I would be disposed to note in this all too brief consideration of an important writer:

(1) He standardized the vocabulary of formal criticism. He sharpened the instruments with which the student of composition should be equipped.

(2) He insisted that the writing of prose is an art. There were those in his time, as in ours, who urged that good writing should be natural and unstudied—that it should be what Wordsworth called "spontaneous utterance." Quintilian pointed out that that is best, even in nature, which is done in the best way possible—even a river flows with most force when it is unimpeded by superfluous rocks. Nothing will ever be at its best except

when the best is brought out of it by art. Vigour is not impaired by beauty. Beauty is the companion of art. Indeed, when the excellence of style is lost by the alteration of words, it will often be found that the qualities for which a work was admired have disappeared. But there he leaves the argument. He does not discuss, except indirectly, the essential question of the relation of language to thought—language as *expression*.

(3) Quintilian had an advantage of which he availed himself. The result is an interesting example of comparative criticism. He was far enough away from the golden age of Latin literature to see it in perspective, and he saw it as a literature different in kind from that which the Greeks had produced. Aristotle had before him none but the Greek models. The Romans in the time of Virgil and Horace were still spellbound by the tradition of Greek pre-eminence, and hoped for no more from Latin literature than that it should imitate and repeat the successes of the ancients, in the ancient manner. Quintilian recognized that, in fact, they had done something more. Working in a different language, they had achieved excellence of a different kind. He compares Greek literature with Roman, the Greek language with the Latin. He recognized that the Latin was a less gracious, a less subtle instrument than the Greek. Therefore, to attain results as great, it must be used differently; it must make up by strength, variety, and metaphor what it lacked in lightness and grace.

Chapter Eight

THE FIRST ROMANTIC CRITIC

HISTORY has been brightened by the belief that the Longinus who wrote the treatise *On the Sublime* (Περὶ Ὕψους) was none other than the Longinus who gave faithful service to Queen Zenobia. The treatise becomes more appreciable if we know its author as the hero of Palmyra, just as Palmyra gains in splendour if we know that the author of the treatise helped to direct its planning. It has seemed one of the lucky happenings in history that the greatest creative writer of the third century A.D. should have had the rare opportunity of turning an oasis in the desert into an Imperial city, whose Greek palaces and temples vied with the greatest in the world; and that it should have fallen to him, an Athenian don, to direct the affairs of a Queen who was as gifted as she was reputed beautiful, and mingled learning with splendour and clemency with statecraft. What a happy chance for a man of letters to guide and inspire a ruling monarch and play the part of artist (if not philosopher) king! And fitting, too—for those who may think this romance was made for a tragic ending—that Zenobia, who had played her spirited part so well, should, at the last, like Joan of Arc, lose courage when threatened by her captors. But Zenobia, unlike Joan, had, in the accredited author of our treatise, a servant willing to be a victim in her place. "Without uttering a complaint," says Gibbon, "he calmly followed the executioner, pitying his unhappy mistress, and bestowing comfort on his afflicted friends."

And then, spoiling the story, come along those scholars

who have denied that Longinus was Longinus at all—or rather, granting, of course, that the hero of Palmyra was the Longinus who lectured at Athens in the third century, who had Plotinus for a contemporary, and Porphyry for a pupil, they will not admit that this was the man who wrote the treatise *On the Sublime*. The allusions to Cæcilius, they say, coupled with the fact that the author quotes no book later than the Augustan period, clearly indicate that Longinus the writer belonged to the early part of the first century.

We might oppose the argument in the spirit of those who advance it, showing that there are a dozen ingenious ways in which Cæcilius could be accounted for; that the allusion to Moses, the "legislator of the Jews," would have been far more remarkable in a writer of the first century than in a writer of the third; and if it is strange that he should have quoted no late authors, it would be no less strange, had he written early, that he should not himself have been quoted—even by Quintilian. Indeed, had he preceded Quintilian, it would have been he, and not the Latin writer, who would have deserved the credit of a pioneer in comparative criticism. Did he not contrast the Roman style of Cicero with the Greek style of Demosthenes?

But here, we think, is a case where we may follow the example of those "godlike ones" who, according to Longinus, were scornful of laboured scholarship (τῆς δὲν ἅπασιν ἀκριβείας ὑπερφρονήσαντες). For we have only to read the treatise sympathetically to be convinced that it was the work of no first-century writer. Surely it is by one who was deeply steeped in the spirit of Plato as revived and interpreted by the Neo-Platonists, a student who, whilst not, perhaps, specially attracted to the logical or ethical side of Plato's work, was moved by his winning style and his emotional approach to literature (not the less so, because intellectual duty made the philosopher condemn it), and who used for his own purpose the Platonic account of the enchantments with which poetry can ravish and lift us out of ourselves. At last, after six centuries of rhetoric, we come to a professed rhetorician who turned again to the passion, the ecstasy, the transport which Plato failed to banish from his writing, but which the Aristotelians could so easily extinguish with syllogisms. Longinus may have paid the conventional tribute to the Aristotelian method handed on by the Professors, but upon it—and this was his special contribution—he superimposed the imagination and insight of Plato.

The essential character of the essay *On the Sublime*, its style, its argument, its implied philosophy, serve to identify its author with the Longinus who in late life became Zenobia's Greek Secretary. The latter was a contemporary of Plotinus (the founder of Neo-Platonism) and probably about eight years younger than him. He lived at the time when Plotinus was bringing Plato back into vogue, popularizing his work in the learned and even the fashionable world, and building on to it a mystical philosophy of his own. We have a direct link between the two men in Porphyry, the second famous expounder of Neo-Platonism, who, after studying under Longinus at Athens, went on to become the pupil of Plotinus at Rome. It is not too much to assume that Longinus introduced this promising student to an old friend whose teachings he admired and whose principles, in the main, he accepted. He, as professor of literature and critic, would not be concerned, like Plotinus, to expound metaphysical theories ; but those theories, if he held them, might be expected to colour his general views about life and literature. And in fact we often find him dropping into sentences and whole passages to which we can find close parallels in Plotinus—though for richness and robustness of phrase Longinus has the best of it. Thus we read in Plotinus' essay *On the Beautiful*:

> The soul, ranking as she does with what is nobler in the order of realities, must needs by her very nature thrill with joy if she see something even remotely akin to her own spirit, and will draw it to her, becoming aware alike of herself and of that which is her own.

And in Longinus we read :

> It was no mean or low-born creature which Nature chose when she brought man into the mighty assemblage of life and all the order of the Universe, and ordained us to be spectators of the cosmic show and most eager competitors ; from the first she poured into our souls a deathless longing for all that is great and diviner than ourselves.

And is there not some community of thought between the saying of Plotinus, that " the body becomes beautiful, by participating in the Reason that flows from the Divine," and Longinus' judgment, that all the greatest writers are " above what is mortal . . . Sublimity lifts them near the great-mindedness of God " ?

In the critic of literature we shall not look for the speculative mysticism, the remote other-worldliness of Plotinus—in the treatise *On the Sublime* it was not his job, perhaps not his inclination, to talk metaphysics. Nevertheless, Longinus reveals an intellectual kinship with the Neo-Platonist which is more than accident. The same impulse, having its root in the same study of Plato, led the one, a philosopher, to the construction of a mystical system, and the other, a literary critic, to a new and startling statement of the functions of literature.

We must remember that Longinus (he of the third century) was a "rhetorician." He had studied grammar, and composition, and analytical criticism, with due attention to the rules of art and the proper use of words, metre and figures of speech. We do not know just in what way he may have specialized as year after year he gave of his knowledge to his pupils. It may have been his duty to expound the structure of a "speech" and all the devices by which the orator or prose-writer aims at "persuasion," with innumerable apt examples and quotations from an orderly store of knowledge; or to explain all the rules of a tragedy or an epic, and the methods by which the poet instructs and pleases.

For "to instruct and to delight"—that throughout the centuries had been the admitted aim of the poet. And "to persuade"—that was the object of the orator or writer of prose. To instruct, to delight, to persuade—all the efforts of all the inspired bards, of all the brilliant historians, eloquent orators, and profound philosophers of the world had been summed up in that formula of three words. After all, they covered no mean field of effort. To Homer it was not a small matter that the minstrel had from the god the gift of making men glad. Nor in the eyes of Aristophanes was it any slight on the poets that they held it their chief function "to make men better in some respect"—surely it was no paltry power to be able to make men wiser or more just. And finally, there was the gift of the rhetorician—to capture men's minds, to lead them, by harmonious language and most skilfully arranged arguments, to an opinion—in a word, to "persuade."

But Longinus was not satisfied. He knew all the "rules" so well that it may have seemed to him, when he was explaining to his pupils the figures of speech and the art of composition, that nothing remained but that they should go and apply the rules, and turn out *Iliads* or *Philippics* by the dozen. This will please. That will persuade. What could be simpler? And what more absurd? For we cannot thus account for the passion of Homer, or the "Demosthenic sublimity." [1] It is not enough. There is something in the experience of literature which the formula has not allowed for.

Longinus, so admiring a student of Plato, would doubtless recall that passage in the *Ion* which I have already quoted:

> The Muse first of all inspires men herself . . . For all good poets, epic as well as lyric, compose their beautiful poems not by art, but because they are inspired and possessed. And as the Corybantian revellers when they dance are not in their right mind, so the lyric poets are not in their right mind when they are composing their beautiful strains . . . For the poet is a light and winged and holy thing, and there is no invention in him until he has been inspired and is out of his senses, and the mind is no longer in him; when he has not attained to this state, he is powerless and is unable to utter his oracles.

What if Plato, who was so wrong in condemning poetry, was after all more right than he knew in thus accounting for its strange power? Perhaps the old popular theory of inspiration had more in it than a rhetorician cared to admit, that theory of "possession" which lifted poet and audience out of themselves, and produced the condition of

[1] *De Sublimitate*, 12, 5.

ecstasy or transport. The Delphic rapture, the divine madness, the very breath of the god breathed into his votaries[1]—may not this provide the clue to an experience which is not pleasure, nor knowledge, nor opinion, and yet is present in all literature at its highest moments? This passion, intensity, exaltation, transport was surely a fundamental condition which the formula had utterly failed to include.

Longinus was not concerned to probe the source of this power. Not for him the "Metaphysic depths" in which Coleridge regretted he had squandered his genius. That field of inquiry he might well leave to such an one as Plotinus. It was not for him to explain the divine cause of inspiration. Sufficient for him, as a critic, that he should recognize it when he found it. Sufficient for him to lay down his thesis that loftiness or sublimity in literature has as its end, not persuasion, but ecstasy—transport—"lifting out of oneself": οὐ γὰρ εἰς πειθὼ ἀλλ' εἰς ἔκστασιν ἄγει.

> The Sublime consists in a certain loftiness and consummateness of language, and it is by this and this only that the greatest poets and prose-writers have won pre-eminence and lasting fame.

And he goes on:

> For a work of genius does not aim at persuasion, but ecstasy—or lifting the reader out of himself. The wonder of it, wherever and whenever it appears, startles us; it prevails where the persuasive or agreeable may fail; for persuasion depends mainly on ourselves, but there is no fighting against the sovereignty of genius. It imposes its irresistible will upon us all.
>
> Where there is only skill in invention and laborious arrangement of matter a whole treatise, let alone a sentence

[1] *De Sublimitate*, 8, 4.

or two, will scarcely avail to throw light on a subject. But the Sublime at the critical moment shoots forth and tears the whole thing to pieces like a thunderbolt, and in a flash reveals all the author's power.[1]

Here then we have the first perfectly definite statement of a doctrine which Joubert could not make more precise when he said : "Nothing is poetry unless it transports" ; which Sir Thomas Browne was to translate into the language of sentiment when he exclaimed, "I love to lose myself in a mystery, to pursue my reason to an *O Altitudo!*" and which De Quincey was to nail down in his distinction between the literature of *knowledge* and the literature of *power*—"The function of the first is—to *teach*; the function of the second is—to *move*." The sublime effect of literature, for Longinus, is attained, not by argument, but by revelation, or illumination. Its appeal is not through the reason, but what we should call imagination (though there is no word in his Greek which will bear this translation.)[2] Its effect upon the mind is immediate, like a flash of lightning upon the eye.

But Longinus had not spent his life as a rhetorician for nothing. He knew that it will not do to make art too easy. He knew the saying of his master, "hard is the beautiful" (χαλεπὸν γὰρ τὸ καλόν).

Little patience as he had with academic poets or pedantic critics, he was not one to discount the efforts of the past or its living value for the present. Though he was the first to expound the doctrines upon which romanticism rests, he turned, and tempered them with what is sanest in classicism. Whilst he pointed the way to the storm and fury of a romantic movement, he himself,

[1] *De Sublimitate*, 1, 3-4.

[2] *Ibid.*, 15, 1. Having used the word φαντασίαι, he says: οὕτω γοῦν εἰδωλοποιίας αὐτὰς ἔνιοι λέγουσι.

with singular critical judgment, set up the danger-posts, and reimposed the classic discipline. Though he was the first great critic to proclaim the efficacy of inspiration, he did not think that beauty comes like a wind from heaven to fill the sails of the poet's ship and drive it without effort across the sea. Just as he laid it down for the critic that "the judgment of literature is the long-delayed reward of much endeavour,"[1] so also he insisted that the poet must study to master the technique of his art. "Nature," it is true, is the first thing. Nature must "supply." But Nature cannot dispense with Art, whose function it is to "regulate."[2]

And he reminds us that faults are not the less faults because they arise from the heedlessness of genius. Though he has little respect for the meticulous accuracy of middling ability, and admires the daring of genius which aims at the summit and makes light of risks, still, he says, he has "observed not a few errors in Homer and the other greatest writers," and hastens to add that he is "not in the least pleased with such blunders."[3]

And so when Longinus comes to discuss the sources of the Sublime, he is not ashamed to name among them those that belong to the art, or artifice, of literature. Here the skilled rhetorician in our author asserts himself, and he discourses upon artifice in the use of figures of speech, and warns us against bombast, puerility or affectation, and the conceits of "frigidity"; and it is pleasing to be reminded that all the improprieties which he names can be traced to one common cause—"pursuit of novelty in thought—an orgy in which the present generation revels."[4] And he speaks, almost conventionally, about

[1] *De Sublimitate*, 6.
[2] *Ibid.*, 2.
[3] *Ibid.*, 33.
[4] *Ibid.*, 5, 2.

the choice of words, the ornaments of style, and dignity of composition.

Such are the sources of sublimity which belong to the domain of "Art" considered from the external point of view. But Longinus is far more interested in that side of it which springs from the "Nature" of the artist, the internal element which *supplies* what artifice can only regulate. Not that the two can be divorced. Just as Ben Jonson was to say that "in all speech, words and sense are as the body and soul," and De Quincey was to speak of language as an "incarnation" of the soul, so Longinus recognizes that "thought and language in literature are for the most part interfolded each in the other."[1] So, though you may separately discuss words, style, structure, which belong to the body of literature, you cannot actually part them from the thought and passion which belong to its soul. And of all the sources of sublimity Longinus puts first grandeur of thought and vigorous, spirited treatment of the passions. It is the quality of mind which determines everything. "For beautiful words are the true and peculiar light of the mind,"[2] and in saying this he anticipates another imaginative critic who was also a student of Plotinus. "As light to the eye, even such is beauty to the mind," said Coleridge. And this "Nature" of which Longinus speaks—this natural creative force which manifests itself in the mind of man, distinguished from the regulative function of art—does it not call to mind that *natura naturans* of which Coleridge speaks when he says:

> Believe me, you must master the essence, the *natura naturans*, which presupposes a bond between nature in the higher sense and the soul of man.

[1] *De Sublimitate*, 30, 1.

[2] *Ibid.*, 30, 1.

There, in Coleridge, we can see the acknowledged influence of Plotinus. Have we not already detected it in certain words of Longinus, which I here insert in their context?

> What then did they see, those godlike ones who set their hands to what was greatest in literature and thought little of meticulous scholarship? Besides much else, this: that it was no mean or low-born creature which Nature chose when she brought man into the mighty assemblage of life and all the order of the Universe, and ordained us to be spectators of the cosmic show and most eager competitors; from the first she poured into our souls a deathless longing for all that is great and diviner than ourselves.
>
> And so, when in thought and contemplation we range over the field of human endeavour, the whole world is not enough, but often our thoughts transcend the borders that hem us in; and any man who will look at life in all its wide orbit, and consider how in all things it abounds exceedingly in what is great and beautiful, will know straightway to what end we were born.
>
> And then naturally we are drawn on to admire, not surely the petty rivulets, however clear and pure they may be, but the Nile, and the Danube, and the Rhine, and most of all the Ocean. Nor are we more amazed at the flame that burns within ourselves, though its light is sure and radiant, than at the heavenly fires, often as they are obscured; nor do we think it more worthy of wonder than the craters of Etna, which gushes forth and brings up rocks and mighty crags from its depths, and sometimes vomits rivers of elemental fire from the bowels of the earth.[1]

Longinus is not often willing to stray into "metaphysic depths." He prefers to speak of the emotions which great literature stirs, the passion it calls forth, the transport or ecstasy to which it leads. "I would confidently lay it down that there is nothing so stirring as noble, inevitable passion, its rapture induced by a kind of madness or divine influence, and flowing forth in

[1] *De Sublimitate*, 35, 2-4.

phrases that are inspired."[1] The *Iliad*, he thinks, owes its supremacy to its action, its dramatic intensity, its speed, its realistic imagery, its heaping of passion on passion's head, whereas the *Odyssey* betrays the old age of Homer by its decline of passion—the poet falls back upon realistic portraiture of life and manners.

And he contrasts the style of Cicero with that of Demosthenes. The voluminous style of the former, saturated with commonplaces, is suitable to scientific disquisitions. But Demosthenes, "in his ability to kindle and rend with his force, his swiftness, his strength, his intensity, may be likened to a flash of lightning . . . The climax of the Demosthenic sublimity is reached in moments of intensity and extreme passion when the reader is completely carried away."[2]

This, then, for Longinus, is the mark of sublimity in literature—literature when it reaches the peak in the domain of creative art—it can transport and lift us out of ourselves by a power which confounds the judgment, eclipses mere reason, and illumines a subject with the vividness of lightning.

Thus assured, Longinus is willing to face the problem which, sooner or later, critical theory was bound to grapple with. What is the criterion of excellence in literature? What is the distinguishing quality and character of great literature, and how shall we know it? Or is there no absolute criterion? Is there no wrong and right? Are there as many excellences as there are tastes?

The question was not complicated for Longinus by the existence of a "popular taste." In his day there was no vast uneducated reading public which had learnt to

[1] *De Sublimitate*, 8, 4.
[2] *Ibid.*, 12, 4-5.

read novels and newspapers before it had learnt the meaning of words or the rudimentary structure of ideas. The thrill of a murder case reported in the papers, the excitement of a detective story, the rapture of a tale of amorous passion which can stir the emotions of every typist in the City—Longinus had not thought of this. εἰς ἔκστασιν ἄγει. How easy to-day to reduce his argument to absurdity. Is it the ecstasy of the true sublime which transforms the face of the anæmic waitress, when some foolish story of love rewarded transports her to the seventh heaven of bliss?

Does that absurd story that thrilled her belong to Fine Art? Is it sublime literature? Does it not lift the little waitress out of herself? Well, the problem does not arise for Longinus, quite like this. He assumes a reading public which has read much, and has read also with effort. More than that, he limits the right to judge to those who have submitted themselves to the discipline of literature—"the judgment of literature is the long-delayed reward of much endeavour."

He presupposes, then, men wise and well versed in the literature of the world, who have not shrunk from taking pains in mastering and understanding it. It is only for such readers that the power of literature to *move* becomes a test of its high quality; and it must be able to exercise this power not only once, in some happy mood of the reader, but again and again. A passage is only really great

> . . . when it makes the utmost demand on the attention, when it forces itself upon us importunately, irresistibly, when it takes so strong a hold on the memory that it cannot be forgotten.[1]

[1] *De Sublimitate*, 7, 3.

Such is the test which the individual reader may apply for himself. But he is willing also to accept the consensus of opinion, not of any one period, but of all periods.

> In general we may consider that passages which always please, and please all readers, contain the beauty and truth of the sublime.[1]

Thought and passion—these are demanded by Longinus in the same spirit in which Matthew Arnold demanded "truth and seriousness." And just as Arnold demands that we should learn "the best that is known and thought in the world," and suggests that we should always have in our minds lines and expressions of the great masters to apply as a touchstone to other poetry, so Longinus refers us to Homer, to Plato, to Demosthenes, to Thucydides. How would they have said it? How would they have given it exaltation? Better still, how would Homer or Demosthenes be affected if we were actually able to take our work and submit it to their judgment? If that is not enough, if we are forward-looking, and plume ourselves on being a little ahead of our time, like the twentieth-century artists who respect nothing but what has yet to be done, suppose—says Longinus, almost as if he had these modernists and futurists in his mind—suppose we add, "How will my writing strike the ages yet to come?"

Not sure and infallible tests, perhaps, but hard ones—tests which at the least should free us from the minor tyranny of the cliché or the major tyranny of the fashionable fad, which at the best should bring us into a spiritual camaraderie with great minds and make the meaner competitions impossible. We cannot at one and the

[1] *De Sublimitate*, 7, 4.

same time write to satisfy a Middle-Western American market, and ask for the approbation of him who brought Priam to the tent of Achilles. We cannot even seek novelty by the use of pungent Joycean slang if we would impress a generation for whom that slang may be meaningless. Some of these brilliant ones of to-day, for whom Homer is a matter of academic culture, who know not Longinus—or rank him with Ruskin—who stride magnificently ahead, by a year or two, of the mediocrities of their time, had their counterparts, no doubt, in the age of Longinus. Those clever contemporaries of his have been forgotten. And if it be said that Longinus himself has not been too well remembered, at least his light burns not less brilliantly for all the centuries that have passed, and it may burn more brilliantly still in the future.

For him, classicism was touched with romance, but not darkened. His romanticism was sane and bright by dint of contact with the classic order. Mysticism was arriving to obscure the ways of life and literature. But mysticism as he translated it was a lamp which could be kept trim and bright in the temple of Athene. He could still teach the decorous rhetoric of the Greeks in the lecturer-ooms of Athens, yet escape from its cramping formalism in the same spirit of adventure as that which led him afterwards to serve Queen Zenobia in the desert. And in the desert—surely under his guiding hand—the old Attic spirit again took material form, and became manifest in the brilliant city of Palmyra.

Chapter Nine

THE DARK AGES

THE gulf which separates ancient literature from modern may be bridged. But its depths have never been satisfactorily explored. The stream of pure literature can be easily followed as it emerges clear and fresh in ancient Greece. Its course can be traced through the earlier centuries of Imperial Roman rule. But then, gradually, it buries itself in the gorge of early Christian and mediæval Europe, coming to view from time to time in fragments of Saxon or French literature, in troubadour and Provençal poetry, in the mystic writings of saints, in remnants of ballad poetry, and prose and verse romance. At last, after devious, hidden wanderings, it comes into the open again at the Renaissance.

The student of pure literature cannot agree with the historian or the historical novelist who may refuse to regard the Middle Ages as the Dark Ages. For the novelist or descriptive historian there is no lack of matter to fill and vary the picture—the service and the pageantry of feudalism, the parallel march of Church and State, the evolution of law, the learned life of the universities, the ambition and devoted sacrifice of the religious orders, the growth of towns, the proud activity of burghers, the splendour of Gothic architecture, and the traditional self-expression of the folk in dance, ballad, tale, or mummery.

There is no lack of life in those centuries which lie between the age of Longinus and the age of the classical Renaissance ; no lack of romance. But the only romance for which literate expression was always possible was that of the religious mystic, which has been called the " romance of religion." Already, when Plotinus was founding his system, the new spirit of an age already impregnated with the Christian doctrine of self-sacrifice was beginning to assert itself. Greek art had always been vividly alive to the affairs of this world. For the Greek critic, form and matter might be distinguished; but they were inseparably one and indivisible in a poem, a picture, a statue. What Walter Pater, I think, has called the "this-worldliness" of Greek art gave it a unique quality—it was a crystal-clear reflection of the world the Greeks lived in—a world in which gods were always like men and men might be like gods—in which natural objects were divine when they were most like nature. There was little mist in the Attic air, till Plato, condemning the "this-worldliness" of the art he knew, opened the way for the invading clouds of the East.

For six centuries these had been accumulating in the Pagan air when Plotinus evolved his mystic system, and handed on to the Christians a metaphysical justification of "other-worldliness." The doctrine of renunciation in its most relentless form was to dominate Christendom for more than a thousand years. For more than a thousand years the irresistible organization of the Christian Church drew into its service most of the intellect, culture, and trained mind-power of Catholic Europe; its all-absorbing authority imposed its discipline upon its members and restricted their devotion to the world-renouncing ideals of the Church.

It is true, there were always worldly priests; but it was not so much the practice as the doctrine of other-worldliness which the Church insisted upon. A priest might make merry on All Fools' Day, but to burn a candle with Roger Bacon on the altar of pure science was an unpardonable sin. A ribald joke might be carved on the walls of a cathedral, but to acknowledge a taste for profane poetry was to admit intercourse with the devil. Early in the sixth century Boëthius defined the position which afterwards had the full support of the Fathers of the Church; he denounced the Muses of poetry as "wantons of the theatre," enemies of wisdom, and destroyers of reason.

Whatever we may say about the development of Christendom, as organized under the Christian Church from about the fifth century to the fifteenth, the fact cannot be denied that it tended to stifle the free, conscious development of the secular arts, and impeded the progress of any continuous stream of literary activity. Here and there its influence was successfully defied or modified, as in the Provençal literature of Southern France and the neighbouring parts of Spain and Italy; and there were many important signs of a more general break-away during the two centuries before the orthodox date allotted to the Renaissance—in the south first, in the north later. But in the main, in Central and Western Europe, it is true to say that secular expression of the art impulses was driven underground during most of the years of the supremacy of the Catholic Church in Central and Western Europe. The literary art, as a pleasurable activity pursued for its own sake, as a part of intellectual culture dissociated from religion, came under its ban.

I say "as a part of intellectual culture"—an important qualification. I do not for a moment suggest that the creative impulses which are an inextinguishable part of human life were stifled, even in the most ascetic period of ecclesiastical influence. Even in its strongest days the Church could not absolutely enforce its discipline except in the ranks of its own clergy, and it could not always do that. But from the earliest time it strenuously opposed the excesses of the Roman *spectacula*, and gradually extended its ban to all that savoured of the theatre—its dances, its pantomime, its play, its songs. St Jerome condemned the reading of comedies by priests. The pronouncements of the Fathers and Councils of the Church against players, jugglers and jesters were held, in a later age, to apply also to minstrels—it was a sin for a clerk to listen to their songs. The censorial attitude of the Church in the twelfth century is well shown in *Aucassin and Nicolete*, when Aucassin, bidden to choose between his mistress and heaven, declares he will go to hell. "Thither go the gold and the silver, and the vair and the grey, and thither too go harpers and minstrels and the kings of the world. With these will I go, so that I have Nicolete, my most sweet friend, with me."

Not all the anathemas of the Church could banish from the mediæval world the song, the dance, the ballad, the popular romantic tale told in prose or verse. The art impulses are universal, not to be denied; but their expression was restricted or discouraged in the broad daylight of current ideas. It was only in so far as the arts directly ministered to religious ceremonial or orthodox religious teaching that they received the blessing of the Church. And the Church, we must remember, had a monopoly of learning. Almost all educated persons were priests; most professional appointments were held by men in Holy Orders; the clergy, being those who preached sermons, wrote books, delivered lectures, taught the young, and instructed lawgivers, comprised within their ranks most of that educated class which, in the main, always controls opinion. Within this trained, self-conscious, intellectual society the free practice of literature and the arts was hindered for a thousand years. Outside, the world might make merry with its harpers and its minstrels, singing its songs, footing its dances, listening with rapture to the teller of tales at the cross-roads ; and even the lesser clergy, defying rules and discipline, might join in the forbidden merriment, or furtively introduce it into sacred precincts. But, in the main, the freedom by which literature thrives was denied to just those who were equipped to carry on its traditions.

What secular literature lacked in the Middle Ages was an informed criticism. What all literature lacked was a free criticism. In learned circles there was no dearth of theological and quasi-philosophical writing ; there was an abundance of devotional writing ; and to the mystics at least the way lay open. But the use of Latin, which was the language of scholars, was a severe handicap to literary expression, and the obligation of religious and doctrinal orthodoxy was a fatal impediment alike to sincerity in authorship and freedom in criticism.

But beyond the circle of the educated, outside, where men were free, if they would, to go to hell with Nicolete—where men wrote and recited in the vernacular, and sang their songs in what dialect or rhythm they chose—all was go-as-you-please, without law, without standard—unreferred to world literature and the art-forms which belong to it. There cannot have been any effective criticism—either the artist's self-criticism, fortified by awareness of the stored art of the world, or the criticism of informed opinion, which accepts and rejects in the light of wide experience. Nature, instinct, intuition, innate fineness of perception and of taste—the faculties without which there can be no appreciation, no æsthetic delight, no valuable criticism—these, no doubt, had full play, as they always have ; these, no doubt, lent their sweetness to folk-poetry and sharpened the edge of the thrill with which it was heard.

But they were not enough for the production of a literature which could hand itself on in a continuous stream. They were divorced from the organized world of coherent thought—there was no contact between the spasmodic thought-products of the popular poet and the trained judgment, the exact knowledge, the intellectual *savoir-faire* of the men who ruled the mediæval world and were able to hand on their scholastic writings as the expression of the age in which they lived.

For secular literature there was no informed opinion, no effective criticism, and therefore no continuous progress in literary art. The building of castles was a part of the world art of self-defence, and so we have the magnificent piles of Norman architecture. The building of churches was an art to which authority lent countenance ; the highest knowledge and technical accomplishment were at its service ; and the result still remains in the monuments of Gothic architecture. But for secular literature there was no recognition, no studied technique, no body of trained opinion, none of that free interchange of ideas which enables each worker to draw upon the whole intellectual fund of his age.

Perhaps it helps us to appreciate better the part that criticism plays in the creative efforts of literature if we note these two facts—that during the thousand years of the ascendancy of the Catholic Church, and especially in such countries and at such times as its authority was paramount, we have a period extraordinarily sterile in creative literature, and at the same time almost destitute of free literary criticism ; and that the same period, in other fields of activity, which were not deprived of criticism—in theology, law, architecture—was not correspondingly poor in achievement. The fact seems to be that there can be no great literature which is divorced from the main stream of intellectual activity; and the main stream, in those days, flowed within banks determined by the Catholic Church. All art activity that burst forth outside was shut off from fertilizing sources of knowledge and the free play of criticism.

Chapter Ten

DANTE

AS if to prove that all generalizations about the "Dark Ages" are false, we have ever before us the figure of Dante. It is not enough to say that Dante is a forerunner of the Renaissance, and that in him we have an early result of a return to the study of the ancients. For what is finest and most spiritual in thirteenth-century Catholicism has left its mark on the *Divine Comedy* and entered into its soul. We recognize in its author an example of what that strangely mingled age might produce under favourable circumstances, an age which seems to present to us so many contrasts of faith, chivalry, splendour, violence, squalor, meekness—in which the flesh and the spirit, the devil and the saint, are thrown, in grotesque juxtaposition, into relief.

Indeed, can we conceive an age richer in the material out of which a dramatist might wish to construct a play, or a novelist a novel—an age which gave scope to so many passions fiercely indulged, convictions passionately held, and subtle hypocrisies in the very precincts of holiness? Some of its social types survived—no doubt, with a difference — into the more sceptical period of Chaucer; and we have them still. But Dante alone —in the thirteenth century, and of it—has been able to express objectively its spiritual experience in the passionate language of poetry.

How was it that he alone was sufficiently near the centre of the intellectual current of his age, and yet sufficiently outside it, to carry out his task? It was part of his good fortune that he came from such a city as Florence, where learning was encouraged among the laity as well as among those who were entering the Church. Perhaps also he may have owed much to his exile, to the wanderings which took him forth into the company of all manner of men, with whom he heard the songs of the minstrels, or read, in his leisure, the poetry of Provence. Amongst them, in many provinces where many dialects of Italian and French were spoken, may he not have learned the superior force of the mother-tongue, the eloquence of men composing in the language they learned in childhood? How much more direct and persuasive than the stilted Latin which scholars so laboriously learned to write!

And yet, whoever his companions may have been in his travels, we may be sure that there was one always with him—the pagan friend, who could not indeed take him, where only Beatrice could take him, to Paradise, but was his guide through Purgatory and Hell. The study of Virgil set him thinking. Why could not men still write like that? Supposing one could find an author of the thirteenth century equally serious, equally impressionable to the spectacle of the moods of nature, the endeavours of men, the tears of things, how could he find fit expression for his thoughts either in the Latin of the schoolmen or the rough dialects of the popular poets?

Dante realized that this was no secondary question—this question of language. It was one to be decided at the outset by every poet, be he Italian, or French, or English. "What language will the poet use?" he asks in the *De Vulgari Eloquio.* For the learned there was always Latin,[1] a flawless instrument of precision for those who could master it perfectly. But even the few

[1] This is surely the meaning of the word "*grammatica*."

who have become fully familiar with it have only done so by schooling and discipline and long study. How much more freely and naturally men write when they use the vulgar tongue which they learned from their nurses! This is the language they used first, the language in which they freely and naturally express their emotions; and it is used by every kind of man. Yet in Italy, as in England and in France, there were many dialects, many vocabularies varying with each locality. How use the language of nature, and yet escape provinciality and meanness?

Dante, then, was confronted with the problem of making, or rather choosing, a language. He decided that it must be that of the vulgar tongue, the vernacular—but with a difference. It must be the language of culture, the language which would be common to men of letters who meet together from all parts; it must be suited for the headquarters of society, art and letters—an Illustrious Vernacular. This instrument of precision which the poet needed should be the mother-tongue, but that tongue purged from its provincialisms, employing words and turns of speech which are not peculiar to any one province or small State, but are common to all.

So far, the problem for Dante assumes a form which does not concern the modern Italian or the modern Englishman, who finds a fixed literary language ready to his hand. But that is only the beginning of the task he has set himself. Granted the use of an Illustrious Vernacular which all Italians can understand—and in England it is the same for Englishmen—nevertheless it still remains for each writer to shape it worthily and in the best possible manner. Dante, as a poet and critic, is intent upon shaping and defining nothing less than an ideal language fit to express the best thoughts of the greatest poet. He has started from the fact that this must be the native tongue, the language in which he freely and instinctively expresses thought and emotion. Yet he is as far as possible from the view of Wordsworth that poetry is just "the spontaneous overflow of powerful feelings," or that the poet will be content with "a selection of language really used by men." Poetry is not, for Dante, "spontaneous utterance." He holds the opposite view. "Poetry and the language proper for it are an elaborate and painful toil." When he advised the use of the Vernacular, he did not mean "the language of common life"; on the contrary, he says, "Avoid rustic language." And he proceeds to examine the kind of words he would admit into his vocabulary.

But not till he has first examined a question prior to this, upon which all else depends. Language for Dante is a powerful and a subtle instrument, without which, fitly used, there can be no worthy literature; but he does not exalt the instrument above that for which it is used. It is a means of expression, but that which has to be expressed comes first in order of thought and importance. Speech, he says, is for a poet what a horse is to a soldier. The best soldiers should have the best horses, and in like manner the best speech is that which is suited to the best thoughts, and can only be used by those "in whom wit and knowledge are found."

In the same spirit, then, in which Aristotle declared that the plot is the first thing, Dante puts first the claims of the poet's *subject*. It is no use asking for a grand style until you have recognized that it can only be employed in the service of a grand theme, as conceived by a man of great intellectual stature. Somewhat arbitrarily, perhaps, he decides that the best subjects are *salus*, *Venus*, *virtus*—but those three Latin words cover no small field—*safety* (of the State), *love*, *excellence* (moral, philosophic, and religious). The first may be compared with the French word *Securité*, and includes all that we may indicate by prowess in war, chivalry, patriotism. Perhaps we should not be far wrong if we said that these three words imply actions arising out of love of country, love of woman, and love of God.

Subject—theme—thought—that is the first element in the higher kind of literature which he calls "tragic." To characterize it he uses that excellent Latin word, a word most expressive, as some have thought, of the essential quality which appears again and again in the typical achievements of the ancient Romans—the word *gravitas*. *Gravitas sententiæ*, weight of meaning or thought—that is the first condition of a poem that is to be written in the tragic style. And to this will necessarily be added certain qualities of verse, of style, of vocabulary (*superbia carminum*, *constructionis elatio*, *excellentia vocabulorum*).

His consideration of the best metrical form is relevant only to composition in a Romance language, more especially the Italian. The best style is that which adds to the lesser excellences—those of correct composition and rhetorical embellishment—that quality of loftiness or elevation which distinguishes the illustrious masters of style. This, in turn, depends in no small measure upon excellence of vocabulary.

Thus Dante is brought back to the subject he had embarked upon—the language suited to the best writers—the Illustrious Vernacular. For the Italian, as for the Latin writers in prose and verse alike, the actual sound of words and their pitch are of inestimable importance in a beautiful line or in a sonorous rhythm. For Dante each individual word is spoken of almost as if it had a separate personality of its own, certainly a distinctive character which it may possess independently of its context. He sets about his task of collecting words as if he were choosing a company of trusty comrades, and there is not one of them which must not play its part worthily in the texture of the poem.

He requires, then, that the vocabulary of his Illustrious Vernacular should be composed of grand words only (*grandiosa*)—words that lend themselves to what Matthew Arnold, borrowing the adjective, calls "the grand manner." He does not hesitate to excommunicate whole classes of Italian words, which are described as childish, effeminate, rough, slippery (or slimy), and rumpled, and leaves only two classes of "urban" words which are fit for his Illustrious Vernacular, those that are "combed" (*pexa*) and those that are "shaggy" (*hirsuta*). The first are "trisyllabic, or very nearly so, without aspirates, without acute or circumflex accent, or double Z's and X's, without the collocation of two liquids, or the position of a liquid immediately after a mute." These are words "which leave the speaker's lips, as it were, with a certain sweetness, as *amore*, *donna*, *disio*, *virtute*, *donare*, *letizia*, *salute*, *securitate*, *difesa*." And to these may be added the "shaggy" words, the necessary monosyllables which cannot be dispensed with, or "ornamental" words which "when mixed with 'combed' words make a beautifully harmonious conjunction."

Such was the exactness with which Dante proposed to sift the vocabulary of the Italian vernacular and leave only those words which would wear like the fast colours in a tapestry. To the English ear this precise, fastidious ruling may seem, if not pedantic, then fanciful and half-playful. But it is worth considering how much we have lost, partly by the natural roughness—the "rusticity"—of our language, and partly by the failure to nurse it, to prune away the coarser elements, and to encourage the use of words whose very sound is a delight. Lacking this constituent element in beautiful language, our poets have had to make the most of other elements, accent, rhyme, alliteration, and robustness of sound, together with the associated thought-elements of imagery, metaphor, simile, and the play of ideas. We lack the rich vowel sounds and the quantitative values of the Latin and Italian. What English verse could produce the lingering regret that sighs in every syllable of that line in the *Georgics*:

> O fortunatos nimium, sua si bona norint,
> Agricolas!

or the still resignation in that line which Matthew Arnold loved to quote:

> In la sua voluntade è nostra pace.

Keats more than most English poets attempts to win his effects through the sheer sounds of words, but how often in his most admired lines there is a cloying sweetness arising from that collocation of liquids which Dante condemned!

> Charm'd magic casements, opening on the foam
> Of perilous seas, in faery lands forlorn.

Betraying his affection for the l's and r's in that last line, he must needs go on:

> Forlorn! the very word is like a bell
> To toll me back from thee to my sole self!

It is all l's and r's, and exhibits in the sound something, perhaps, of that effeminacy which Dante shunned.

But an English poet enjoys the use of many Latin words and names, and may make good play by combining the excellent shaggy words, which are English, with "combed" words, which are Latin. Thus :

> To sport with Amaryllis in the shade,
> Or with the tangles of Neaera's hair.

And there have been poets, like Rossetti—who was half Italian by birth and more than half Italian by sentiment—who have endeavoured to use the English tongue according to the genius of the Italian. Note how in this stanza from *The Blessed Damozel* most of the names are words which have a Latin origin, and even the English word "handmaidens" must be pronounced in a foreign way if we are to get the full value from the line :

> "We too," she said, "will seek the groves
>   Where the lady Mary is,
> With her five handmaidens, whose names
>   Are five sweet symphonies,
> Cicely, Gertrude, Magdalen,
>   Margaret and Rosalys."

Chapter Eleven

EMANCIPATION

WE have already seen that a distinction must be made between two essential processes of literary criticism. There is, firstly, that of the artist who, in the act of making an image or a representation of life, is thereby, consciously or unconsciously, criticizing life itself. He does not *copy* nature simply, even when his method is purely " representational." He gives us his rendering of nature, and his rendering is at one and the same time *less* than nature—for only reality itself is equal to reality, with which art cannot compete on its own terms—and *more* than nature, in that he has put into it *himself*.

I have already suggested (in Chapter Two) that art must begin as a rudimentary attempt to define or criticize reality. The first art impulse may have other elements mixed in it, but this is one of them. When this purposive element is lacking, we may see results which are beautiful, as in the accidental scrawling of a child, or the musical notes of a bird ; but these are to be regarded as beauties of nature rather than beauties of art. They lack that essential of all art, however rudimentary, however subtle and complex—namely, its characteristic as a criticism of life.

But as it develops, the artist becomes also increasingly self-conscious about his art. He comes more and more to consider his methods, to study what it is he wants to create, what effect he hopes to produce upon others, what devices he may employ to win this effect, what tools and medium will suit his purpose. The man of letters must study language, arrangement of words, rhythm, metre, rhyme, imagery and other technical problems, and this study may be infinitely complicated by all sorts of considerations about the function and purpose of literature. Thus he has become a critic in the secondary sense. Whilst essentially a judge or critic of life, or his impressions of life, he has become, in the second place, a judge or critic of expression, and all that relates to the methods or effects of expression.

So this function of criticism in the secondary and more usual sense of the term is separate from the artistic or creative criticism, in the primary sense; and it may be exercised both by artists and by those whose creative effort is restricted to the appreciation of the works of others. A body of opinion about art and its forms grows up and diffuses itself through the whole cultured community. Such opinion constantly tends to become standardized, though the standard may vary from age to age, and year to year, and man to man. A jargon is soon created; men expert in the use of the jargon become accredited critics; and a new class of literature known as criticism comes into being. But all the time the artist himself never ceases to be a critic in the second as well as the first sense of the term; a critic of life, he is also a critic of methods and technique; and he seldom fails to contribute to that general body of opinion—the intellectual currency of an age, which affords so much comfortable security when it is stable, and so much excitement when the exchange rates run violently up and down.

The critic in the second sense cannot come into being until he has before him works of art on which to exercise his judgment; and he does not come into being in an important sense until he has before him important examples of art. We might suppose that a highly creative age would be a highly critical age. And in a sense it always is and must be. The fact that far the most interesting body of critical writing about poetry has been the work of poets is enough to show that the period of most intense creative work coexists with the period of the most active critical work. But if we speak of criticism in a narrower sense, when it is engaged in collecting, formulating, classifying, explaining, then a highly "critical" period, like the late seventeenth and early eighteenth century, is one in which the stimulus to creative energy appears to be low. Matthew Arnold's view that the critic, in building up sound opinions, in spreading the best ideas about life and art, is well engaged, during periods of depression, in preparing an atmosphere from which a new epoch of creative activity will emerge, is comforting to the self-esteem of the critic. At all times, it is true, he will be busy spreading ideas. But will these always be the "best ideas"? He will always be sowing seed, some of which will fall on fertile soil. But the trouble is that he may sow bad seed; anæmic sprigs of his planting may contrive to grow in the too well-weeded ground. The critical industry of the Alexandrians in antiquity or the neo-classicists in modern Europe, divorced from the demonic energy of creation, had a numbing effect upon contemporary letters, and did not prepare an atmosphere for anything better than itself.

History, I think, shows that criticism is most potent in spreading the best ideas when it actively co-operates with the best creative effort. If it is not written by the men who are artists, it is written by men who are in close sympathy with them, who understand their impulses, who share their ideas, who have the knowledge to propagate principles impregnated by the creative spirit. The true critic is an ally of the artist. He comes into the field ready to break a lance with any opponent on his behalf. He is an enemy of the false, the pretentious, the meretricious because he is intent upon clearing the way for what he conceives to be genuine and real. He flourishes on the same soil as the artist. He manures and tills it. He prolongs the life that he cares about, and nurses its progeny.

Criticism that is not itself-based upon the originative art impulse can produce nothing, lead to nothing, prepare nothing. A mistaken conception of its character has perhaps arisen from some popular untruths about the origins of the Classical Renaissance. Some of us have been taught from childhood that the Renaissance owes its origin to the revival of the study of the ancients, and that this was brought about by the downfall of the Greek Empire at Constantinople in 1453, and the consequent flight of the Greek scholars with their books to the hospitable shores of Italy.

A picturesque conception of the Renaissance, which is true enough for mythology, and contributes to our natural pleasure in assigning dates to events which changed the world—1066, 1453, 1789, 1914. But if the critical study of the ancients could really account for the outpouring of art and letters in the fifteenth and sixteenth centuries, why had it never produced such a result among the Byzantine Greeks, who had been living for centuries in the possession of this priceless culture ? The study of the classics did, of course, give direction to the movement known as the Renaissance, but it did not call it into being. And it is a significant fact that the neo-classical criticism did not dominate Europe until the most vital forces of the Renaissance were already spent.

In the fourteenth and fifteenth centuries the activities

of intellectual Europe were becoming more than the Catholic Church could shoulder. Moreover, when the Church suffered glaring abuses within its ranks it lost much of its authority; men began to neglect its restraints, to impose new restraints, and dare things forbidden—the Puritans of the world seeking a new religion under which to restore the old severities, the adventurers in life and art setting out to explore the world for more constructive activities. Petrarch and Boccaccio, John Ball and Wycliffe, Chaucer, Langland, Huss, and finally Columbus, each in his different way testified to the right of the individual to feel, act, think and believe for himself—to pursue openly paths that had been forbidden.

The new impulse to freedom manifested itself in every form of activity. It led to voyages of discovery, to scientific and mathematical inquiries, to the invention of printing. It led in like manner to the reading of the Bible—that was one revelation—and to the reading of the classics—that was another. Lectures in Greek were being given in Italy long before Constantinople fell. A certain Aurispa travelled to Constantinople in 1423 to study Greek and collect Greek books. It was not the arrival of the exiled scholars in Italy which produced the revival of learning. Rather it was the good fortune of these scholars to find a revival waiting for them.

And there is one important fact which should not be overlooked. We have seen that though mediæval scholasticism discouraged the formal—the respectable—cultivation of most of the arts not connected with religion, it never succeeded in stamping out the popular arts; it never killed song, story-telling, romance. The popular ballad and the romance held their own all through the ages when more finished forms had no chance to exist. Here was a vast reservoir waiting to be tapped. The first English printers of the fifteenth century began to give wide circulation to material they had found to their hand, romances of English, French, or German origin such as *Reynard the Fox*, *Robert the Devil*, *The Famous Historie of Fryer Bacon*, and *The Noble Parentage and the Achievements of Robin Hood*.

The great literary creations of Elizabethan England were certainly no slavish imitations of the Classics or even of Italian literature. They cannot be attributed to the steady preparatory influence of a criticism based upon the methods and ideals of the Greeks. They are the result of a continuous growth of literary work during the fifteenth and sixteenth centuries made possible by the gradual removal of restraints upon the Press. They were modified, of course, by Greek, Latin, and Italian influences, and by the talk of men who had travelled and studied. Though the great Elizabethan writers were men who had either had a classical education, or had come under the influence of Classical scholars, they had not yet acquired the habit of thinking that their experiments in the English tongue must be exclusively modelled upon the ancients. That was yet to come. At present they were rather disposed to carry on existing English traditions, which in the case of drama had been handed on from the old Morality and the early Tudor play ; and though romance writers were disposed to turn to Italy for their plots, they modified, borrowed, and invented to their hearts' content. The playwrights, the romancers and the poets were romantic through and through, right down to and including the time of Spenser, Marlowe, Chapman, Ben Jonson, Shakespeare.

So the great Revival of Letters should be thought of,

not as a movement produced and inspired by reverence for the rediscovered Classics, but as an escape from mediæval bondage, a long process in the emancipation of the arts, hastened, and made brighter and sweeter, by the intelligent reading of ancient literature. Even in the last quarter of the sixteenth century it was still necessary to assert the right of poetry to exist for its own sake. Ideas die hard. The Roman Church had discouraged the Muses because they were wantons, because they had a power and an influence which, not being hers, could only be those of the devil. When the Church itself was discredited, the Muses did not at once become respectable. When the Roman Church ceased to be Puritan, Puritanism reasserted itself as a separate force in English life. It is a remarkable fact that as late as about 1581 Sir Philip Sidney should still think it necessary to write an *Apology for Poetry* (published 1595).

It may be said that Sidney is not attacking the prejudices of his own time ; that he is merely attacking the argument of Plato, Greek meeting Greek. To which we may answer that he does not seriously deal with the argument of Plato, and does not touch his fundamental position, which is philosophic. On the other hand, he definitely indicts the views of poetry current in his day. "From almost the highest estimation of learning," he says, it "is fallen to be the laughing-stock of children." And he speaks of the learned who inveigh against poetry.

> And first, truly to all them that professing learning inveigh against Poetry may justly be objected, that they go very near to ungratefulness, to seek to deface that, which in the noblest nations and languages that are known, hath been the first lightgiver to ignorance, and first Nurse, whose milk by little and little enabled them to feed afterwards of tougher

knowledges: and will they now play the Hedgehog, that being received into the den, drave out his host? or rather the Vipers, that with their birth kill their parents?

Sidney speaks throughout as if the learned and respectable opinion of his time was hostile to poetry—so hostile, indeed, that it was worth his while to write an *Apology* to show that poetry does not deserve this scorn, and that it has the very qualities which that respectable opinion would respect: namely, that it instructs, that its purpose is moral, that it is consistent with correct religion.

And in order to help his case he weeds out the poetry which does not deserve the name. He pours scorn upon the "mongrel Tragicomedy" of his time—the "gross absurdities," which are "neither right Tragedies, nor right Comedies": "mingling Kings and Clowns, not because the matter so carrieth it": thrusting in "Clowns by head and shoulders, to play a part in majestical matters, with neither decency nor discretion." He exposes the false view that "there is no delight without laughter," and blames writers who "stir laughter in sinful things; which are rather execrable than ridiculous: or in miserable, which are rather to be pitied than scorned."

Let us frankly recognize, he means, the faults of writing which masquerades as poetry, but do not let us make true poetry chargeable with those faults. And so we return to his main argument, that poetry which is really poetry is "honest," and does not deserve to be made "the laughing-stock of children." Science, history, philosophy, morals, are all under a debt of gratitude to the poets who went before "with their charming sweetness" to draw "wild untamed wits to an admiration of knowledge." "Let learned Greece, in any of her manifold Sciences, be able to show me one book before Musæus,

Homer, and Hesiodus: all three nothing else but poets. . . . The philosophers of Greece durst not for a long time appear to the world but under the masks of poets. So *Thales*, *Empedocles*, *Parmenides* sang their natural Philosophy in verses: so did *Pythagoras* and *Phocylides* their moral counsels: so did *Tyrtæus* in war matters, and *Solon* in matters of policy: or rather, they being Poets did exercise their delightful vein in those points of highest knowledge, which before them lay hid to the world."

He pays a higher tribute—as we should think it—to poetry when he shows that the poets have not only been scientists, historians, philosophers, but that the calling of poetry is one which has never failed to command the highest admiration. Even in the body of the work of Plato the philosopher, "though the inside and strength were Philosophy, the skin as it were and beauty depended most of Poetry." Among the Romans a poet was called *vates*—a diviner, foreseer, or prophet—"so heavenly a title did that excellent people bestow upon this heart-ravishing knowledge." And may he not even presume to say that "the holy David's Psalms are a divine Poem"?

> For what else is the awaking his musical instruments; the often and free changing of persons; his notable *Prosopopæias*, when he maketh you as it were, see God coming in his Majesty; his telling of the Beasts' joyfulness, and hills leaping, but a heavenly poesy, wherein almost he sheweth himself a passionate lover of that unspeakable and everlasting beauty to be seen by the eyes of the mind, only cleared by faith?

Thus carried away by the critical instinct of a poet, Sidney is better than his argument. Having set out to appease the censors of his time, to prove that even if poetry could delight it was not therefore a "wanton of the theatre," to convince them that it conformed to their didactic standards and satisfied their schoolmasterish demand for edifying knowledge, we find him declaring in spite of himself that it stands supreme in its own right, and that the glory of the Psalms of David was nothing else but the glory of poetry. While, like Horace, he still maintains that "delightful teaching is the end of Poesy," he is already beginning to put more emphasis on "delight." It may be that he was ready to go even further, and that he would approve the judgment (recalled for us by Professor Saintsbury) uttered by the Italian, Minturno, in 1559—"It will be the business of the poet," said this critic, using words which recall the doctrine of Longinus, "so to speak in his verses that he may teach, that he may delight, that he may *move*."

For all his desire to commend poetry to the good opinion of the pundits, for all his willingness to borrow their standards and worn jargon, Sidney, too, knew that poetry can "move." "I never heard the old song of *Percy* and *Douglas*," he writes, "that I found not my heart moved more than with a Trumpet."

Chapter Twelve

BEN JONSON

LITERARY fashion naturally runs from one extreme to another. Under its influence every excellence may be turned by mediocrity into a fault, freedom degenerating into insolence, restraint or reverence into servility. The sound judgment which denounces insolence starts the reaction which ends in servility; and *vice versa.* The history of literary fashion and its attendant criticism presents a see-saw, on which we rise into fantastic heights of bombast or dreaminess, and dip down into the puerilities of grammar. Now we admire the dishevelled genius who claims inspiration for his madness, now the suave serf of academic culture. The few who remain amid all changes in possession of their right minds — men such as Ben Jonson, Dryden, Lessing, Goethe, Matthew Arnold—must needs turn the current back from the excess of the moment. Unwittingly, they sometimes help to force it towards the opposite, and equally objectionable, extreme.

Thus Jonson, in resisting the unruly romanticism of his time, helped the reverse movement towards neo-classical pedantry. But this was not because he failed to recognize the greatness of his age or to appreciate the poets who had taught him so much. The same fire which moved the greatest of the Elizabethans burned also in him. He, too, knew the rapture of Anacreon's madness—*secundum Anacreontem insanire.* But the very magnificence of the Elizabethan age had its dangers, and even its absurdities. The pent-up force of centuries seemed to burst forth with volcanic splendour, and tear to pieces the trim doctrines of scholars and budding neo-classicists. Within a few years of the time when Sidney was trying to appease the disciplinarians, all authority was being flung to the winds except that of the Bolsheviks of literature, who were disseminating among themselves their own doctrine of force, extravagance, wit, passion, and contempt for bourgeois restraints. Genius was a justification for every fault. Passion was the motive force that urged the wings of fancy. Nature was exalted to the point where it could dispense with art. The impetuous roughness of Chapman, the torrent of Marlowe's eloquence which mingled fantastic brutality with sweetness, the unrelieved pressure of thought, passion and poetry in the tragedies of Shakespeare —in all of these the romantic splendour and carelessness of genius were set up for examples, which mediocrity could not follow without disaster.

Ben Jonson was well aware of the strength and the weakness of this age in which his young manhood was spent. He agreed that "that is worse which proceeds out of want, than that which riots out of plenty." "The remedy of fruitfulness is easy, but no labour will help the contrary." Assuredly "want" was not the failing of the Elizabethans—no need to prescribe for anæmia. The excess lay in the opposite direction. While "we should take care our style in writing be neither dry nor empty, we should look again it be not winding, or wanton with far-fetched descriptions." Shakespeare he loved, and did "honour his memory, on this side idolatry, as much as any." But he was not therefore blinded, as others even in a later age have been, to his shortcomings.

I remember the players have often mentioned it as an honour to Shakespeare, that in his writing, whatsoever he penned, he never blotted out a line. My answer hath

> been, "Would he had blotted a thousand," which they thought a malevolent speech. I had not told posterity this but for their ignorance, who chose that circumstance to commend their friend by wherein he most faulted. . . . He was, indeed, honest, and of an open and free nature; had an excellent fancy, brave notions, and gentle expressions, wherein he flowed with that facility that sometime it was necessary he should be stopped. "*Sufflaminandus erat*," as Augustus said of Haterius. His wit was in his own power; would the rule of it had been so too.

None of us to-day will read malevolence into this criticism, or reproach Jonson because he loved Shakespeare this side idolatry. "There was ever more in him to be praised than to be pardoned." But if at any time it behoves a critic to speak with complete frankness about faults, surely it is when he discerns the faults of the greatest; for the world is always ready to confuse the "vices" with the "virtues," and to commend its idol "by wherein he most faulted." The composed poetic spirit of Ben Jonson reacted in protest against the extravagances of an age which admired ungoverned and therefore imperfect self-expression, which was prone to bombast, rodomontade, reckless violence, cloying sweetness, imagery for the sake of imagery, the alluring sound of words for the sake of their sound. Under the urge of this unbridled and admired expressionism the lucky discernment of genius might carry the author to felicitous and even immortal passages, but when inspiration failed it left him at the mercy of verbiage and absurdity—as sometimes in Shakespeare, in Marlowe often.

In a world in which he saw chaos, Jonson endeavoured, in the light of ancient learning, to reimpose the classic order. One contemporary figure stood out for him above all others, that of a man stately, aloof, cold, uncannily wise, terrifically self-possessed—his Dominus Verulamius —Bacon, the scholar, the statesman, the scientist, the logician, the grave essayist. "No man ever spake more neatly, more pressly, more weightily, or suffered less emptiness, less idleness, in what he uttered. No member of his speech but consisted of his own graces." This admiration for Bacon, a man whose intellectual integrity no Time-Spirit could touch, an embodiment — in the sphere of letters, if not of politics—of strength exercised with restraint, is a clue to the spirit in which Jonson looks for the proper excellences of literature.

Seeking principles of order, restraint, harmony, he takes his stand upon the precepts and the examples of the Greeks. Reading him side by side with those stilted critics who were already making their voices heard on the Continent, and were soon to turn the classics into text-books and to manacle the poets with gyves forged out of a pedantic reading of Aristotle and Horace, we may feel that Jonson is perilously near to the neo-classicism of Boileau, Racine, and Le Bossu. But whilst the latter reflected the too staid decorum of the age in which they lived, Jonson was preaching decorum in an atmosphere of riot. He stated, and, under provocation, over-stated the values of ancient example, which the critics of the next generation, without any such excuse, exaggerated to the verge of parody. Jonson dwelt upon the Greek principle of "nothing too much" (μηδὲν ἄγαν) when he was surrounded by writers who "commonly seek to do more than enough." He pleaded for "election and a mean," for proportion, fitness, propriety, for "a strict and succinct style" wherein "you can take away nothing without loss." With such maxims, which had not in his time gained the currency of platitude, he countered the doctrine that mere profusion is genius, protesting against "the scenical strutting and furious vociferation" of the *Tamerlanes* and *Tamer-chams* of his time. But he was not content to reassert the general principles which underlie the practice of the Greeks. Though he admitted that the laws of poetry were not invented by Aristotle; that none fulfilled them more perfectly than Sophocles, who lived before Aristotle; that no Greekling "durst ever give precepts to Demosthenes"; still, it was Aristotle who "understood the causes of things." "What other men did by chance or custom he doth by reason; and not only found out the way not to err, but the short way we should take not to err."

"The short way not to err"! Is not this the very jargon of the neo-classics, foreshadowing submission to a sovereignty which was soon to become an intolerable servitude? Jonson restates the doctrine of the *Poetics*, only diverging from it to dot "i's" which Aristotle never dotted, and to impose the Unity of Time more emphatically than did the master. The difference between epic and drama, the meaning of fable or plot, the "wholeness" of an action, its dimensions—all of these are explained in language which is little more than a paraphrase of Aristotle.

He accepts the classic order, not, as Winckelmann did in a later age, in a deeply critical spirit, seeking to discover in the forms of ancient art the profound spirit which they embodied; not probing the mind of those older poets to discover the nature of their feeling for the beautiful or the true which led them to preserve so austerely certain types of poetry, as in like manner it led the sculptors to limit their range of expression through the human face. But then, in the England of Jonson's time, classicism had neither been grossly exaggerated, nor put upon its defence. His interest was not in probing the methods of the Greeks, but the methods of the Elizabethans. Enough for him that the former had an authority which he could enlist without fear of challenge. His main concern, in a literary circle which seemed to know no standards, was to impose some unquestionable standard of excellence, even if it were a superficial one; to introduce discipline, where there was none; to set limits, where hyperbole was the besetting sin; to strengthen, by curbing; to make art a matter of conscience as well as impulse. Conscience, perhaps, is just what he means. He compares "custom of speech, which is the consent of the learned" to "custom of life, which is the consent of the good." Thus he insists that there is a right and a wrong in art just as there is a right and a wrong in moral conduct.

I do not mean that his discussion touches what we call the problem of "art and morality." His is an argument by analogy—just as there are standards in morality, so there are standards in art; just as there are excellences of character, habit, conduct, so there are excellences proper to the poet. He dwells much on what we might call "conduct" and "conscience" in the practice of literature, and asks what the poet "is or should be by nature, by exercise, by imitation, by study."

Thus the first quality that he requires in a "poet or maker" is "a goodness of natural wit, ingenium," a "perfection of nature." Thus endowed, he is "able by nature and instinct to pour out the treasure of his mind." Or if we should care to use the language of theology, it is as if he said that the poet is what he is by the Grace of God; he is born of the Elect. The poetical rapture, the madness which inspires him, is not of his own power, but of divine origin :

Frustra poeticas fores sui compos pulsavit.

(1) Natural endowment, then, is the first, the essential thing ; but secondly, and thirdly, and fourthly Jonson makes demands which fall strictly within the sphere of "conduct."

(2) This "perfection of nature" is not enough by itself. We must add "exercise of those parts, and frequent." His opinion runs with that of Dante, not Wordsworth. Poetry is not "spontaneous utterance." Rather, it is—in the words we have quoted from Dante—an "elaborate and painful toil." "It is said of the incomparable Virgil that he brought forth his verses like a bear, and after formed them with licking." Just as the rhapsodic humanitarian rhetoric of the first decade of the twentieth century was distasteful to fastidious ears, so the vapid mouthings of some of his contemporaries to Jonson ; he distrusted facility, shoddy ornament, thoughtless fluency. "The best writers in their beginnings . . . imposed upon themselves care and industry ; they did nothing rashly ; they obtained first to write well, and then custom made it easy and a habit." For Jonson there was no Royal Road to success in literature. "Hard is the beautiful" was an old motto which his contemporaries had scorned ; but it was his task to remind them of the ancient truth which one age forgets, another exaggerates out of all proportion. He demands that the literary artist should make his appeal to what Walter Pater was to call "the scholar and the scholarly conscience." And just as the latter said : "The attention of the writer, in every minutest detail," is "a pledge

that it is worth the reader's while to be attentive too, that the writer is dealing scrupulously with his instrument," so Jonson : "things wrote with labour deserve to be so read."

(3) Pursuing his examination of what I have called literary "conduct," he finds the third requisite of his poet to be imitation, *imitatio*—"to be able to convert the substance or riches of another poet to his own use."

(4) And the fourth—"exactness of study and multiplicity of reading, *lectio*, which maketh a full man." Here again we see the student of Bacon.

For Jonson, the calling of poet or man of letters implies a certain life which may be lived by the Elect alone, and by them only upon the condition that they will enter upon it humbly as novices, and submit themselves to an austere regimen, shaping themselves in accordance with the most excellent patterns, and finding therein the maxims which are to guide their conduct. For him it is a matter of the first importance to the State to "take care of the commonwealth of learning." Schools are "the seminaries of State ; and nothing is worthier the study of a statesman than that part of the republic which we call the advancement of letters."

Yet, intent as he is upon discipline of the mind imposed both from within and without, he is far too good a poet to rest content with precepts, maxims, ready guides to literary conduct. He is not in love with the grammarians. "To descend to those extreme anxieties and foolish cavils of grammarians, is able to break a wit in pieces, being a work of manifold misery and vainness, to be *elementarii senes*." He does not want literature to become a department of schoolmastering. "I am not of that opinion to conclude a poet's liberty within the narrow limits of laws which either the grammarians or philosophers prescribe."

The authority of Aristotle, as he writes these words, seems to be slipping away from under his feet ; and all the more dangerously when he declares that "to judge of poets is only the faculty of poets ; and not of all poets, but the best." He does not long let us forget his feeling that the excellence of literature springs from what is excellent in the personality of the author. With poet and painter alike "Nature is more powerful in them than study." Expression, as we should call it—self-expression—is the business of art from beginning to end ; and he puts it in memorable words : "In all speech, words and sense are as the body and the soul. The sense is as the life and soul of language, without which all words are dead."—"Language most shows a man : Speak, that I may see thee."

And so the tempered wisdom of the poet, who is a critic, demanding standards and restraints, must be read side by side with the passionate declarations of the critic, who is a poet, that the mad divinity of genius should be allowed wings to fly away with its rider, and "utter somewhat above a mortal mouth." But for those who would claim this licence too easily, he is ready with the curb.

Whether it is to be the curb, or the spur—how are we to know ? The answer, in the last resort, he has already given : "To judge of poets is only the faculty of poets."

Chapter Thirteen

NATURE METHODIZED

SHOULD it not be with bared head and every outward show of reverence that a critic of criticism approaches the age of Prose and Reason—the age of criticism *par excellence*, covering the long period from the middle of the seventeenth century till near the end of the eighteenth? This, above all others, was an age of respect for learning and authority, when literature was at last reduced to law and order, and its rules interpreted by men "born to judge." It had but to be granted that the ancient writers did all things better than the rest of the world, and that the moderns could only excel in proportion as they successfully imitated them; and it followed that he who knew best the rules of the ancients was best qualified to discern the merits of a modern. To challenge the authority of the classics was to separate oneself from culture. It was a mark of civilization to submit to the laws of Aristotle and Horace, as codified by the French:

> But we, brave Britons, foreign laws despised,
> And kept unconquer'd, and uncivilised;

Corneille, Racine, Boileau and Le Bossu, by example or precept, laid down the rules of correct writing, and woe to the writer who ignored them! The fashion swept over England, which by no means "kept unconquer'd," and subdued the noblest minds to the orthodox pattern of tameness and correctness, and an outward show of elegance, dignity, proportion, moderation.

No mere accident, this, of taste in letters. Its causes lay deeper than I can here attempt to trace them. If the passions of religious warfare could be allayed, if the fury of the romantic temperament could be hushed, if reason, decorum and good sense could radiate their benign light from the Court of Louis XIV. and shine in reflected glory in the baronial antechambers of England, we may suspect influences, deeply rooted in social history, but beyond the scope of this inquiry. Here I can only note that this damping down of the literary furnaces had taken place. Shakespeare had gone. Corneille reigned supreme in his place. The invention, passion, curiosity, adventurousness, and experimental effort in which the released forces of the Middle Ages had broken out with explosive violence, were now looked askance at — they appeared as the wildness of a disordered mind—Nature without Method —the inferior, brutish thing, which it was the business of criticism, built up on the good manners of the classics, to expose and suppress.

The critics, in those days, sharpened their weapons. It was a good thing, perhaps, that they did so, for there was much grammar yet to be learned ; and the harm which they did in suppressing genius must have been slight, for they, too, were the product of their age—an aristocratic age—which, since it could tolerate this criticism, naturally could not stimulate a more forceful art. The most that the criticasters could do, as experts in the vetoes of fashion, was to discourage or obscure erratic genius from time to time. (Blake, for example, was effectually obscured for the better part of a century.) The Alexandrians, in a duller age, had done useful work in settling the rudiments of critical grammar. The neo-classical critics added much that is essential to "culture," and fixed all the important truisms without which we can hardly begin to-day to discuss the art of literature.

In England, neo-classicism, borrowed from France, never assumed so noxious a form as it did in its country of origin.[1] Though parallel influences were at work in England, the disease was far less virulent. Even the critics, who followed the French, expressed themselves with more humanity. Addison, who wrote a bad play in which every rule of Boileau was observed, wrote discriminating criticism far beyond Boileau's reach. Pope's *Essay on Criticism* is strictly in accord with *L'Art Poétique* of Boileau, but there is human sense in it. We cannot, however, acquit him of echoing the jargon of the Frenchmen :

> Those *Rules*, of old discover'd, not devised,
> Are nature still, but nature methodised.

Or :

> Learn hence for ancient rules a just esteem ;
> To copy nature is to copy them.

or the excellent Greek adage, which loses some of its quality when it is repeated *ad nauseam* :

> Avoid extremes ; and shun the fault of such
> Who still are pleased too little or too much.

But we begin to wonder to what extent Pope is talking with his tongue in his cheek when he appears to yield himself to Boileau :

> Thence arts o'er all the northern world advance,
> But critic-learning flourish'd most in France ;
> The rules a nation, born to serve, obeys ;
> And Boileau still in right of Horace sways.

Boileau ! *Le Législateur du Parnasse !* The bigoted apostle of neo-classicism, the tinkling echo of Horace, the

[1] In neither country, of course, could the best talents be ruined by so superficial an influence.

opinionated pedant, the maker of correct and execrable verses, the suitable protégé of Louis XIV., the rhymester who moulded the literary opinion of France for a century or more and established the dull fashion which was handed on to grown men in England, as Paris fashions are handed on to English women to-day. Allied with him were a few, greater men than he, whose practice accorded with his theory—Corneille, Racine, La Fontaine—and fellow-students of the art of criticism, like Rapin and Le Bossu. Famous by reason of his fierce abuse, powerful through the support of *le grand monarque*, respected for his honesty and obstinate persistence, Boileau had the authority of a sergeant-major in a circle which delighted in the military discipline of letters. To be a Warrant Officer in the literary army of the King who built Versailles—that was the rôle which exactly suited him. He was a master of the technique of parade-ground literature, a relentless expert in squad-drill who could be counted upon to lick any unpromising poetic recruit into shape and make him a good private in the ranks. He excelled, in that he left nothing in doubt. The rules of poetry were as precise as Infantry Drill regulations. There was one, and one way only in which you should write an epic, a drama, an eclogue, an elegy, an ode, just as there is only one way in which you should "Left Turn" or "Form Fours." The prescribed way was that in which Homer, Virgil, Horace, Theocritus and the other ancients performed their various movements; any deviations from these were wrong. For each poetic form there was its appropriate formula, and Boileau wrote it down in rhyming couplets.

He admitted, of course, the nobler virtues; he patronized them, and put them in their place. Like Rapin or Le Bossu, he was willing to pay lip homage to "Nature"

—so much was due to their master, Horace. "Never must we deviate from nature." "Let nature, then, be your only study," is his advice to authors who aspire to honours in comedy:

> La nature, féconde en bizarres portraits,
> Dans chaque âme est marquée à de différents traits.

But it was "nature" with a difference — nature "methodized." (Rapin, and all the criticasters, favoured this expression.) For Nature has a way of "distributing the talents" among authors, and may not poets misconceive their genius? They must submit themselves therefore to the correctives of "good sense" and of Reason:

> Quelque sujet qu'on traite, ou plaisant, ou sublime,
> Que toujours le bon sens s'accorde avec la rime.

And:

> Aimez donc la raison. Que toujours, vos ecrits
> Empruntent d'elle seule et leur lustre et leur prix.

Such, then, is the wise advice proffered and repeated. "Aimez la raison," and "Tout doit tendre au bons sens." Avoid the excesses of insensate excitement, of verses monstrous—sham diamonds which Italy foisted upon the world. Restraint is the first lesson of writing. Avoid "sterile abundance." Nothing too much! Let everything be in its place, and the beginning and end respond to the middle. Take the classics for your model, and copy them to the letter. If you would write an eclogue, shun the extremes of the pompous and the abject, and follow Theocritus and Virgil:

> Entre ces deux excès la route est difficile.
> Suivez, pour la trouver, Théocrite et Virgile.

If your talent lies in Elegy, Tibullus and Ovid will be your exemplars; if in satire, follow Horace, Lucilius,

Persius, and Juvenal ; if in Tragedy, Epic, or Comedy—but here Boileau gives us a whole Canto to set forth once again the rules of Aristotle and Horace, with some arbitrary additions.

We have, of course, the famous trio of the Unities, Action, Time, and Place, the first of which was required by Aristotle, the second recommended by him, the third added in excess of zeal by the neo-classical critics. With amazing optimism Boileau presents his recipe for filling a theatre, and keeping an audience seated till the end—submit to the rules of Reason, and give us in your Tragedy a single action, which occurs in one place, and in one day :

> Mais nous, que la raison à ses règles engage,
> Nous voulons qu'avec art l'action se ménage ;
> *Qu'en un lieu, qu'en un jour, un seul fait accompli*
> *Tienne jusqu'à la fin le théâtre rempli.*

Avoid the incredible, remembering that the true is not always the probable ; shun low conditions of life ; choose heroes pre-eminent in valour and in virtue ; do not select a subject too charged with incident. But with these old rules he is not content. Boileau plunges at full tilt into the war of the Ancients and the Moderns, commanding his poets not to bring God or the devil, saints or prophets into their themes, but to cling to pagan subjects ; not to think that the terrible mysteries of the Christian faith can lend themselves to the bright ornaments of art. Leave Pan his flute, and the Fates their scissors, and to the Tritons their empire of the seas. Even when we would choose names for our heroes, has not antiquity left us names born for poetry :

> Ulysse, Agamemnon, Oreste, Idoménée,
> Hélène, Ménélas, Pâris, Hector, Énée.

Why, then, be so absurd and ignorant as to choose "Childebrand," whose harsh, outlandish sound is enough to make a whole poem burlesque and barbarous?

And so our lawgiver runs on. He is content to leave no detail in the metrical form of the verse to the taste of the poet. A word ending in a vowel must not be followed by a word beginning with another vowel. Let each line be so divided that there is a pause at the hemistich—with what results we may see in his own mean couplets, and in the monotonous lines of the misguided writers who followed his advice. It decreed the death of poetry, as Théodore de Banville said, creating a verse as lifeless, automatic, and dull as the steps of a soldier on the march.

Is it strange that this dull, meticulous, really stupid criticism should not merely have been acclaimed, but should have come to stay? Forty years later it was said that "Boileau still in right of Horace sways," and in France his reputation was scarcely assailed till Chateaubriand took the field against him. For a full hundred years this little strutting pedant, tricked out in the dress of ancient writers whose works he was temperamentally incapable of appreciating, imposed himself as a dictator of taste upon the cultured world; and much of his jargon is still the jargon of polished persons alive to-day.

The truth of the matter is that Boileau is a type which is always with us, and probably always will be. He and his kind live among the dry bones of literature, a tribe of intellectual busybodies who proclaim trifles to be great matters, as someone has said, lest it should appear that to trifles they have given their lives. We may be grateful for such prettiness as survives their flight from beauty. For them, art has nothing whatever to do with life. It is a matter of *ornements égayés*, delicate things which shrink from the touch of mystery, the penitence, or punishment, of religion, the horror of evil, the "low circumstance" of poverty. A snake or odious monster so treated as to please the eyes, the tragedy of a "bleeding Œdipus" which can draw tears from us "for our diversion"—these provide the innocent sentiment dear to Boileau. For him, the terror of tragedy is turned to sweetness; pity is charming: and when I am touched, I must be pleased. The poet's usage will conform to custom. He must be mannerly in his selection of themes and his use of plot, lest the etiquette be broken, and the easy security of sound rules be threatened. The parlour manners of literature which can be taught in the nursery and enforced under fear of the lash in the grammar-school—these are the theme of Boileau's teaching.

He sharpened all the little tools that were necessary for the writing of a literature which was to be primarily a craft, with professional critics as instructors. Poetry was to conform to trade-union rules, which, having once been set up, none dare violate on pain of expulsion from the union of letters. The last word lay with the critics. They might wrangle among themselves, but only on the common ground of the sanctity of the rules. Boileau was eminently qualified for the job of organizing secretary.

This was the man whom even in England Roscommon followed, Addison obeyed, and Pope eulogized. If his authority was not as fatal to this country as to France, that perhaps is due in great measure to the healthy sense of humour which distinguishes our robust eighteenth century—to the common sense which was a very different thing from the *bon sens* of Boileau. Here we had no Academy to insist on uniformity of practice, and Swift was not outlawed because he called criticism "a malignant deity" who "dwelt on the top of a snowy mountain in Nova Zembla," where she was found "extended in her den upon the spoils of numberless volumes half-devoured." Even Pope, who so deftly tightened up his verse to the strict fashion of the time, was for ever writing impish things which all but let the cat out of the bag :

> We poets are (upon a poet's word)
> Of all mankind, the creatures most absurd.

Chapter Fourteen

DRYDEN

AN age steeped in the grammar of criticism was for the most part content to follow Boileau. To-day, most of us can find more profit in the study of John Dryden, who had no belief in quack prescriptions for the cultivation of genius, and offered nothing to the would-be poet or critic who lacked native wit and judgment. Having a deep affection for English literature, having also the courage of his own convictions, he was incapable of stomaching the puerilities of Boileau. Such finicky criticism, with its precise rules and definitions, bore no correspondence to the variety of life, or the abundance of genius.

In Dryden it found a solitary opponent. This great poet and perhaps greater critic, who produced such finely discriminating studies of the poets, broke new ground as a student of the principles of literature. He penetrated more deeply than any modern had yet done into the problem of the character of poetry, and the function and meaning of a work of conscious art. In reading his essays and prefaces we find him aware of poetry in its threefold capacity—as the proper business of the poet, as the object of the critic's appreciation, and, for society, as a force operating in its midst. In his work we have not only criticism, but criticism becoming aware of itself, analysing its objects with sympathy and knowledge, and knowing what kind of thing it is looking for.

He clears the ground for himself by brushing away all the arbitrary bans upon freedom of composition and freedom of judgment. He refuses to be cowed by the French playwrights and critics. He sees no reason why tragi-comedy should be forbidden because it mingles mirth with serious plot, nor will he join in blaming "the variety and copiousness" of the English plays, with their "underplots or by-concernments," because they do not conform to the French ideal of singleness of plot. He ridicules the "servile observation of the unities of time and place," which needlessly limit the scope of the dramatist and often force him to resort to absurd contrivances. Even to Aristotle he refuses to render slavish homage. "It is not enough that Aristotle has said so, for Aristotle drew his models of tragedy from Sophocles and Euripides: *and, if he had seen ours, might have changed his mind.*"

That, in the seventeenth century, was a revolutionary saying. Thus to question the authority of the ancients, to suggest that there might be another good way of writing tragedies beside that of Sophocles and Euripides, to hint that, after all, the plot may not necessarily be the chief thing, "though it be the foundation," of a tragedy, and to call in question the singleness of theme, the sacrosanctity of the unities, and the proper ubiquity of Pity and Fear in tragedy—to dare all this, as Dryden did, was audacity indeed. Should it succeed, it would knock the bottom out of neo-classical criticism and its principles.

Dryden had not only read and digested Sophocles and Euripides, Theocritus and Virgil; he had also read and digested Shakespeare, Ben Jonson, and Fletcher. He found them worth reading. He found that their tragedy had upon him the effect of the tragic, their comedy the effect of the comic. Yet they were not Greek. By no device of casuistry could their technical methods be said to be those of the Greeks. "Other wits, as suitable to the nature of tragedy, may be found in the English, which were not in the Greek."

Dryden thus opens a new field of comparative criticism. Up to now, post-Renaissance critics had been content to compare modern literature with Greek and Latin, but always on the assumption that the latter were models for all time and in all languages. Long before, Quintilian, comparing the excellences of Latin with the excellences of Greek, declared that the Latin language, being different, called for different treatment, by which the Latin might acquire strength, weight, and fullness to compensate for the superior grace, subtlety, and propriety of the Greek. But Dryden went much further. He found a difference more deeply rooted than that of language alone. The state of development, the character, the taste of a people undergo profound changes. He anticipated Taine in pointing out that each age or nation has its own genius; the climate counts for something; the disposition of mankind varies at different times and places, and involves variations in taste and in art. Shakespeare and Fletcher enjoyed a success in their age comparable with that of Sophocles and Euripides in theirs:

> And one reason of that success is, in my opinion, this, that Shakespeare and Fletcher have written to the genius of the age and nation in which they lived: for though nature . . . is the same in all places, and reason too the same, yet the climate, the age, the disposition of the people, to which a poet writes, may be so different, that what pleased the Greeks would not satisfy an English audience.

For the first time Dryden introduces the notion of literature as an organic force which develops with the development of a nation, expressing the impulses of each new age in a manner suited to its growth. "It is not enough that Aristotle has said so." Art is a dynamic not a static force. It must speak to the spirit of each succeeding period. Dryden may not go quite so far as to say, with Frederick Schlegel, that "literature is the comprehensive essence of the intellectual life of a nation," but he does say that it is to "the disposition of the people" that the poet writes.

What, then, is this relation between the people, to whom the poet writes, and the poet himself? ("Art for Art's sake" had not been invented in Dryden's time, and he, like all men before him, and most after him, presupposed an audience whom an author addresses, a reader for whom he writes, a kindred soul, it may be, who is to be stirred to communion.) The old formula had come down to him through the ages—"To *teach*, and to *delight*"—to which Longinus had added the third term "and to *move*." Sidney, as we have seen, had been worried by that necessity of "teaching," or "instructing," and to satisfy the correct opinion of his time had compromised with "that delightful teaching which is the end of Poesy." Dryden is more direct. "Delight is the chief, if not the only, end of poesy; instruction can be admitted but in the second place; for poesy only instructs as it delights." And he frankly "confesses" his own aim as a poet: "My chief endeavours are to delight the age in which I live."

At last, then, we are rid of the old tangle of art and morality, and have a clear admission of the truth that it is not the business of the poet to set out to preach—that is the preacher's business. It is the business of the poet, as a poet, to cause delight.

That in itself would have been no inconsiderable

admission to make in one jump. But in making it Dryden goes further, and corrects and qualifies his statement, removing from the "pleasure" view of poetry the defect from which it has suffered along with all other purely hedonistic doctrines. He implies that there is pleasure and pleasure, delight and delight; and he qualifies the pleasure which is the end of art by naming the influence which Longinus dwelt upon—εἰς ἔκστασιν ἄγει—it transports:

> 'Tis true, that to imitate well is a poet's work; but to affect the soul, and excite the passions, and above all to move admiration (which is the delight of serious plays) a bare imitation will not serve.

So far, then, Dryden has said that it is the function of a poet to imitate, and to imitate in a certain way—namely, with a view to giving pleasure or affecting the soul. But that is not a sufficient definition. A play "is supposed to be the work of the poet," and the poet, therefore, in imitating nature, is not content merely to reproduce an exact copy of life, but, being a poet, will change it in the handling. For this reason a playwright will prefer to use verse instead of prose, and similarly, rhyming verse instead of blank verse, because prose "is too near the nature of converse," and blank verse is nearer than rhyme.

> There may be too great a likeness; as the most skilful painters affirm, that there may be too near a resemblance in a picture: to take every lineament and feature, is not to make an excellent piece; but to take so much only as will make a beautiful resemblance of the whole; and, with an ingenious flattery of nature, to heighten the beauties of some part, and hide the deformities of the rest.

So art does not aim at mere copying, but at making "a beautiful resemblance of the whole." It cannot be a mere imitation, for it is the work of a poet, or maker, or creator, whose concern it is to produce something that is beautiful. No Realistic or Naturalistic doctrine could have satisfied Dryden ; for, on his presupposition that the artist is concerned with the beautiful, and with producing pleasure through the medium of beauty, he cannot be interested in the representation of life, just because it is life, but only in the representation of life, so far as it is beautiful. According to Dryden, the artist aims at making something more beautiful than life. In anticipating the conclusion of Coleridge that "simulations of nature," such as waxwork figures, are "disagreeable," he arrives at it by a somewhat different argument. Dryden eschewed mere nature because of its imperfection. Coleridge despaired of repeating it, because of its perfection. "What idle rivalry !" exclaimed Coleridge. How can an artist hope to recreate or equal nature? He can only endeavour to make, out of material drawn from nature, something that is his own, shaped in accordance with principles of his own creative imagination.

Dryden, unlike Coleridge, introduces no metaphysical doctrines to explain the shaping processes of art. He has in his mind no elaborate theory of the Imagination with which to interpret the vision of the poet. He is content to assert what he observes, that the poet does not leave things as he finds them, but handles them, treats them, "heightens" their quality, and so creates something that is beautiful, and his own.

> In general, the employment of a poet is like that of a curious gunsmith, or watchmaker : the iron or silver is not his own, but they are the least part of that which gives the value : the price lies wholly in the workmanship. And he who works dully on a story, without moving laughter in a comedy, or raising concernment in a serious play, is no

more to be accounted a good poet, than a gunsmith of the Minories is to be compared with the best workman of the town.

Here there is no appeal to disputable doctrines of metaphysics to explain the source of inspiration or the nature of the poetic process. None the less, there is much in Dryden's view that would satisfy the demands of the metaphysic of Coleridge. For him, as for the later critic, it is not by observation of life that poetry is formed, but by the shaping of the raw material of observed life in the light of imagination, and under the curb of the judgment. *Imagination* now springs into its recognized place in the language of criticism, though Dryden uses the words "fancy" and "imagination" with little if any difference of meaning; where he writes "fancy" we are justified in reading "imagination."

Thus he says that "imagination in a poet is a faculty so wild and lawless, that, like an high-ranging spaniel, it must have clogs (rhyme) tied to it, lest it outrun the judgment"; and he continues: "the fancy then gives leisure to the judgment to come in."

Again, when he says "fancy is the principal quality required" in a poet, he means what we mean when we say *imagination*. And he goes on: "Judgment, indeed, is necessary in him; but it is fancy that gives the life-touches, and the secret graces to it: especially in serious plays, which depend not much on observation. For, to write humour in comedy (which is the theft of poets from mankind), little of fancy is required. . . ."

Here Dryden uses the word *fancy* almost exactly as Coleridge uses *imagination*, implying the faculty by which the poet creates. Sheer realism, slavish representation, in so far as it is a mechanical copying of life, in which the photographic machine does everything and the artist nothing, is a mere theft from nature—it is not life transmuted by imagination. It is, in Dryden's view, a denial of the proper function of the artist, who disposes, and beautifies under the guidance of a power within himself—the imagination—the image-making power. He does not work by fixed precepts and rules, which lead to "dearth of plot, and narrowness of imagination"; rather, we discern his true method in the example of Shakespeare, who "needed not the spectacles of books to read *nature*; he looked inwards, and found her there."—"It is fancy that gives the life-touches."

Dryden offers no explanation, metaphysical, psychological, or pathological, of the mysterious operations of this transmuting, creative fancy, or imagination. But, after all, why should he? He is not explaining or accounting for things. He is giving evidence—he is declaring facts drawn from his own experience as a poet, and from his experience as a reader.

And so when he says that "the story is the least part" of the "work" and of the "graces" of a poem, he should not be understood, I think, as Professor Saintsbury supposes, to be challenging the verdict of Aristotle who declared that "the plot is the first thing." For he goes on to qualify his statement: "I mean the foundation of it [the story], before it is modelled by the art of him who writes it." What he is concerned to prove is that the plot is nothing till it has become the subject of treatment; the raw material is a slight matter; everything depends on what results after the poetic faculty has been at work upon it. But if by "plot" we understand the theme as conceived by the poet, then Dryden is not in the least disposed to belittle it. Indeed he is scarcely less insistent than Matthew Arnold on the need of choosing a " fit subject." He even relapses for a moment into the conventional language of his time when he declares that the argument, the characters, and the persons should alike be " great and noble," lest the poet be dragged down by the meanness of his material.

Drawing together, then, some of the principles which we discover in the writings of Dryden, we see that he rejects the authority of the lawgiver in literature, whether he be an Aristotle, a Horace, or a Boileau—not because such a lawgiver may not correctly define the practice of great artists at this or that period of history, but because ages, nations, tastes differ, and a technique which may be right for one age may be wrong for another. To the temper and taste of his age the creative writer cannot be indifferent, for his main concern is to give pleasure.

There is no question of writing just to please himself; that notion had not yet arisen.

He clears away the ancient stumbling-block of criticism, the doctrine that the aim of the artist is to instruct or " make men better in some respect." In asserting that the aim of the artist is, not to teach, but to please, he implicitly distinguishes between literature as an art and literature which is didactic. Instruction may result from the reading of poetry, but is not its end; for " poesy only instructs as it delights."

But the pleasure which a work of art produces is of a certain kind—it is that which consists with a sense of the beautiful. Dryden does not for a moment consider the possibility that the end of art can be dissociated from beauty. For him, as for Aristotle, it goes without saying that when you speak of poetry, or art, you are speaking of beauty ; and if you speak of the pleasure of poetry, you mean a pleasure arising out of the beautiful.

How, then, will Dryden's poet attain his end—the making of something which will cause pleasure through beauty ? By imitation, or representation, certainly, as all critics from time immemorial had agreed. And yet not just representation. The poet is a ποιήτης—he is a creator. He selects, alters, refashions, like a " curious gunsmith " working on iron. This raw material on which he works assumes a new form, a new life, under his handling—" it is fancy which gives the life-touches "—and becomes the thing conceived by his imagination, and regulated by his judgment. The latter is apparently the faculty by which he knows the limits of his material and his tools, and the means appropriate to his artistic end. It keeps genius within the borders of reason and common sense.

We may regard this power of the Imagination, recognized, if undefined, by Dryden, as the special faculty of the poet or originative artist, whether he be, as Aristotle says, εὐφύης or μανικός—endowed with some gift of nature, or inspired by madness. It includes the old idea of rhapsody or exaltation associated from the earliest times with the gift of song—the inspiration breathed into its possessor by the god impelling him to outbursts of winged, beautiful words. It needed the " regulation " of the judgment, for whilst it was originative and original it was also turbulent and wayward, a Pegasus straining to whirl its rider to dizzy cloud heights unless tightly held under the curb.

For each poet it was something distinctive, peculiarly his own, an element inherent in his character, by virtue of which he made his personal contribution to letters. This faculty of genius was one thing in Shakespeare, another in Jonson, and yet another in Fletcher. It is an intimate part of personality which impresses itself upon the author's writings so that we esteem them for the personal qualities which are his. Thus it was that "Shakespeare writ better between man and man; Fletcher betwixt man and woman." "The one described friendship better, the other love; yet Shakespeare taught Fletcher to write love, and Juliet and Desdemona are originals." "The scholar had the softer soul; but the master had the kinder."

These are qualities of character and personality, attributes of a man of genius which issue in the distinctive flavour of his works—human elements which penetrate and give life to the formless matter of literature. For Dryden, the qualities which distinguish the works of Shakespeare and Jonson are personal. The excellences of the one and the other, the qualities of imagination arising out of character, are named and contrasted. "Shakespeare was the Homer, or father of our dramatic poets; Jonson was the Virgil, the pattern of elaborate writing; I admire him, but I love Shakespeare."

Chapter Fifteen

THE LOGIC OF TASTE

FOR modern Englishmen, though not perhaps for Frenchmen, the eighteenth century, much as we esteem it, fondly as some may seek to modernize it in popular productions at the theatre, is a very long way off—further, surely, than the Elizabethan age, and perhaps as distant as Henry James would make it in *The Sense of the Past*, or Mr Squire and Mr Balderston when they give us *Berkeley Square*. We have seen in Dryden something of our modern selves, where he introduces the Elizabethan imagination into a theory of criticism—or rather, into those various scraps of theory which admit of being pieced together into a whole. Dryden has projected on to his critical screen some pictures which come back to memory when we read Coleridge. Yet we go but a few years beyond him—a little further into the country of "Prose and Reason"—and we find ourselves moving in a circle where notions, utterly different from Dryden's, predominate—notions governed on the one side by "Nature Methodized," the clichés fixed by Rapin and Boileau, and on the other by the philosophy of John Locke. The "imagination" turns up again, a thin simulacrum of itself, product of a forced union between the "imagination," so precisely defined by the psychologists, and the more potent faculty known to Dryden and the Elizabethans. This mongrel progeny lacked the precision of the one, and the vital force of the other.

We may study the use of this word, already pigeonholed in the vocabulary of æsthetic criticism, in Addison, or in Burke—Addison referring us to Locke, and Burke, on one occasion, to Addison. In each case the argument is cast in the mould laid down by Locke, who in his turn, of course, owed much to Hobbes. Why Mr Basil Worsfold, in his book on *Principles of Criticism*, should suggest that Addison opened new paths of discovery in his disquisitions on the Imagination I am at a loss to understand. Addison merely applied the jargon, made familiar in his time by students of Locke, to the language of æsthetic criticism; and Burke, later, was still under the spell of this widely read philosopher who was already out of date for those acquainted with Berkeley and Hume. Happily, there are many penetrating judgments which last longer than the metaphysical or psychological theories in which they are wrapped, sometimes piercing through them, or emerging triumphantly when the theories are worn out. Philosophical endeavour expresses itself in this way and that at various stages of human effort, in forms which are accepted like fashions in dress, and pass away like them. But elements of pragmatical truth within them, more deeply rooted in personality, may often survive, and prove superior to logic. In an Addison these elements may be as thin as the argument. In Burke the matter is more solid.

Both of these speak and think in the philosophical language of Locke. Addison does no more than apply his psychology, somewhat loosely and naïvely, to the processes of the mind which occur in the appreciation of art. Burke, with a stronger grip, pursues a similar but more systematic inquiry in his essay on *The Sublime and the Beautiful*.

Addison's account of the Imagination is derived from Locke, but we can find the gist of it, earlier, in Hobbes's *Leviathan*, where we read:

Concerning the Thoughts of man . . . the Original of them all, is that which we call *Sense*; (For there is no conception in a man's mind, which hath not at first, totally, or by parts, been begotten upon the organs of Sense.) The rest are derived from that originall. . . .

After the object is removed, or the eye shut, we still retain an image of the thing seen, though more obscure than when we see it. And this is it, the Latines call *Imagination*, from the image made in seeing; and apply the same, though improperly, to all the other senses. But the Greeks call it *Fancy*; which signifies *apparence*, and is as proper to one sense, as to another. *Imagination* therefore is nothing but *decaying sense*; and is found in men, and many other living Creatures, as well sleeping, as waking.

This "decaying sense" is rather a poor material out of which to construct the creative imagination of the artist. But even Hobbes finds means of strengthening this flimsy stuff of thought; and in Locke the secondary ideas assume greater importance, being caused not only by recalling original ideas of sense in our minds, but by the conjoining of ideas as originally presented to form new and infinitely variable ideas. Addison converts the argument to his own purpose, choosing to apply the word Imagination to the perception of visible objects, as well as to the secondary ideas which flow from them. He desires the reader:

. . . to remember, that by the Pleasures of the Imagination, I mean only such Pleasures as arise originally from Sight, and that I divide these Pleasures into two kinds: My Design being first of all to discourse of those Primary Pleasures of the Imagination, which entirely proceed from such Objects as are before our Eyes; and in the next place to speak of those Secondary Pleasures of the Imagination which flow from the Ideas of visible Objects, when the Objects are not actually before the Eye, but are called up into our Memories, or formed into agreeable Visions of Things that are either Absent or Fictitious.

Burke, more properly, restricts the word Imagination to the second order of ideas, and does not confine these to ideas derived from the sense of sight. He distinguishes three powers of the mind: (1) that which is conversant about externa lobjects — namely, the senses; (2) the imagination, which represents at pleasure "the images of things in the order and manner in which they were received by the senses, or in combining those images in a new manner . . ." ("to this belongs whatever is called wit, fancy, or invention, and the like"); and (3) the judgment, or reasoning faculty, which is chiefly concerned in "finding differences."

For Addison the imagination is (1) the perception of Nature at first hand, and (2) the *mental* representation of ideas derived from those original perceptions; and this he somewhat obscurely confounds with the *objective* representation of these ideas in works of art. Under the first head he declares that the pleasures of the imagination, arising "from the actual View and Survey of outward Objects," proceed from the sight of "what is Great, Uncommon, or Beautiful." Why we should take delight in these qualities is explained by the writer, who recognizes the handiwork of a prudent Deity. The Supreme Author of our Being, it seems, was careful to form our souls in this way: (1) in order that we may take pleasure in the contemplation of the Divine Greatness; (2) that the pleasure annexed to the Uncommon may encourage us in the pursuit of knowledge; and (3) that by pleasure in the Beautiful all creatures may be tempted to multiply their kind, or find "Creation more gay and delightful."

Addison finds no more difficulty in explaining the pleasure of the imagination when it is concerned with derived ideas, or works of art. It arises from the twofold satisfaction of comparing a copy with the original, and from the variety and added liveliness which we experience from the manifold combinations of ideas which are not found thus combined in nature. "The Poet gives us as free a View of an object as he pleases, and discovers to us several parts, that either we did not attend to, or that lay out of our sight when we first beheld it."

I shall not pursue Addison's examination of the questions, why tastes differ, why descriptions which cause pity and fear can afford us pleasure, and why words have so great a power. His essays on this subject have little importance except as a connecting link between the philosophical use of the word Imagination, and its use in æsthetic criticism. His attempt to identify these two uses revealed confusion rather than originality of thought. He passes loosely from one use of the word to another, now meaning by it simple apprehension, now mental representation, now objective representation, and confusing them all with that undefined but sufficiently intelligible meaning accorded to it in the parlance of Shakespeare and Dryden. The "lady's philosopher" discoursed on all things, and by an accident stumbled on a word already known to æsthetic criticism, and the same word known to psychology; and with journalistic readiness assumed that they referred to one and the same thing.

Burke is more exact, and more luminous. A detailed examination of his essay is outside the scope of the present work, but he raises certain issues which should not be neglected, as when he asks whether there are any fixed standards in taste, as there are in reason—whether we can fitly speak of a "logic of taste." "If taste has no fixed principle . . . it must be judged a useless, if not an absurd undertaking, to lay down rules for caprice, and to set up for a legislator of whims and fancies."

In raising again this question of the validity of criticism Burke doubtless had in mind the arguments of Longinus, and determined to examine the matter from the psychological point of view current in the eighteenth century. The question he is asking is the recurring one—How is it that there is so great a variety of tastes in regard to literature and art? Is there any reason for supposing that one literary judgment is more valid than another? We do not differ in our opinions as to what is sweet, or soft, or round, or as to the pleasures that may arise from such sensations; if one man prefers beef to mutton, we do not challenge the correctness of his taste. Why then do we set up claims to judge of the excellence of a work of art, and assume that such judgments are valid for others? Is there any common measure between the opinion of one man about a picture or a poem, and the opinion of another man? What value has a work of art apart from the opinions which may be formed of it, and, if none, why do we consider that one opinion is better than another? Are we to assume that there is a standard of taste just as there is a standard of reason in regard to truth and falsehood, and, if so, to what principles are we to refer it?

Burke addresses himself seriously to this question, and concludes that taste is not a "separate faculty of the mind"—in other words, that art has not a separate world of its own, that it is not engaged upon a subject distinct from the rest of life and employing faculties peculiarly its own. We need not suppose that poets and critics

> from Heaven derive their light,
> These born to judge, as well as those to write.

Examining the three constituent elements which, in his philosophy, make up the knowing power of man—Sense, Imagination, Judgment—he considers to what extent each of these is the same for all men. In regard to the first, the pleasures of all the senses—sight, hearing, etc.—are "the same in all, high and low, learned and unlearned." Similarly in regard to the imagination—which, for him, is no more than the power of representing images of things perceived by the senses, or of "combining these images in a new manner." Since it can only vary the "disposition of those ideas which it has received from the senses," it follows that there must be "as close an agreement in the imaginations as in the senses of men."

The stuff of imagination, then, is the same for all, and its delight consists in tracing resemblances, whereby new images are produced offering fresh food to the imagination; whereas the judgment, concerned always in finding differences, offers no food to the imagination, but on the contrary restricts it and throws stumbling-blocks in the way. Whence, then, the differences of taste? If the stuff of the imagination is the same for all, how is it possible that tastes should vary, or that one should be better than another?

Burke answers that the difference is one of degree, not of kind. Some have greater sensibility to ideas, and have given them closer and longer attention; by which he appears to mean that they have a richer knowledge of life, and an ampler material from which to feed the imagination. But experience of life is not enough. They must also have experience in art. Before a man can take discriminating pleasure in the resemblance which a statue bears to its original, he must have seen many statues. Even then, when he has thus increased his experience, it will not be his taste which will have altered—his satisfaction in the best statue will be no greater than his earlier satisfaction in the worst. It will be merely that his *knowledge* has improved, that his judgment has been brought in, to dissipate the enchantment and "tie us down to the disagreeable yoke of our reason."

The pleasure of art, in Burke's view, consists in tracing or recognizing resemblances, and is the same for all men except in so far as this power of recognizing resemblances may be limited by greater or less knowledge of those ideas which resemble one another. There may be want of knowledge of the objects which are to be represented—that is one way in which the imagination may be defective. There may be want of knowledge of examples of art, which, had they been known, would have made it impossible for the judgment to accept a crude resemblance—that is another cause of inferior taste. In such cases the critical judgment steps in, not to enhance enjoyment, but to limit it.

But in another passage he virtually admits that there are pleasures (other than that of pride) which accompany the use of the judgment. For he recognizes, after all, that the subject-matter of the imagination—the stuff, as we might call it, of which it is compounded—is "not confined to the representation of sensible objects"; it includes also the manners, the characters of people, and much that comes "within the province of the judgment, which is improved by attention, and by the habit of reasoning."

Burke is evidently getting beyond his premises. In his effort to bring in the judgment, he is now constrained to say that imagination is "not confined to the representation of sensible objects," though he has just affirmed the contrary, and has clearly asserted that the imagination can do no more than "vary the disposition" of ideas derived from the senses.

The argument bristles with difficulties which he does not remove. What does he mean by "sensibility," when we merely have ideas of sense, or have them not? Is he not giving a *qualitative* value to the term, which by definition appears to be merely *quantitative*? Again, why should we wish to limit the imagination by the tiresome use of the judgment, if blissful ignorance can pursue the flight of fancy to its dizziest and most delightful heights? Is he not really giving to the *judgment* an æsthetic value of its own, and asserting an element of *truth* in the relation between ideas, an element inseparable from the satisfaction of art? And again, like Addison, does he not fail to distinguish between the representation of ideas in the mind, and their objective representation in art?

He leaves these questions unanswered. His psychology is inadequate for the problem before him. But Burke as an artist-critic is much more satisfactory than Burke as a philosopher. As an artist he recognizes that art is concerned with all the matters of life that concern all men, and that the practice of it depends not upon a separate faculty but a deeper sensibility to life and a profounder attention to it. From this it follows that he does not regard the artist as a different kind of man from ordinary men, but as more of a man; genius is not abnormality, but abundance. His account of the various elements which evoke in us fearful astonishment in presence of the Sublime, or love in presence of the Beautiful, leaves us unconvinced. But he drops the conventional attitude of his time when he comes to consider how it is that we find pleasure in the painful experiences of tragedy. He discards the contemporary view that pleasure arises from the reflection that we ourselves are in no danger of sharing the pain which awakens our tragic pity. He prefers to regard the emotions of tragedy as a strenuous form of activity, an "exercise of the finer parts of the system," a pleasurable surmounting of difficulties comparable to an exertion of the muscles. Perhaps, after all, "pleasure" and "pleasurable" are not the words that matter most when we seek to explain the satisfaction derived from the arts.

So we see that the psychologists of the eighteenth century, like the psychologists of to-day, were very busy in discussing the functional processes of art. Such discussions, though in conformity with logical theory, or carefully based upon experimental science and consistent with the last word in the science of psychology, cannot, even at the best, give us more than an account of the *processes*; they do not thereby account for the character of the experience, or argue away with psychological vanishing tricks the conviction of significance and meaning. Burke begins to be most impressive when he abandons the philosophical language of Locke, and talks common sense with the poet. He recognizes that the method of art is constructive, and that the judgment, by itself, is destructive, its only pleasure being that of "pride and superiority, which arises from thinking rightly." Art in its very nature is creative. It is synthetic, not analytic. The power which is purely analytical is dumbfounded when it seeks to account for a power which is synthetic, or creative. It may indeed "account" for it; but in so doing it looks under, and over, and round, but never *at* the secret it sought to discover; in its scientific retorts it burns up the life whose principle it set out to isolate and reveal, and exposes no more than the charred remnants of forms that have been deprived of their vitality. What in its fundamental nature is constructive, alive, organic may have all its separate elements dissected by analytical philosophy; but it cannot be explained. For creation can only be described in terms of creation; the positive, in terms of positives; life, in terms of life.

Chapter Sixteen

CLASSIC AND ROMANTIC

WHAT, after all, does this famous distinction between classic and romantic come to? Up to now I have kept the question at arm's-length, though the reader may have seen it closing in upon me. I am not sure than I can honourably decline the conflict any longer. Close ahead now, from the viewpoint of the discursive eighteenth century, lies the period of noise, stir, conflict, upheaval with which the modern epoch begins. The old landmarks were to be thrown clattering to the ground. In a few decades the appearance, thought, sentiment and literature of the world were to be radically transformed. In one aspect, this change manifests itself in the speed and fury of the French Revolution. In another, not quite so quickly, but more permanently, in the industrial and scientific revolution. In another, in the awakening of the mass consciousness of nations in flamboyant forms of altruism, humanitarianism, Egalitarianism. In yet another, in the literary and artistic revolution known as the Romantic movement.

It seems, looking back upon it, as if this change in the habits and mentality of the world came upon it suddenly, deafeningly. At one moment all civilized human beings in Western Europe appeared to be reposing in a placid atmosphere where life flowed on according to long tradition, and all men were content with old-fashioned ways. At another moment, but a few decades later, everything has altered; the very language has become different; the way of thought, the approach to problems, the jargon of philosophy, criticism, politics, society—all have undergone a radical change—we have been lifted as by magic into the modern world.

All that happened on one side of the dividing line has the flavour of the antique ; all that happened on the other side is vibrating with modern thought-currents and modern words. To the old way of thought and expression belong Corneille, Pope, Addison and even Johnson—to the new, Lessing, Goethe, Coleridge, Wordsworth, and the solitary Blake. In point of time, these groups overlap, but in character they might be separated by centuries. The first belong to the past, the second to the present.

"Classic" and "Romantic"—before we attempt to get to closer quarters with these terms, a few relevant historical facts should be called to mind.

The style, mental attitude, and achievement of Jean-Jacques Rousseau entitle him, I think, to be described as the first striking literary phenomenon in what is called the Romantic movement. Yet it is not literature which Rousseau challenges, but Society. His life and writings were a protest, not against classical literary standards, but against the stereotyped order of the world. He demands, not the freedom of the artist, but the freedom of man. "Man was born free, and everywhere he is in chains."

His style of writing, it is true, is a new thing in French literature. It is free, impassioned, of the heart ; it is romantic. But his romanticism challenged nothing less than society in all its aspects—government as it was constituted, law as it was administered, religion as it was imposed by the hierarchy, customs and conventions as maintained in the interests of the *status quo*—nothing less than the fixity and established authority of the European system. Against the old gods of custom and privilege he set up the claims of Reason, the rights of Man, the freedom of the individual to remake society in the light of his ideals. His doctrines swept France, and prepared the way for the Revolution. The French Revolution and the literary Romantic movement were products of the same intellectual ferment.

But in the long view, the exciting events which occurred so dramatically in the eighteenth century appear only as culminating incidents in a vaster European movement which began at least as early as the fifteenth. The proper contrast to the twentieth century is not the eighteenth but the thirteenth century, and the critical moments in the long transition between the two occur, firstly, around the year 1500, and secondly around the year 1800. In the mediæval period we have Europe dominated by the Roman Catholic Church and the Feudal System—a society which looked askance at change, discouraged science, suppressed free thought, and imposed the strictest limits to artistic invention. In the later and modern period we find society characterized by ideals of just the opposite order. In the centuries of transition between the two, the ingrained human forces of enterprise and innovation fought their eternal battle with conservatism and authority. First the Roman Catholic Church, then any established Church, then any organized Church became the objects of attack or more damaging indifference. The king, the aristocrat, the plutocrat, and the privileged person one after the other became targets of criticism. Things which had existed through the centuries began to disappear, at first slowly, then very quickly. The factory system supplanted cottage industries. The rural population migrated to the towns. Buildings were hurriedly thrown up and pulled down. Bad roads were replaced by good roads, and these by railways, and these again by arterial motor roads. Bows and arrows and lances gave place to clumsy firearms, and these to quick-firing guns, high explosive, poison gas, and bombs. Aeroplanes came, and airships, and other things more marvellous. The news of the world's doings, once slowly carried by messengers or by rumour, is now disseminated by newspaper, telegram and wireless. What need to pursue the story? A world in which things went on as they had always gone on, under an authority which claimed divine sanction, was replaced by a world of perpetual change in which individual initiative and enterprise receive unbounded admiration.

The earlier break-away from the old order—that of the fifteenth and sixteenth centuries—was characterized by religious changes, by enterprise in geographical discovery, by rapid, though necessarily gradual, progress in science, and by outbursts of romantic activity in literature. But each movement towards what we may call the Left was checked by reaction towards the Right. In England, when the Roman Church went under, the monarchy held up its head proudly, and the Anglican Church flourished with it. When the monarchy went under, the aristocracy prospered abundantly, and summoned to its side the adventitious aids of a political constitution, a respectable Church, a subsidized Press, and a patronized literature. In France a despotic monarchy regained the hold which in the sixteenth century it had nearly lost, and gathered the aristocracy round it; and the Court of Versailles exhaled the combined odour of sanctity and culture. At last the too long bottled-up forces of the modern spirit burst forth in the explosion of the Revolution, which awakened sympathetic echoes in every country of Western Europe.

Here I am only concerned with the literary aspects of these forward and backward movements in the social life of the world. I have already shown how, in his *Apology for Poetry*, Sir Philip Sidney somewhat bashfully defended the cause of what I may now call modernism, and tried to prove to the satisfaction of the orthodox that even poetry is respectable. We have seen how the Elizabethan dramatists cast off the shackles and asserted their freedom with an exuberance which wearied the fastidious, and made their vogue a short one. Ben Jonson sounded the warning note. Rapin and Boileau, in literary criticism, led the final counter-attack, and swept all before them. Sheltering under the revered name of the classics, the critics of the Age of Prose and Reason steadily advanced and held all their gains. It was as if by some ironic cunning of the Time-Spirit that the classics, first summoned to the aid of those who rebelled against mediæval repression, were afterwards successfully used to crush the rebels ; they were actually enlisted on the side of aristocratic authority, pedantic restraint, and critical convention. The first terrific outburst of the Renaissance was followed by a pause, a retreat, a consolidation of positions, a prolonged rest. During such a period the brass-hats always come into their own. The neo-classicists had their way.

Thus in the see-saw of the world movement the contending forces of Classicism and Romanticism rose and fell. But it is already clear that the ancient classics and so-called classicism are not the same thing. Homer and Virgil do not lose their fascination for those steeped in romanticism. The fire of Æschylus did not burn for Pope or Addison, and the humanism of Euripides can have roused few responsive echoes in the heart of Boileau. Yet the neo-classical writers effectively called in the ancients to help them in their task of restoring literary law and order, and of stabilizing the forms and standards of the poetic art. They paid little attention to the gradual, organic growth of drama on Attic soil, and to the fact that the distinctive form which it achieved there in the climax of the fifth century belonged to just that society, at that period, in that part of the world, and could never be reproduced again, in just that way, at any other time or place. They studied its methods, its rules, its technique ; but because they too often studied these without attempting to penetrate to its spirit, they arrived at the rules only, and forgot the poetry and drama. Thus classicism fell into the hands of those whom Walter Pater describes as "praisers of what is old and accustomed, at the expense of what is new"—"critics who would never have discovered for themselves the charm of any work, whether old or new . . . who would never really have been made glad by any Venus fresh-risen from the sea, and who praise the Venus of old Greece and Rome, only because they fancy her grown now into something staid and tame."

Here, then, as Pater sees it, was something spurious, a mockery of beauty in the praises of those who gave it false values. It was a travesty of classicism which passed itself off for the real thing, and brought discredit on it, just as all that is narrow in reaction injures the prestige of the finer conservatism. Pater contrasts this "misleading" idea of the classical with its authentic charm. "The charm of what is classical, in art or literature, is that of the well-known tale, to which we can, nevertheless, listen over and over again, because it is told so well. . . . The 'classic' comes to us out of the cool and quiet of other times, as the measure of what a long experience has shown will at least never displease us."

That, certainly, is not an over-statement of the case for the true "classic," and it would be far too modest if in these words he was describing the art of the Greeks. But he is thinking not of what the Greeks were, but of what their influence has been in the modern world—the qualities of beauty which we have in mind when we contrast the "classical" with the "romantic." In that sense, external beauty will always be the inalienable attribute of the classic, and though it is not absent in the romantic, the emphasis is altered. "It is the addition of strangeness to beauty," Pater suggests, "that constitutes the romantic character in art"—"it is the addition of curiosity" to the "desire of beauty."

The "classic" spirit, then, has its true character; and there are also the perversions of it. Its qualities, when aimed at by meaner minds, become defects. And this is true also of the "romantic"; its brilliant qualities pass into the faults of the exaggerated, the grotesque, the sloppy. But these perversions of type, all the more because they are exaggerations, help us to see the deep-lying distinction between the "classical" and the "romantic" in art. It is not simply a distinction between ancient and modern. There was romanticism, mysticism and grotesque fantasy in ancient literature also. It is a distinction between tendencies, between forms of objective expression which were especially admired by the cultivated Athenian, and forms of self-expression more congenial to the individualists of the north. Perhaps we may compare it with the difference between the Mediterranean Sea, round whose shores classicism has prospered, and the moody northern oceans familiar to Teutons and Scandinavians.

The Greeks saw all their deities in human form. They loved to personify them alike in worship and in artistic representation. Form, outward form, is the first distinctive element in classicism, and on this beauty of outward appearance, with its attributes of symmetry, balance, order, proportion, reserve, it takes its stand. And as contrasted with this the romantic tends to emphasize the spirit which lies behind form—not the formless, but the freedom which is not content with any one form, but experiments, and expresses itself now in this, now in that way, as the spirit dictates. The first tends always to emphasize the "this-worldliness" of the beauty that we know; the second, its "other-worldliness." For the first, then, "the proper study of mankind is man," whilst the second, in its pursuit of the soul, looks for it in strange and unknown places, and in the wilder scenes of Nature:

> Huge cloudy symbols of a high romance.

The one seeks always a mean; the other an extremity. Repose satisfies the Classic; adventure attracts the Romantic. The one appeals to tradition; the other demands the novel. On the one side we may range the virtues and defects which go with the notions of fitness, propriety, measure, restraint, conservatism, authority, calm, experience, comeliness; on the other, those which are suggested by excitement, energy, restlessness, spirituality, curiosity, troublousness, progress, liberty, experiment, provocativeness.

But just because the ancient classical writers were something more than "classics," it was necessary, if their works were to become a real inheritance of the new world, that they should be studied by minds which, being neither too crude nor too stale, could know them as they were. A rare genius such as Dante could penetrate to the soul of Virgil. But the scholars of the Renaissance, Italian, Spanish, French, English, equipped with so slender a basis of native culture, and amazed at the treasure-trove of finished classical literature which lay before them, could not be expected in the earlier readings to learn more than its simplest and most rudimentary lessons; and it was not surprising, as experimenters in the modern tongues gained confidence, that those who had learned these simple lessons should rebuke the more boisterous innovators, and should insist, as Jonson did, on the need for restraint and rule. And we have seen how, at last, the stale spirit of the grammarian came to dominate both the study of the ancients and the criticism of contemporaries.

What was needed in a grown-up age was a study of the classics in the romantic spirit of re-discovery and curiosity. Perhaps it is not really so amazing that this profounder discovery of the beauty and meaning of Greece should come from uncouth, untutored, and as yet unconventionalized Germany. Here the fantastic romance of the old Middle Ages was not yet dead. Here, in the University towns, relics of mediæval scholasticism were to be found side by side with the modern learning, and already in the middle eighteenth century a few young intellects, fired with the new spirit of German nationalism, and zestfully ready to emulate and defy the arrogant culture of France, were tilling the ground for the intellectual ferment of the Romantic movement, as Rousseau was tilling it for the French Revolution.

At the time when the new spirit of exploration and romance was awakening in these younger minds, Johann Joachim Winckelmann was already devoting his life to the re-discovery of Greek culture. In spite of restricted conditions of work, his laborious and passionate study of the painting and sculpture of the Greeks brought him, as we must think to-day, nearer to them than any modern had come before. In his endeavour to probe the secret of their message and their art, he was destined to sing the praises of the classics as no neo-classicist had ever done, and in a spirit romantic enough to help the Romantic movement, whilst actually laying the basis of that sound culture which turned Goethe in his later years back to Hellenism.

"There is but one way for the moderns to become great, and perhaps unequalled," he says, in the *Essay on Grace*; "I mean, by imitating the Ancients."

For a moment that has the all too familiar ring of neo-classicism. But Winckelmann is writing in the atmosphere of scholastic Germany. It is an exclamation of passionate protest against obscurantism, in favour of that sanity and comeliness which he had discovered in long study of Greek painting and sculpture. The sheer love of physical beauty among the ancient Greeks was the trait above all others that drew him to them, and he dwells upon this as revealed in their games and even in the stern regime of the Spartans. He studies with minuteness the manner in which the Greeks of the best period, as contrasted with those of a decadent age, portrayed the human form idealized and beautiful. He notes how in the sculpture of this period "the profile of brow and nose of gods and goddesses is almost a straight line." "The form of real beauty has no abrupt or broken parts." In the human face, "it consists in the soft coalescence of the brow with the nose. This uniting line indispensably accompanies beauty." And in his exact diagnosis he points out how the "eye-bone is magnificently raised" and the "chin thoroughly vaulted," contrasting with the admired models of "degenerate modern times," when "the eye-bone becomes roundish—the chin mincingly pretty."

He was, certainly, preoccupied with the exact details of outward form. But how else, after all, can sculpture be studied? Winckelmann was far from content to take examples of classical art as tradition or custom might present them. In the spirit of painstaking research and inquiry in which the scholars of Germany were soon to distinguish themselves, he set himself to study examples, to compare them, to question them, and above all—as best he could with the meagre opportunities open to him, and no doubt with many mistakes—to distinguish between the later examples of ancient work which had too readily been accepted as models, and the authentic Greek of the best period. In studying these last with affectionate precision he felt that his search for "the form of real beauty" was rewarded.

He is no less exact in his analysis of the perfect form than Boileau had been in his analysis of the perfect tragedy. But he is upon a different quest. His search is for a beauty of a different order. The form is still that which matters supremely—for art is form, and can only present itself through a medium that is objective, external, discernible through the senses. But already the very language of art, as he uses it, is changing. He, a classicist surely, is only able to be so superb a critic of that order because some spirit from the early Romantic movement has already touched him, so that he is able to bring to the study of the Greeks the spiritual curiosity which they themselves possessed abundantly. He endeavours to put himself into their actual frame of mind. He observes how physical beauty, both in their life and in their art, attracted them ; how they devoted themselves no less in their gymnasiums than in their studios to the attainment of it ; and how the stubborn material of art was thus, through art, translated into terms of the emotion which they valued most.

It was not for any paltry reason that they insisted on the simplicity of straight lines, unbroken parts, and bold, grave features. A sculpture, like a poem, was an outward thing which was to convey an inward feeling—though, for them, the inward and the outward were inseparable. Art was a matter of the spirit revealed as form, the artist submitting himself to the conditions which his medium required. He did not closely distinguish, as Lessing did, between the different methods of approach and treatment imposed upon the poet and the sculptor by reason of the difference of their media. But he did exactly study the demands of the artist's medium, because it was through a given medium that he sought to arouse a beautiful emotion.

He does not ask, as a modern might ask, and as indeed some Greeks asked, whether any or every emotion might not be conveyed in an artistic form. He is insistent rather on that nobility and fine emotional satisfaction which the greatest Greeks did in fact endeavour to present or convey. Hence the simplicity, the detachment, the calm splendour of Attic sculpture as of Attic drama. "The more tranquillity reigns in a body, the fitter it is to draw the true character of the soul, which, in every excessive gesture, seems to rush from her proper centre, and being hurried away by extremes becomes unnatural."

"The true character of the soul"—this is not the language of Boileau. The critic of the classics is still concerned with the forms of expression, but only because they are expressive and convey spiritual emotion. And if Winckelmann must still be ranked on the side of the classical, and not of the romantic school, that is because he has transferred his reserves, his demands for a limit, his restrictions, to the spiritual order of things, not because he has dropped them; and also, we should add, because his companions in this reserve are the classic Greeks themselves. Yet it is not a narrow field of emotion to which he would ask the artist to confine himself; but rather, he asks that in revealing it he should never squander his power in showing more than an object, which never changes, can bear, or in so cheating the imagination that it is surfeited at a glance. There may be joy, and sorrow, and terror, but these emotions of a moment cannot spend all their force in a beautiful object which is to remain beautiful for ever.

> In the countenances of antique figures joy bursts not into laughter; it is only the representation of inward pleasure. Through the face of a Bacchanal peeps only the dawn of luxury. In sorrow and anguish they resemble the sea, whose bottom is calm, while the surface raves.

By going back, not to the doctrines of the ancients, but to their works, by endeavouring to relive their life and see the world as they saw it, Winckelmann rescued classicism from the pedants. They, in their academic way, had seized upon the formal rules, and so had lost the formal values. Winckelmann restored the Greek spirit to the Greek body. Keenly aware of its poise, its symmetry, its grace, its restraint, he showed it as alive and buoyant and, in that the artist knew the limits of expression, not therefore less passionate, nor less spiritual. The Greek artist, sensitive to life, exposed to the tumult of passion which, to Sophocles, seemed "a frantic and savage master," clung all the more ardently to his ideal of beauty. That ideal, as Winckelmann reveals it, is a healing harmony of the mind, a tranquillity which makes ecstasy complete. This harmony of the mind the sculptor sought to express in harmony of body, the poet in harmony of verse, the dramatist in harmony of action. For Winckelmann the problem of art was the problem of form, resting upon the prime conception that the body is nothing without the spirit, and the spirit nothing without the body.

Chapter Seventeen

PAINTING AND POETRY

WINCKELMANN has shown how the half-opened mouth of Laocoon, emitting no more than a suppressed sigh, revealed grandeur of soul in a hero racked with bodily pain. Yes, says Lessing, but Virgil's Laocoon cried aloud, and the Philoctetes of Sophocles shrieked and moaned, and filled the camp with imprecations. What does this difference mean? Is the grandeur conceived by the sculptor different from that conceived by the poet? Or should we conclude that there is something in the nature of his art which compels the sculptor to represent one thing, the poet another?

Gotthold Ephraim Lessing, a man more cosmopolitan in his interests than Winckelmann, a poet, a dramatist, a journalist, a student of the classics, and an omnivorous reader of modern literature, including English, wrote and published his *Laocoon* in the seventh decade of the eighteenth century. It was a time when German thinkers were beginning to examine problems of art and literature afresh; to question the hypotheses upon which critical theory had been built up; endeavouring to discover values of art in terms of emotional experience. Some were disposed to release the artist from all restrictions of rule, and to see in the painter, the poet, the philosopher, and the historian men engaged on the one common task of expressing universal truth, even at the expense of beauty. Art, says Lessing, has in modern times been allotted a wide sphere:

> Its imitations, it is said, extend over the whole of visible nature, of which the beautiful is but a small part:

truth and expression is its first law; and as nature itself is ever ready to sacrifice beauty to higher aims, so likewise the artist must render it subordinate to his general design, and not pursue it farther than truth and expression permit. Enough that, through these two, what is most ugly in nature has been changed into a beauty of art.

Truly there is no new thing, and no new theory, under the sun—even in the twentieth century we have encountered similar arguments set forth with an air of novelty. Lessing scarcely pauses to confute them. He is intent upon showing that there are certain limits to expression which are thrust upon the artist by the nature of his medium. His task at the moment was to distinguish the arts by the specific effect each is capable of producing.

The man who first recognized that there is a likeness between the various arts, and that the painter of a picture is engaged upon the same sort of task as the composer of a poem, was the discoverer of Fine Art as a class of human activity. The invention of the nine Muses —though their guardianship extended beyond the arts proper, and did not include all of them—was a primitive and indistinct recognition of the artistic faculty. The common property which unites all the arts was named once and for all by Plato—they are modes of imitation. From that time on critics had no difficulty in recognizing certain principles which were said to enter into every work of art: it was an imitation or representation of reality in various media (words, musical sounds and visible shapes drawn, painted or chiselled) in such a way as to create an illusion of reality and produce an effect of pleasure or satisfaction; and some added, In accordance with the universal laws of beauty.[1]

[1] In modern times there are theorists who accept none of these principles.

The fraternity of the arts being thus defined and established, it has been a delight at all times to poets, painters and musicians to compare one another's methods and to enjoy the comradeship of various craftsmen who are found to be sailing in the same boat and engaged upon the same adventure. Critics have found it profitable to observe the common ground on which poet and painter move. Aristotle laid down certain principles common to all works of art; a picture and a poem must alike conform to the laws of beauty, each being a whole, or an organism, composed of parts arranged in order, and of such a magnitude as to produce the due effect upon the mind of spectator or audience. And he compared poetry with painting in so far as each is concerned with the representation of character—Polygnotus painted men as nobler than they are, Dionysius drew them realistically. And just as he contrasted poets who succeeded in the delineation of character with those who failed, so he contrasted the paintings of Polygnotus with those of Zeuxis.

The comparison of one art with another gives to critics some of the delights of artistic creation. If it be true, as Burke says, that the pleasure of art consists in tracing or recognizing resemblances, here is an admirable opportunity for the critic to combine with his more chilly exercises the luxurious sense of creative effort. Moreover a generous impulse is satisfied if he can endow the poet with the excellences of the painter, the painter with those of the poet. Plutarch approved the saying "poetry is a speaking picture, and picture a mute poesy"; and Ben Jonson repeats the quotation, and declares "it was excellently said."

But no need to go back to Plutarch and Ben Jonson. Living in our Europe to-day is a famous philosopher and critic of criticism who comes near to obliterating all fundamental distinctions between one art and another. I should do an injustice to Signor Benedetto Croce if I attempted to sum up his position briefly at this stage of our inquiry—that is a question for a later chapter. But that I am not far wrong in classing him among those for whom "poetry is a speaking picture, and picture a mute poesy" seems to be confirmed in the view taken by Miss A. E. Powell in her very able account of Croce's *Æsthetic*, in the light of which she examines the romantic theory of poetry.[1] She introduces the view of Lessing as an example of the point of view which is controverted by Croce. (It is only fair to say that in a concluding chapter she puts her finger precisely on the spot—or rather, one of the spots—where Croce's theory of art fails to account either for the practice or enjoyment of it; and therein reinforces the argument by which Lessing, who understood art, if not philosophy, had already in advance given his reply to Croce.)

> Croce [she says] combats the idea that the different arts represent the impressions of different senses. The poet can produce visual or tactile impressions. "And it is a curious illusion to believe that a painter gives only visual impressions. The bloom of a cheek, the warmth of a young body, the sweetness and freshness of a fruit, the edge of a sharp blade, are not all these impressions which we receive even from a picture?" Lessing attempted to show that "bodies with their visible properties are the peculiar subjects of painting . . . actions are the peculiar subjects of poetry," and this because painting can only represent a single moment of time, while poetry, in describing bodies, must give in temporal sequence what has been received as a single impression. . . . Art has nothing to do with sequence in time or juxtaposition in space. Painter and poet express, not the material detail

[1] *The Romantic Theory of Poetry*, Arnold.

> of the practical world, but their own single states of mind. If the painter represents an action, he does not petrify one instant, as does the photograph of a moving person. He gives the whole movement, unifying in his representation a multitude of impressions. He gives, in fact, himself as impressed by the action, his own mental reproduction of it. To him, as to the man who acts, it is single. So, in Lessing's instance of the *Laocoon*, the shriek plays just the same part in the statue as it does in the poem.

The slip in that last sentence touches the root of the matter. The shriek does not play the same part in the poem and in the statue. In the statue there is no shriek at all—no more than a sigh can be emitted from the half-opened mouth. Suppose we grant that the *subject* treated is the same for the poet and the sculptor, and that the state of mind contemplating the subject is the same. In such a case the external expression—and it is that alone of which Lessing is speaking, whereas Croce is speaking of the internal expression—is and must be different. The suffering of Laocoon cannot find the same kind of expression when described in the poet's narrative as when shown in statuary. Nor is the real distinction which Lessing draws touched by the reply which the exponent of Croce would doubtless make; the latter, challenging the hypothesis, would declare that the state of mind which finds expression in sculpture cannot be the same as the state of mind which bursts into poetry: that it is a poetic mind which is expressed in the one, a sculptor's mind which takes form in the other. That may be true, but it does not diminish the essential value of Lessing's distinction—that poetry tolerates and will only tolerate certain modes of expression, painting and sculpture, others. That is to say, poetry is not a speaking picture; painting is not mute poetry.

Lessing is dealing with a practical artistic issue, not with a problem in the philosophy of æsthetics. He presents various facts based on the evidence of artistic experience. We should expect the theorist either to explain these facts, or to produce other and more relevant facts; but merely to contradict them, on the basis of theory, is to be bold to the point of arrogance, and not less so if the theorist is asserting something which the critic was not concerned to deny.

What are the facts to which Lessing calls attention? I anticipate, what I must explain more fully, when I say that he adduces a series of examples from Painting (under which he comprehends the plastic arts generally), of which the Laocoon sculpture is a type, and from Poetry (and kindred literary arts), of which Virgil's *Laocoon* or Sophocles' *Philoctetes* may be taken as types. In each case he shows that a certain mode of representation is and must be employed in order to produce the fullest effect upon a spectator or listener.

That is one order of facts to which he appeals. The second is general, and throws light upon the first. A painting represents objects as related to one another in space, in a single moment of time. A poem presents words which must follow one another in a sequence of time. To his argument it does not matter whether the painter's or poet's state of mind is or is not already a perfect expression; it does not matter whether or not that state of mind is independent of space and time. What is for him relevant and certain is, that a picture, no matter what it expresses, is spatial; that a poem, no matter what it expresses, is a sequence of words in time. That, as he is prepared to show from experience, affects the manner in which the artist in each case attempts to produce his effect.

Here, it is true, we do touch upon an assumption which Lessing does not seek to justify, for its truth seemed self-evident. He takes it for granted—he even lays it down as an axiom—that a work of art is designed to produce an effect. A picture is made to be looked at; a poem is made to be read. It is by the effect it produces on us that we judge it, and it is this effect which the artist seeks to produce. To him it would be idle to suppose that an artist is concerned only with his own "state of mind"; it is the successful *communication* of that state of mind which means success or failure in his task. Again and again he speaks of "the effect" of the artist's art. "Material beauty arises from the harmonious effect of numerous parts." Of a certain passage in Homer he says: "What can *impart* a more lively idea of beauty?" and adds: "What Homer could not describe by its constituent parts he forces us to acknowledge in its effect." The poet's aim is not merely to have clear and lively intuitions, but he must also "awaken in us conceptions so lively that . . ." And he attributes to Aristotle an especial regard "to that necessity of art, namely, of being intelligible to all." Indeed "illusion . . . is the principal end of poetry," and for that reason Sophocles is profoundly concerned, not only with the perfect expression of his own impression of Philoctetes, but "the impression which Philoctetes' cry makes" upon the spectators; and for the same reason it is not enough for the sculptor to apperceive the sufferings of Laocoon—he must "*exhibit* in the body the pain and workings of the poison."

To those who think that in extracting such passages from Lessing I am labouring the obvious, I reply that in this twentieth century such emphasis is not unnecessary. The nineteenth-century doctrine of Art for Art's sake had its truth and its falsity, but its falsity was more easily assimilated and applied than its truth, and has impregnated much modern art with its follies and perversities. To-day it is more necessary than it was in Lessing's time to assert that a work of art exists to be appreciated; that its aim is to communicate—to be intelligible; that a picture or a poem or a novel is not something to be thrown out impertinently in a "take it or leave it" spirit, but should be a work in which nothing has been left unstudied to ensure that its appeal may strike home to others, and that it may convey its full message to tutored and sympathetic minds.

Expression, then, as the artist conceives it, is not an activity confined to his own consciousness, or designed to meet only his own spiritual satisfaction. For him, it is only successful when it renders his meaning intelligible, when it makes his state of mind clear to others, when it carries the thought-content expressed over the threshold of somebody else's consciousness. Expression for the artist is communication; and if this were not so there would be no means by which the critic could judge the value of his work. The practical problem, then, with which every kind of artist is concerned is the manner of externalizing his theme—the poet externalizes his thought in a poem, the painter in a painting. The poem and the painting are the objective means by which his message is to be conveyed to all the world. The technical part of his work, therefore, becomes a matter of first-rate importance; for he has not merely to consider how his meaning may sound or look to himself when expressed, but how his rendering will accurately convey it to others.

So the artist cannot afford to neglect any knowledge

which will help him in his craftsmanship. If he is a painter, it is well that he should know the limits of painting. If he is a poet, he should know where it may be a danger to attempt to paint in words. This is the practical æsthetic question to which Lessing gives his attention in the *Laocoon*.

The group of sculpture now in the Vatican at Rome —a magnificent plastic treatment of the subject which Virgil had handled in the *Æneid*—offered a unique example for Lessing's comparative criticism. The poet tells the tale of the two prodigious serpents rising from the foam of the sea, advancing with hissing mouths and voluminous curves across the land, enfolding Laocoon's children in their double embrace; and describes how the monsters seize Laocoon himself in their huge coils, clasping his waist, encircling his throat, their tall necks towering above him, while he strains with his hands to tear away the knots, and the heavens resound with his shrieks.

Lessing, who assumes that the ancient sculptors had taken their theme from Virgil, notes several points in which their treatment diverges from his. They removed all the coils from the sufferer's body and neck to the thighs and feet. They exhibit him, not clad in his priestly garments, as in Virgil, but naked. They did this because the poetic account which excellently satisfies the imagination was no picture for the artist—whose object it was to "exhibit in the body the pain and workings of the poison." "A garment in poetry is no garment; it conceals nothing." But the sculptors, for whom every lesser aim was subordinate to beauty, refused to suppress the beauty of an organic body beneath the convention of drapery.

The difference is best illustrated by Laocoon's shriek

which Virgil described, the sculptors suppressed, and Lessing has immortalized. This amazing cry rings in our ears as a sound, and seems to rise up before us as a shape through all the importunate pages in which the critic-poet develops his argument.

Did the sculptors reject it, because a cry at the sensation of bodily pain was unbecoming to the noblest of men? Not so; the Greeks had no such feeling.

Or was it because any expression of intense pain is an unbeautiful thing? Again, not so, for the extremity of Laocoon's suffering, expressed in a shriek which rent the sky like the bellowing of a wounded bull, can fill the imagination in Virgil's narrative, and satisfy the demand for beauty.

Does it not rather appear that what was possible, and indeed excellent, in the poem would be impossible, because ugly, in marble?

Lessing reminds us that the Greek artists painted nothing but the beautiful. They did not paint to afford evidence of their skill, or to give bare representation of objects merely because they were real. "Among the ancients beauty was the highest law of the plastic arts," and for that reason they abstained entirely from expressing those passions which required the ugliest contortions of the face. "Rage and despair disgraced none of their productions; I dare maintain that they have never painted a Fury." And for that reason he thinks that in Timanthes' painting of the sacrifice of Iphigeneia he showed the sorrowful faces of the bystanders, but concealed the too sorrowful face of the father; and this not because he despaired of rendering it, but because the grief becoming to Agamemnon could only have been expressed by ugly contortions. Such grief did not admit of being softened into sorrow ; nothing was left but to conceal it.

In like manner the sculptors of the *Laocoon* arrived at the highest beauty compatible with the hero's bodily pain. "Only imagine the mouth of Laocoon to be forced open, and then judge ! Let him shriek, and look at him ! . . . The mere wide opening of the mouth . . . is, in painting, a spot, and in sculpture a cavity ; both of which produce the worst possible effect." To avoid this hideous contortion of the face they softened the shriek into a sigh, and were content to express his full agony in the tension of trunk and limbs.

But Lessing is prepared for the arguments of those who would say : Surely truth is more important even than beauty ! What right has the artist to violate nature in order that he may maintain his idea of the beautiful ?

To which he replies that there are other considerations also which "compel the artist to put certain limits to expression." From the nature of the medium through which he works he can never present an emotion at its highest intensity. Out of ever-varying nature he can only make use of a single moment, and this must be one that can stand the test of long and repeated contemplation.

> Now that only is a happy choice which allows the imagination free scope. The longer we gaze, the more must our imagination add ; and the more our imagination adds, the more we must believe we see. In the whole course of an emotion there is no moment which possesses this advantage so little as its highest stage. There is nothing beyond this ; and the presentation of extremes to the eye clips the wings of fancy, prevents her from soaring beyond the impression of the senses, and compels her to occupy herself with weaker images . . . Thus, if Laocoon sighs, the imagination can hear him shriek ; but if he shrieks, it can neither rise a step higher above nor descend a step

> below this representation, without seeing him in a condition which, as it will be more endurable, becomes less interesting. It either hears him merely moaning, or sees him already dead.
>
> Furthermore, this single moment receives through art an unchangeable duration; therefore it must not express anything of which we can think only as transitory.

Lessing's position, then, comes to this, that the medium in which the painter or sculptor works compels him to present only that which we can bear to have constantly before our eyes, "a thing of beauty and a joy for ever." It must not be hideous, lest it offend. It must not be purely transitory, for it endures. It must not present the moment of greatest intensity, and thus baulk the imagination. He maintains that "succession of time is the department of the poet, as space is that of the painter." "Subjects whose wholes or parts exist in juxtaposition"—namely, "*bodies with their visible properties*" —are the "peculiar subjects of painting"; whereas "subjects whose wholes or parts are consecutive"—namely, actions—are the "peculiar subject of poetry." And in illustration of his view he argues that Homer describes nothing but progressive actions. He never enters into any "description" of a ship. His ship has generally but a single characteristic; it is "hollow" or "swift" or at most the "well-rowed black ship." But in the successive *actions* of sailing, setting out, and hauling up, Homer heaps detail upon detail. Lessing pertinently asks, if the works of Homer were entirely lost, could the richest collection of pictures imaginable give us the ideas which have been imparted by the *Iliad* and the *Odyssey*?

If, then, there is much in the domain of progressive action which the painter must renounce, there is much also that the poet must renounce. He must not paint—must not, that is to say, present a multitude of things which are to be apprehended simultaneously by the eye. Description is not his true domain. Lessing does not say this—as a philosopher might—for the sake of self-consistency and theory, but because the study of poetry leads him to it. He gives many instances to show his meaning, among them Ariosto's description of the bewitching Alcina in *Orlando Furioso.* Here the poet describes one by one the various charms which make Alcina beautiful—her yellow hair, long and knotted, her roseate cheek, her ivory brow, her black, arched eyes, her incomparable nose, her mouth, teeth, neck, breasts, arms and hands. Put each and all of these features in a painting, and the result may be the picture of a woman of entrancing beauty. But the catalogue in the telling leaves us cold. It does not and cannot produce in our minds an image of physical beauty. The words are incapable of conveying "those soft emotions of the blood which accompany the actual sight of beauty."

Are we, then, to conclude that to the painter is denied all that range of expression which belongs to *action* and *movement*—events which succeed one another in time; and that the poet (or the novelist) must renounce *description*, or the detailed portrayal of circumstances which co-exist at a single moment? To be forced to the latter conclusion might be shocking indeed to admirers of the "great descriptive writers" and the magic of their "word-painting."

But perhaps such critics, should they be persuaded, may find that they were not altogether wrong in their approval, though they may have failed to analyse the artistry which won it.

Lessing does not deny that the painter or sculptor may portray a body in movement ; but should he do so, it will be a body arrested at one moment of its movement. What could be more intensely active than the body of Laocoon himself and the coiling serpents ? We could multiply instances indefinitely. I have before me at the moment of writing the print of a somewhat conventional picture illustrating

> Haste thee, nymph, and bring with thee
> Jest and youthful jollity.

What could be more necessary to such a theme than the suggestion of the restless, dancing movement of arms and legs, what more appropriate than the gay whirling of light drapery seen rising or falling in the air ? The suggestion of movement, of action, is essential to such a subject. But all this, being presented at one single instant of time, is subject to the law that any trace of bodily exertion which, though tolerable in an actually moving body, is intolerable in an arrested body, should be eliminated in a picture. There is nothing in the nature of painting which denies that the imagination may fly to preceding actions or anticipate what is to come ; but nothing should actually be there which we cannot be glad to find there for ever.

Or take such a case as Blake's *Reunion of the Soul and Body*. What could be more fiercely energetic than these passionately moving bodies, that of the Soul whose every line suggests headlong descent through the parting clouds, and that of the Body whose stretched limbs betray the irresistible eagerness with which its owner has bounded forwards, the extended arms revealing the rapture with which he is about to clasp his beloved ?

A picture, indeed, of energy and movement incarnate. *Incarnate* in the literal sense. Bodies, said Lessing, are the proper subject of painting. Blake, too, has had to choose a single moment, and he, like the sculptors of the *Laocoon*, has refrained from choosing that of highest intensity, but has selected one immediately preceding it. Just as Laocoon is revealed, not when his suffering finds vent in a shriek, but when his lips are but half-opened, so, in Blake's picture, it is the instant preceding that of the fullest rapture which is arrested, and fixed for ever in his picture. The painting admits only of that one chosen moment on which the eye can linger, and satisfy, without sating, the imagination.

Lessing's argument stands or falls upon his assumption that the value of a work of art depends on its capacity for producing an effect upon us, the effect desired by the artist. This, he maintains, may be produced in painting by elaborate description, but cannot be so produced in poetry and kindred literary arts. He quotes Horace and Pope in evidence of his view, the former declaring that when the poetaster can do nothing more, "he at once begins to paint a grove, an altar, a brook meandering through pleasant meads, a rushing stream, or a rainbow." And in like manner Pope, who desires that he who would worthily bear the name of poet should renounce description as early as possible :

> Who could take offence,
> While pure Description held the place of Sense ?

But does it follow that the poet is shut out from that whole domain of beauty which the painter can unfold in description ? Surely not. Lessing's point is, not that certain desired effects are utterly denied, but that they will be attained by quite different means. Poetry is not painting that speaks. When Homer desires to interest the reader in the shield of Achilles he does not describe it in its finished form, but in the successive actions in which the god forged and hammered and adorned it. And so, again, when Homer brings Helen before the Trojan elders, he knew that he could not make us see her beauty by describing its several parts. " Paint for us, ye poets, the delight, the affection, the love, the rapture which beauty produces, and you have painted beauty itself." Often, too, the poet can come up with the artist by changing beauty into charm. " Charm is beauty in motion." With the painter it becomes grimace. " But in poetry it remains what it is, a transitory beauty that we would gladly see repeated."

We might cite a hundred instances from English literature of the manner in which the poet conveys the effect of personal appearance without describing the constituent parts. What could be more expressive, yet less precisely descriptive, than Milton's introduction of Delilah.

> But who is this? What thing of sea or land?
> Female of sex it seems,
> That so bedeck'd, ornate, and gay,
> Comes this way sailing
> Like a stately ship
> Of Tarsus, bound for th'isles
> Of Javan or Gadire,
> With all her bravery on, and tackle trim,
> Sails fill'd, and streamers waving,
> Courted by all the winds that hold them play,
> An amber scent of odorous perfume
> Her harbinger, a damsel train behind.

That, for the purposes of literature—not dressmaking—may be contrasted with a kind of reporting that is supposed to appeal to women : "The bride wore a gown of ivory taffeta, and a veil of Limerick lace over white tulle. . . ."

If we look closely at examples from that great body of English literature devoted to what is called "descriptive writing," I think we shall discover that it succeeds precisely in so far as it is not purely descriptive, and that it fails when it is so. Part of the tediousness which some readers find in the introductory passages in Scott's novels is due to the fact that he has been too artless in this respect. Some "descriptive" writers who have successfully won their effect and aroused our imaginative interest have done so precisely because they have conveyed by other means that which they could not effectively have painted. Sometimes they have conveyed their impression through action, as Lessing recommends, but also by many other devices, not mentioned by him, which are suitable for engaging a reader's attention. At the disposal of the writer are all those impressions which, when added one to the other in the sequence of narrative, can be held together by the imagination ; and these include not only actions, but all self-sufficient ideas which the mind can immediately absorb, and may be readily conjured up by metaphor, simile, personification, comparison (comparison, for example, with vivid impressions of hearing, touch or smell) and allusion (especially to any "scene" that is already very familiar, whether in nature or in a well-known picture). Thomas Hardy, in his "descriptive" passages, is seldom content to "paint" a scene. He shows us things moving, breathing, appearing ; there is as much that can be *heard* as *seen* in such passages ; and he delights also in recording the effect left on the mind of a spectator. Here is an example from *Far from the Madding Crowd* :

> Between this half-wooded, half-naked hill, and the vague, still horizon that its summit indistinctly commanded, was a mysterious sheet of fathomless shade—the sounds from which suggested that what it concealed bore some humble resemblance to features here. The thin grasses, more or less coating the hill, were touched by the wind in breezes of differing powers, and almost of differing natures—one rubbing the blades heavily, another raking them piercingly, another brushing them like a soft broom. The instinctive act of humankind was to stand and listen, and learn how the trees on the right and the trees on the left wailed or chaunted to each other in the regular antiphonies of a cathedral choir; how hedges and other shapes to leeward then caught the note, lowering it to the tenderest sob; and how the hurrying gust then plunged into the south, to be heard no more.

Again, when Joseph Conrad best succeeds in "description," it is where he is least content to "paint" just objects which are visible to the eye, where he loads his picture with suggestions of impressions made upon the mind, suggestions sometimes of sensations of smell or hearing or touch, sometimes of scenes remembered and called up by the imagination, sometimes conveyed through implied personifications of the relentless forces of nature. Take this from *Heart of Darkness*:

> Going up that river was like travelling back to the earliest beginnings of the world, when vegetation rioted on the earth and the big trees were kings. An empty stream, a great silence, an impenetrable forest. The air was warm, thick, heavy, sluggish. There was no joy in the brilliance of sunshine. The long stretches of the waterway ran on, deserted, into the gloom of overshadowed distances. On silvery sandbanks hippos and alligators sunned themselves side by side. The broadening waters flowed through a mob of wooded islands; you lost your way on that river as you would in a desert, and butted all day long against shoals, trying to find the channel, until you thought yourself bewitched and cut off for ever from everything you had known

> once—somewhere—far away—in another existence perhaps. There were moments when one's past came back to one, as it will sometimes when you have not a moment to spare to yourself; but it came in the shape of an unrestful and noisy dream, remembered with wonder amongst the overwhelming realities of this strange world of plants, and water, and silence.

It is tempting to go on from one example to another. But the reader, if he is interested, can do that for himself, and discover where this or that "descriptive" writer has succeeded, and where, and why, he has failed. And the more we study examples the more sure we shall be that Lessing was right when he showed why the laws of poetry are not the laws of painting. It may be that the separate province of each cannot be defined in terms of feeling or intuition. But in terms of expression, yes. A practitioner in one art may doubtless borrow much that belongs more obviously to another; but he cannot borrow its medium; by the medium he uses he is bound. He defies its limitations at his peril.

Chapter Eighteen

INSPIRATION

THE Romantic movement may profitably be studied as a *phase* in the growth of literature and criticism. The student of principles will be as much interested in what it led to as what it was. A modern critic who seeks only to discover how far it expresses a complete, or fully satisfying, state of mind about art and life will almost certainly come away disappointed or irritated. It is more fruitful, I think, to study it as a stage in development, like that of young manhood, through which the cultured world had to pass before it could become fully adult. This is not a fanciful view. Goethe in his own personal experience lived through all the ardours of romanticism, and put it aside in later life ; he was the richer for his experience, but no longer the victim of its illusions. Coleridge himself, though in essentials he remained a romantic till his death, nevertheless passed right through the growing pains of romanticism to conclusions similar in many ways to those arrived at by Goethe. But when we have said that, let us add that the young adolescent's impressions of value may have as much claim to respect as the second thoughts of the adult. What would the latter be if these impressions were expunged from his memory ?

Just as an active young man, in the years following puberty, begins to purge his mind of the second-hand ideas imposed on him in childhood, and welcomes with open arms the questionings and reconstructions of philosophy, so it was in the storm and stress of the romantic upheaval. The pressing task of the moment was to dispose of encumbering ideas—ideas which had to be cleared out of the way before there could be any further advance. European literature had suffered, as early Greek literature did not, from the tyranny of the dead languages. Classical criticism, helpful as it had been at an earlier stage, became an obstacle to progress. We may put the position thus :

Formal criticism among the ancient Greeks was based upon the practice of a living Greek literature.

The literature of the post-Renaissance world was worried by a criticism, not based on its own literature, but on Roman-Greek literature.

The Greek writers were exposed to a criticism which was based upon native examples, which reflected their own genius, and embodied their own standards.

The moderns, on the contrary, in the seventeenth and eighteenth centuries, were asked to conform to standards of criticism based on an ancient and alien tradition.

The Romantic movement had the effect of clearing this encumbrance out of the way once and for all. It did not kill the classical spirit. But it freed it from artificiality.

We have already seen that this movement was only one aspect of the revolution which was violently changing the life of men from one end of the civilized world to the other. The social and intellectual change which had its first central epoch at the Renaissance reached its second climax at the end of the eighteenth century. It appeared in the growth of science, the application of science to industry, the transference of population from the country to the towns, the accumulation of new fortunes, the breakdown of caste and the differentiation of classes, the development of new studies, such as economics and sociology, and the appearance of a new philosophy and a new literature. External changes, following one upon another with amazing rapidity, stirred the mind and the imagination, and generated intellectual and spiritual changes. The world became conscious of its own movement. Rousseau expressed the social and democratic impulse towards freedom. The makers of verse revolted against cramping verse-forms. In philosophy, Kant denied that the mind was dependent upon objects, or that knowledge was confined to impressions of sense.

> This may well be called the age of criticism [wrote Kant], a criticism from which nothing need hope to escape. When religion seeks to shelter itself behind its sanctity, and law behind its majesty, they justly awaken suspicion against themselves, and lose all claims to the sincere respect which reason yields only to that which has been able to bear the test of its free and open scrutiny.
>
> In metaphysical speculations it has always been assumed that all our knowledge must conform to objects. . . . The time has now come to ask, whether better progress may not be made by supposing that objects must conform to our knowledge.

The literary critic must take some account of these various manifestations of the Time-Spirit. To understand romanticism, he must see at one end of the human scale the pure intellectual element—Kant, Fichte, Schelling turning the mind inwards upon itself, making the reason supreme, or showing the divine reason operating through the individual consciousness. At the other end of the scale were such patent realities as the industrial system, and human beings protesting against it. The great artist stands always in some individual relationship to these two manifestations of the life of his time, the external world moving around him, which is his material, and the intellectual or philosophical accounts of this world which have in some measure impressed themselves upon him, whether they have been the subject of explicit study or not. These two influences combine to determine his perceptions and conceptions at every stage of his awareness to contemporary life, and precisely in proportion as he really belongs to the age in which he lives.

The stirring of the new criticism in Germany made artists and critics peculiarly aware of the manifold possibilities of art. Freed from the restricting channels in which it had so long flowed, it now seemed that there was nothing that literature might not do, no activity which it did not embrace. Frederick Schlegel declared that "Literature is the comprehensive essence of the intellectual life of a nation." He denied that it is possible to put literature in one world and life in another. Their world is the same. He spoke of four bonds which "serve to unite the family of mankind and direct their movements"—the power of money or commerce, the power of the State, the power of Religion, and the power of the Intellect. Literature, as he saw it, was co-extensive with "the whole of man's intellectual life," and included poetry, history, speculation, wit and eloquence. Literary criticism, then, could be nothing less than a comprehensive study of the intellectual life of mankind.

We see the same eagerness in the youthful Goethe to be a master in every branch of knowledge, to be experienced in every activity, in order that he might be complete as man and as poet. The demand which the romantic made upon life and art was for experience, a fuller and wider scope for the realization and assertion of his individual spirit. He put the individual first and foremost, with his claims, his rights, his untrammelled freedom. Therefore it began as a cry for release, release from every kind of rule imposed upon him by authority from without. Whilst the poet's demand for experience led him into new, little-trodden ways, towards the delights of Nature praised by Wordsworth, or the strange recesses of the spirit explored by Blake, his claim to be free from arbitrary authority led him to look inwards for the rules which were to determine his art. The German philosophers seemed to provide the clue for which they were searching, enabling them to find, each in his own consciousness, all that was needed to justify their intuitions; or, if that were not enough, enabling them to trace to an inner source, to God-in-them, feelings which were thus sanctified as spiritual vision.

But the Reason which they exalted was not the Reason of Kant. Blake was frankly aware of the divorce between his mysticism and the methods of pure Reason. All the intellectual gymnastic of Coleridge failed to effect a satisfactory union of that Reason, which for Kant was the faculty concerned only with concepts, and the Imagination, which shaped its world through perceived images. The romantics faced the world confident that they were in possession of a faculty which was neither sense-perception nor reason—though they might call it "Reason in her most exalted mood." It was variously called vision, intuition, imagination, and was based upon inspiration, intimation, illumination, rapture, ecstasy. It was a faculty of perceiving truth immediately through the mind. By it they looked at the world, and saw the world revealed as truth—the fundamental essence of things, not, as in Plato, far aloof from the material world, but in or through it radiantly disclosed:

> Ye Presences of Nature in the sky
> And on the earth! Ye Visions of the hills!
> And Souls of lonely places!

Their faculty of imagination was the power which represented the world of nature and material things, read and transfigured by the spirit. Theirs was a vision whose authenticity was attested by inner conviction, by the ecstasy or illumination which was the mark of genius and the guarantee of truth.

Poetry and the arts were their proper sphere. For it was only in the forms of art that truth could be presented immediately, without the interposition of logical method; it was only through these forms that the same guarantee of truth—the emotion which arises from the beautiful—could be conveyed from the artist to those who contemplate his work. As Nature itself was the expression of the artistry of God for those who had the eyes to see, so a picture or poem directly conveyed the conceptions of its author.

It was in Germany especially that the intellectual revolution was consciously realized, and fought out systematically between the romanticists, who asserted the supremacy and freedom of the individual spirit, and those who, following in the steps of Winckelmann, tried to restate in more modern terms the claims of classicism. German Romantic criticism gave currency to the nineteenth-century tradition of a poetry which combined within itself inspiration and intuition—inspiration, in that it drew its force from some mightier cosmic force beyond itself, of which it was only the vehicle—intuition, in that the poet gazed into life, and by direct vision saw life in its true forms, and re-created it thus. Not, indeed, that the view of poetry as inspired had ever been wholly lacking since the god of his grace gave to the Homeric poet "the gift of wondrous song." Even for Plato it was an inspired and magical thing, though the ecstasy that it induced was for him a kind of divine madness, perhaps even an inspiration of the devil. For Longinus, too, poetry was illumination. "A sublime thought, if happily timed, illumines an entire subject with the vividness of a lightning flash." Never had that conception of a poet as an inspired prophet been wholly forgotten. Even the eighteenth century continued to speak respectfully of "inspiration," but it was that of a very decorous muse, curbed by pedestrian rules. But with the romantic poets the vatic view became once again a matter of passionate belief, based upon a passionate experience. And when once this view got into the air, and became a part of current thought, it was sure to be, in an intellectual age, subsumed under philosophy; the "inspiration" view had to be given a philosophical sanction; and because philosophers are social human beings before they are philosophers, it became, perhaps, a driving force behind new philosophical systems.

From the nature of their faith the romanticists launched upon the world the man of genius, the artist divinely inspired, including that strange phenomenon which loomed so large in the Victorian imagination—the Great Man. Little wonder that he was Great. For he was deemed to speak with the voice of God.

Chapter Nineteen

THE ROARING FURNACES

I

WHEN I first read Professor Saintsbury's account of the prosody of the romantic poets I had the feeling that for him the whole movement was just a question of a new use of metres. As his subject was Prosody, he was of course justified in stressing this single aspect of romanticism. The effect of his book is to show that in this, as in every other respect, the poets of that troublous period were innovators. They were innovators in the use they made of accent and metre, just as they were in intellectual and emotional issues. For the monotonous, syllabic metre of the formal eighteenth-century poets, says Professor Saintsbury, they substituted "equivalent feet," in which the number of syllables and the accent were freely varied. Wordsworth and Coleridge were fully conscious of the vivacity they thus imparted to poetry.

William Blake was equally conscious of it, and in the preface to *Jerusalem* (printed 1804) he is perfectly explicit about it:

> When this Verse was first dictated to me I consider'd a Monotonous Cadence like that used by Milton and Shakespeare, and all writers of English Blank Verse, derived from the modern bondage of Rhyming, to be a necessary and indispensable part of Verse. But I soon found that in the mouth of a true Orator, such monotony was not only awkward, but as much a bondage as rhyme itself. I therefore have produced a variety in every line, both of cadences and number of syllables. Every word and every letter is studied

> and put into its fit place; the terrific numbers are reserved for the terrific parts, the mild and gentle for the mild and gentle parts, and the prosaic for inferior parts; all are necessary to each other. Poetry Fetter'd, Fetters the Human Race; Nations are Destroy'd or Flourish in proportion as their Poetry, Painting, and Music are Destroy'd or Flourish.

"Poetry Fettered." In theory as well as in practice the Romantic movement began with the smashing of fetters. In enthusiastic fury Blake denounced the verse forms which had become traditional. He poured his contempt upon all that he associated with classicism in art and in criticism. "We do not want either Greek or Roman models," he says in the Preface to *Milton*, "if we are but just and true to our own Imaginations." In fragments on Homer and Virgil he irritably declares: "It is the Classics, and not Goths nor Monks that Desolate Europe with Wars": "Grecian is Mathematic Form . . . Gothic is Living Form." The whole jargon of neo-classical criticism had evidently wrought upon his nerves. He cannot be patient with it. In his favourite Scriptural language be asserts that "Israel delivered from Egypt is Art delivered from Nature and Imitation"[1]; and in the Homer fragment he is in the mood to attack any doctrine that is handed down in the name of Aristotle—"Unity is the cloak of folly"—"Goodness or Badness has nothing to do with character."

Such outbursts reveal the fierceness of his reaction against conventional thought and customary morality, against blind laws which extinguish individuality, energy and spiritual delight. The great tragedy for him, as Messrs Maclagan and Russell have said, was "the parting of Reason and

[1] Among the statements printed round the *Laocoon* engraving.

Imagination." The "Reasoning Power," divorced from the Imagination, was :

> An Abstract objecting power, that negatives everything,
> This is the Spectre of Man, the Holy Reasoning Power,
> And in its Holiness is closed the Abomination of Desolation.

Under the influence of this "Body of Death around the Lamb of God" he saw "Imagination denied, Genius forbidden by laws of punishment" and "loveliness as a dry tree."

His ambition was to sweep the encumbrances out of the way and release man's natural energy. "Energy," he said, "is eternal delight." He sought to make his "furnaces roar," in order that "Enthusiasm and Life may not cease." Art, for him, could not be a game of play. It could not be a side-issue, a means of mere pleasure, or a vehicle of formal instruction; it must be something that should "move" in the fullest sense of the term ; it was a vision of fundamental living realities discerned, not by the Reason, but through the eye of the mind. Denying the validity of ideas imposed by custom, asserting that of his own perceptions, he did not hesitate to bring those perceptions into relation with the divine ordinance of the universe, and to declare that his vision was a vision of truth.

I must not here attempt to discuss his mystical doctrines, or to reconcile such statements as "Energy is the only life and is from the Body" with "Man's perceptions are not bound by organs of perception." But we may note sayings such as these : "He who sees the Infinite in all things, sees God"—"Christianity is Art"—"Human Imagination . . . is the Divine Vision and Fruition"—"I come in Self-annihilation and the grandeur of

Inspiration. . . . To cast aside from Poetry all that is not Inspiration"—and this from *Milton*:

> These are the destroyers of Jerusalem . . .
> Who pretend to Poetry that they may destroy Imagination,
> By imitation of Nature's images drawn from Remembrance.

My business in this work is not to consider what this or that poet did, but what principles of art he asserted and brought to the light of conscious criticism. If, then, we should ask Blake what principles the poet should observe, he answers that no formal rules or external literary laws have any authority. The artist's only warrant must be looked for within himself. Of many of his own poems he declares that they were "dictated" to him—dictated by spirits. In this most literal sense he held that "inspiration" could come to the aid of a poet; when he was thus inspired, "Imagination," or the Divine Vision, was the faculty which he used. Energy and delight accompany this expression of the Divine Vision; and we may conclude that the evocation of this vision in those who contemplate a work of art accounts for their delight in it, and what we call the impression of beauty.

Blake claims for the poet, not that it is his aim to please, or to give rational instruction, but to reveal—to reveal, that is, what is given to him as true. This may mean two things, and in Blake's practice it does mean two things. It means, in the more satisfactory examples, that he presents through the sensible forms of art that which his "mind's eye" sees—a world of reality, not as it can be judged by the reason, but apprehended in imaginative experience. This is very different from attempting to express in art an explicit account of a system of the universe. When the poet attempts the latter it is fair to say that he is confusing the task of the artist with the task of the philosopher or theologian. And this Blake, with the true mystic's disposition to interpret his feelings in terms of theology, often does. "Mysticism," said Goethe, "is the scholastic of the heart, the dialectic of the feelings." When Blake gives way to his impulse to expound, he lays himself open to Miss Powell's criticism, when she complains that what he is portraying "is knowledge, not Art"—and that "he regards Art not as an expression of the individual, but as the representation of eternal truth."

But when Blake ceases to expound, to argue, to prove, to persuade—to perform those didactic tasks which we have already distinguished from that of the artist—and is content to *show* us his world, to present, to reveal that in experience which is significant to him, then he is behaving as a poet. Nor is it a just objection to this portrayal of his imaginative world that it lends itself to interpretation, by himself or by another, in the logical terms of a metaphysical or mystical system. The deep feeling which accompanies poetry may be ascribed by him, as it is by most of the romantics, to a transcendent order of reality. But that has nothing whatever to do with the quality of the poetry, which remains poetry if its appeal is immediate, its method not logical. A work of art may stimulate logical judgments, or be specially consistent with certain logical judgments rather than others. But its own method is never that of logic.

And here, precisely, Blake's theory is better than his poetical practice. For he does assert, once and for all, that art depends upon vision, perceptions and the feeling of energy accompanying it, and not upon ratiocination; it is immediate, not discursive. Painting and engraving did not offer the same temptation to wander from the path.

Thus whilst his poetry is marred by the mystic's practice of mingling imagery and dogmatism, his graphic work more consistently reveals his true artistic genius. There, the artist is seldom confounded with the prophet and preacher.

His example should help to convince us that prophecy, as such, has nothing whatever to do with poetry.

II

From the blurred theories of Blake we turn to the more explicit principles of Wordsworth, set forth in the Prefaces to *Lyrical Ballads*. Wordsworth proceeds from the same starting-point — dislike of the artifice and restricted forms of approved eighteenth-century poetry. He too expresses the break-away from formal authority. Disgusted by the "gaudiness and inane phraseology of many modern writers," he castigates poets who "separate themselves from the sympathies of men, and indulge in arbitrary and capricious habits of expression, in order to furnish food for fickle tastes, and fickle appetites, of their own creation."

Just as Blake turns from literary artifice to "Enthusiasm and Life," to Inspiration, to the inner light of the Imagination, so Wordsworth turns to the inner evidence of vivid sensation and spontaneous feeling. "All good poetry is the spontaneous overflow of powerful feelings." He, too, discards Aristotelian doctrine. For him, the plot, or situation, is not the first thing. It is the feeling that matters. In his own poems "the feeling therein developed gives importance to the action and situation, and not the action and situation to the feeling." And just as Blake's Imagination was justified because it was inspired, so for Wordsworth strong feeling carried its own passport; it revealed "primary laws of our nature." In the *Lyrical Ballads* he proposed to make "incidents and situations interesting by tracing in them . . . primary laws of our nature: chiefly, as far as regards the manner in which we associate ideas in a state of excitement." But his innate artistic sense leads him to qualify these words: primary laws are to be traced "truly"—"though not ostentatiously." He, too, betrayed uneasiness when he appeared to be setting the teacher to instruct the singer.

His aim was to find the best soil for the "essential passions." In eschewing artifice, he looked for simplicity. He thought the problem was solved by the deliberate choice of subjects from "humble and rustic life." He had found poets extravagantly preoccupied with the affairs of nymphs and goddesses. Why not portray the deep emotions of village girls and peasants? He was guided by a sound instinct when he said "avoid poetic diction." There was a healthy realism in the demand that the poet should use "the language of men," "the language of prose when prose is well written"; and that he should aim to "keep the reader in the company of flesh and blood." But the flesh and blood of a yokel are not more human than the flesh and blood of a townsman. The emotions of a rustic are not more profound because his experience is narrow. In rightly condemning a too specialized language of poetry, Wordsworth advocated a language that was always in danger of becoming "trivial and mean." In proportion as he confined himself too exclusively to characters chosen from "humble and rustic life," he confined himself to persons for whom many essential elements in human experience were lacking. It was emotion which he sought to display.

But his principle lessened the range without deepening the quality of emotion. It is when he most strictly obeys his own injunctions that he writes his least satisfactory poems. The end he had in view could have been better attained by the portrayal, not of crude rustic persons, but simple, sharply defined characters in which a few qualities were deeply graven—heroes like Œdipus, or Lear, or Giles Winterbourne—characters set in some clear emotional relationship with the "beautiful and permanent forms of Nature."

In his romantic detestation of artifice, Wordsworth committed himself to the doctrine of artlessness. "Poetry is spontaneous utterance." Yet Dante had said that "Poetry and the language proper for it are an elaborate and painful toil." Wordsworth advocated a language that was to be the "language of men," and especially of men in "humble and rustic life." Dante, on the contrary, had said "Avoid rustic language." Write in the Vernacular, but let it be the "Illustrious Vernacular." Longinus, too, had required "a certain loftiness and excellence of language"; and the contrast to this was "puerility."

But we must remember that while Wordsworth, like other romantics, demanded spontaneity, it was not that of a careless or thoughtless person. "Poems to which any value can be attached," he says, "were never produced on any variety of subjects but by a man who, being possessed of more than usual organic sensibility, had also thought long and deeply." That also was the view of Coleridge. The poet was a man of great sensibility whose mentality was already shaped, before the moment of inspiration, by deep and habitual reflection. The pondering had already been done. The situation which was to affect him poignantly, awakening vivid emotion, would pass through the "intellectual lens" of his imagination to his fully prepared consciousness. Without further pondering, the response of the emotions sufficed to show that the Imagination had truly functioned. It was in that crisis of the mind when sensation was vivid, when the faculties were taut and keen, when the whole of the poet's being trembled at the perception of beauty in the world about him, that he had the moment of his highest experience:

> . . . the hour
> Of splendour in the grass, of glory in the flower.

The state of awareness of spiritual significance in common things was for Wordsworth the consummation of poetic experience, the *summum bonum* of the poet's life. This is the characteristic romantic view. And because they consciously held this view it was natural that the romantic poets, in their less happy moods, should tend to dwell too luxuriously on their own emotions, describing them from within, rather than the facts of life which evoked them. In these introspective moods we find them writing subjectively, rather than objectively, and laying themselves open to the charges brought against them in the Crocean argument of Miss Powell, when she says that it is the business of the poet, not to be passive to impressions, but to express them; not to wallow in emotion, but to purge it away in the spiritual energy of intuition.

They are often guilty. But when they are, it is not because they are carrying out the avowed principles of Wordsworth or Coleridge — it is from a degenerate misapplication of those principles. When Keats writes:

> My heart aches, and a drowsy numbness pains
> My sense, as though of hemlock I had drunk

he gives us an intolerable example of sickly preoccupation with his own emotions. But the vivid experience for which Wordsworth looks is far more happily expressed when the poet recovers himself, in the following perfectly objective lines :

> That thou, light-wingèd Dryad of the trees,
> In some melodious plot
> Of beechen green, and shadows numberless,
> Singest of summer in full-throated ease.

Coleridge, as we shall see, was as emphatic as Goethe in condemning the subjective exhibition of emotion, and pointed out that the man of genius chooses "subjects very remote from the private interests and circumstances of the writer himself." Any excess, of course, can shelter under a doctrine of "spontaneity." But in the professed theory of Wordsworth and Shelley, while there is much which explains, there is certainly nothing which demands, the subjective attitude to experience.

It is true they rated experience, personal experience, very high. I think we may go so far as to say that Wordsworth valued art for the sake of experience, rather than experience for the sake of art. There was nothing he prized so much as the state of mind experienced in his happiest contemplation of Nature, and nothing he so much wished to hand on through his poems. We may clearly recognize and assert about Wordsworth, that the experience of the poet in contact with Nature was of supreme value to him ; and it was this certainty of its supreme worth which made him deem it a divine intimation. But this does not mean that the experience was best expressed by analysing his feelings of the moment. On the contrary, just as it was called forth in him by the contemplation of Nature, so the poet would surely evoke it in others by showing them the same objects as had moved him, if possible under the same light. To extract in art the utmost value from a vivid experience is consistent with a wholly objective artistic method.

The romantic poets started from an interest in life, rather than art. It was the worth-whileness of their impressions of life which mattered for them more than anything else, and it was this, they held, which gave value to poetry. A supremely interesting, and primarily emotional, state of mind, arising from the contemplation of life, was postulated as a condition of art. If they had been confronted with Croce's "expression of impressions" they would not have quarelled with the demand for "expression," but they would have laid all the emphasis on the quality of the "impressions." The "impression" was the first important thing that happened to the poet. It was the only important thing which finally repeated itself in the mind of the reader. The point that drew their insistent attention was its quality, its worth-whileness —the desirables which poetry could communicate.

III

Shelley's reasoned account of poetry naïvely justifies much that Matthew Arnold condemned in him. The "beautiful and ineffectual angel, beating in the void his luminous wings in vain," provides a defence of himself in his *Defence of Poetry*. "Poetry," he says, "in a general sense, may be defined to be 'the expression of the imagination'; and poetry is connate with the origin of man. Man is an instrument over which a series of external and internal impressions are driven, like the alternations of an ever-changing wind over an Æolian lyre, which move it by their motion to ever-changing melody." It is the divine mind which thus stirs the poet to effortless song, and impels him, he knows not how, to create "the very image of life expressed in its external truth." A poem is "the creation of actions according to the unchangeable forms of human nature, as existing in the mind of the Creator, which is itself the image of all other minds." More than any other romantic critic he presents the poet moving in a world of other-worldliness, creating things in the image of his own spirit, and man in the image of an abstract God.

It is the feeling of ecstasy which he, like Wordsworth, values supremely; and the presence of that feeling is for him the sign of inspiration and truth. Blake said that his poems were "dictated" to him; Shelley, that they were breathed into him by "some invisible influence":

> A man cannot say, "I will compose poetry." The greatest poet even cannot say it; for the mind in creation is as a fading coal, which some invisible influence, like an inconstant wind, awakens to transitory brightness. . . . When composition begins, inspiration is already on the decline, and the most glorious poetry that has ever been communicated to the world is probably a feeble shadow of the original conceptions of the poet.

When we read that, it will not do to say simply that Shelley is wrong. For Shelley is giving us evidence of what he felt to have happened in his own case, and as evidence we must accept it. Our question is, what does that evidence mean? Certainly, that the feeling of illumination or rapture with which his creative mood started was more intense than his feeling when he was distracted by the labour of composition. Certainly, also, that what he hoped to communicate to others in the poem was precisely that feeling of illumination or rapture which began to fade as he wrote. And surely most lovers of poetry will go with him in wishing that the sense of that brightest moment of his dawning intuition might be the very impression which his poem will impart. But Shelley affirms that in his own case this was not possible; that he could give only of his second best; that the spirit of his finest mood could never be fixed for ever in the created work.

Now is this an essential defect in poetry, or is it a defect in Shelley's way of going to work? Is it not possible that he has neglected some part of his proper task? He has himself provided the answer. It is when he echoes the views of Wordsworth, that poetry is "spontaneous utterance." "I appeal to the greatest poets of the present," he says, "whether it is not an error to assert that the finest passages of poetry are produced by labour and study."

Shelley thus admits his view that poetry should be a sort of sublime bird's song given forth with "unpremeditated art." But it was a greater than he who said that it should be an "elaborate and painful toil." Dante did not say that feeling, emotion, ecstasy come with pain and forethought. He, too, might have agreed that they come, unpremeditatedly, like the inconstant wind. But he did say that to transmute these into the language of art there must be pain, toil, elaboration. The view of Shelley and Wordsworth, based upon a doctrine of happy inspiration, makes poetry too easy for the poet. Theirs was a theory which dangerously panders to laziness, commending the poet when he yields to sensuous temptation and soars with the too easy and "ineffectual" flight of the angel. Too much belief in divine assistance led them to neglect the fact that the poet has to sit down and face squarely the hardness of the beautiful, and address himself to the technical job of expressing his feeling in recognizable terms of life, giving objective form to his ideas. Art has to be true to life—the life about us—as well as true to feeling—the feeling which is peculiarly the artist's. It is a part of the poet's job to discern with perfect clearness just what that is in Nature or in action which has or might have evoked the feeling that he thought worth while, so that he may set it forth again in imaginative language, for all who have eyes to see. Because it is his task to communicate, as well as to experience, he cannot afford to neglect any aid which work, thinking, technique can put at his disposal.

There we have the weakness of the Romantic poets, to which their conscious theories led them. But these defects later generations could avoid. The gigantic positive achievement, which is inseparable from their theory, stands, a monument for ever. They successfully maintained that poetry—or art—is the proper vehicle for the feelings. They declared once and for all that poetry could never be cleverness, never be prosody, never just correctness or the observation of rules. It can never be what the man with no " music in his soul " can judge by a foot-rule or a book of grammar. It can never be compassed by learning. It can never consist in conceits, or fancies, or artifice of any kind, and will never deserve its name if it does not express perceptions of life received with conviction. From all those ingenuities and insincerities they rescued poetry, if not for ever, at least until affected people arrived with the jargon of "Art for Art's sake," or still cleverer people who persuade us to accept fascinating jig-saw toys for poetry. The Romantic poets did not think it enough to astonish. They thought it necessary also to "move."

" It will be the business of the poet so to speak in his verses that he may teach, that he may delight, that he may move." Thus Minturno, whose words I venture to repeat. This third term in a definition of poetry—to " move "—was definitely added by the Romantic poets.

Chapter Twenty

THE ESEMPLASTIC IMAGINATION

I

COLERIDGE did not say with Jonson that "to judge of poets is only the faculty of poets." He was content to ask that a spectator should "judge in the same spirit in which the Artist produced, or ought to have produced." To enable the reader to do so is his avowed object in the *Principles of Genial Criticism.* Much of his life was devoted to critical theory, and even to "delving in the unwholesome quicksilver mines of metaphysic depths"; but, like Lessing's critical genius, he had "within himself the evidence of all rules." In later life, when he complained that "the feelings of the heart" were unawakened, and he sought refuge in intellectual researches, he availed himself of the evidence afforded him in that "blessed interval, during which my natural faculties were allowed to expand, and my original tendencies to develop themselves: my fancy, and the love of nature, and the sense of beauty in forms and sounds."

He seems to have felt that to become a critic was all that a "mismanaged sensibility" left him—the second-best with which he consoled himself. But there are solid gains to set off against the loss. The result, for criticism—embodied as it is in a curious jumble of writings, scattered and often unfinished—affords the most complete exhibition of the within and without of poetry that has ever been given—the poet observing his own experience, the critic subsuming that experience under principles, and the whole strangely intermingled with the verdicts of a fastidious and catholic taste. Before we have finished with him we discover two Coleridges: one, the poet, the friend of Wordsworth, the transcendental philosopher-critic who seeks philosophic grounds for the romantic conviction; the other, a many-sided humanist and connoisseur of letters, with unbiassed and unfaltering taste delivering pure judgments about the poetic art.

The two sides meet. They meet again and again. They even dovetail into one another with surprising success. The humour of Coleridge in his second capacity is sufficiently present to his romantic other self to save it from extravagance. His practical judgments about art, governed by his sense as a poet, are generally in harmony with his more "abstruse researches," governed by his intellect. That fact should put us on our guard against his logical critics. They may successfully pick holes in his logical reasoning, but that will not altogether dispose of his principles. His technical statement of his metaphysic may be faulty. But sound fruit does not come from a tree which is wholly rotten.

The bent of Coleridge's mind was not determined by those German thinkers whom he was afterwards to find so congenial. The world, which was ready for German transcendentalism, ready for Wordsworth and Shelley, ready for the intense passion of revolution, found, in the young Coleridge, an apt interpreter of its spirit. Looking back upon his youth, in the *Biographia Literaria*, he recalls that he felt but little sympathy for the writings of Mr Pope and his followers, or "that school of French poetry" which, he admits, was "condensed and invigorated by English understanding." He was equally dissatisfied with the artifice of this school, and with the quest for "mere novelty"—"the desire of exciting wonderment at his powers in the author." More to his taste were the poems of Bowles and Cowper, the first, then living, poets "who combined natural thoughts with natural diction; the first who reconciled the heart with the head."

The union of heart and head. There he already strikes the keynote. Nothing without that is ever to be *essential poetry* for him. When, as a young man in the early twenties, he concludes "that, not the poem which we have read, but that to which we *return*, with the greatest pleasure, possesses the genuine power, and claims the name of essential poetry," we are reminded of Longinus, whom at that time he probably had not read. Coleridge finds that it was "a continuous *under-current* of feeling" which evoked his genuine admiration in a great poet, and the lack of it which disgusted him with those who "sacrificed the heart to the head," or "both heart and head to point and drapery."

He was already of this mind when he first came to know William Wordsworth. One dramatic moment in the first year of this friendship awoke in him the conviction which thenceforward dominated his critical attitude:

> While memory lasts, I shall hardly forget the sudden effect produced on my mind, by his recitation of a manuscript poem. . . . There was here no mark of strained thought, or forced diction, no crowd or turbulence of imagery. . . . It was not however the freedom from false taste . . . which made so unusual an impression on my feelings immediately, and subsequently on my judgment. It was the union of deep feeling with profound thought; the fine balance of truth in observing, with the imaginative faculty in modifying the objects observed; and above all the original gift of spreading the tone, the *atmosphere*, and with it the depth and height of the ideal world around forms, incidents, and situations, of which, for the common view, custom had bedimmed all the lustre, had dried up the sparkle and the dewdrops. . . .
>
> This excellence, which in all Mr Wordsworth's writings

> is more or less predominant, and which constitutes the character of his mind, I no sooner felt, than I sought to understand. Repeated meditations led me first to suspect . . . that fancy and imagination were two distinct and widely different faculties, instead of being, according to the general belief, either two names with one meaning, or, at furthest, the lower and higher degree of one and the same power. . . . Milton had a highly *imaginative*, Cowley a very *fanciful* mind. If therefore I should succeed in establishing the actual existences of two faculties generally different, the nomenclature would be at once determined.

Thus we are introduced to the first conception of that theory of Imagination which became the cardinal element in Coleridge's principles of criticism. And here let us mark the fact—and beg the attention of destructive philosophic critics who bring their professional heavy guns to bear upon him—that this conviction in his mind did not begin as a deduction from metaphysical principles. It was, in the first place, a practical conviction drawn from experience, from his working knowledge of and feeling for poetry and nature. Years later, after prolonged wrestling with the problems of metaphysics, he thought himself into a philosophical justification and explanation of it. But in expounding his system he did less than justice to himself and his readers. He discoursed of it in lectures which have been lost. There are scrappy allusions to it in his letters. He elaborately leads up to it in long discursive passages in the *Biographia*, but as he approaches the crucial chapter which was to set forth his theory in full, he breaks off abruptly, giving no more than an epitome, in a few sentences, of "the main result." With the characteristic clumsiness of his later life he leaves us to piece together his metaphysical doctrine as best we can.

But he has left us in no doubt about what I have called

the practical conviction, which entered deeply into his mind before he attempted a metaphysical account of it. And this, which is an experience-fact, is perhaps what will have most weight with us, and may stand where the ingenuity of a system may fail.

Let us see how the problem arose for him. He read the "faulty elder poets" and his contemporaries with perfunctory admiration, or without admiration. He found them lifeless, or brainless, or both. He could not discern in them that continuous "undercurrent of deep feeling" which the greater poets had evoked.

Then, in one memorable hour, a poem recited by Wordsworth brought home to him in a flash what he had been seeking to realize. Surely it was by some faculty of the soul that things could be so represented as to be thus both felt and understood. No mere heaping together of lifeless images, no mere juxtaposition of ideas—no mere "arbitrary bringing together of things that lie remote"—could account for the indissoluble one-ness of this perception of beauty and conviction of truth. The psychologists had dissected the human consciousness and shown nothing there but a collection of impressions, images, notions—all dead, cold, and empty. The "fanciful" poets had called upon memory and the mechanical power of associating ideas, and ingeniously presented us with "aggregates"—not living images. But when a poet like Wordsworth handled the material which nature presents—that very material which, mechanically received through the senses, is just sensation and no more — something happened to it. It was itself, but it became different. It assumed a form. It became beautiful. The heart warmed to it. The understanding embraced it. For this experience, as Coleridge understood it, was more than mere feeling, emotion, passion. Its unique quality lay in the fact that it gave satisfaction also to the reason. It was a union of opposites. It bridged the gulf—unbridgable by the intellect—between perception and understanding. The power which the poet had exercised in thus revealing the "beautiful and permanent forms of nature" was the "shaping spirit of Imagination," a unifying, creative faculty —"this beautiful and beauty-making Power."

There are those who would dismiss this introduction of the Reason as the arrogance of an artist seeking to flatter his intuitions. But let us take Coleridge on his own ground. He sought to make room for the fact that a sublime object derives its sublimity from the spectator's awareness of significance in it. That notion of significance could not be accounted for by any analysis of the separate sensations of which the vision appeared to be composed. Therefore, though it arose from an impression that is *given*, it could only be by some power in the soul that a character was discovered in it. He attributed it to a faculty of the soul, which gives what it receives, and receives what it gives—and this act, a volitional act, of bringing to nature something which it was capable of accepting, or of voluntarily accepting from nature that which the imaginative mind was so constituted as to receive, implied, for Coleridge, a "common ground" between nature and the spirit, between the symbol and the mind which could recognize it or create it :

> O lady ! we *receive* but what we *give*,
> And in *our* life alone does nature live !
> Ours is her wedding-garment, ours her shroud !
> And would we aught behold of higher worth,
> Than that inanimate cold world allow'd
> To the poor, loveless, ever-anxious crowd :
> Ah ! from the soul itself must issue forth

A light, a glory, a fair luminous cloud,
Enveloping the earth !
And from the soul itself must there be sent
A sweet and powerful voice, of its own birth,
Of all sweet sounds the life and element !

II

Coleridge set himself to investigate philosophically the "seminal principle" of the Imagination, and to discover the nature of that faculty of the soul by which the poet expresses himself through the forms of art. Metaphysics has no place in the present work, which is concerned with the principles of literature examined from a lower plane of truth. I must try, therefore, as best I can, in a few paragraphs, to indicate the part in consciousness which Coleridge allotted to the "Esemplastic Imagination" ("*Esemplastic* . . . εἰς ἓν πλάττειν, to shape into one"). In Kant he found that the imagination played a subordinate part, merely synthesizing the *data* of sense, giving it forms which could be taken up in the higher synthesis of the understanding. The imagination was a link between the world of sense and the conceptual world of the understanding. But though this faculty could reproduce and combine the particulars of sense, it could only hand on forms drawn from the raw material presented to it, how or whence we know not, in sensation.

Coleridge allotted a wholly different part to this faculty. He refused to accept the view that ideas of sense are imposed upon the consciousness from without, rather than determined by it ; or that the Reason, at the other end of the scale, is incapable of absolute knowledge. The root difficulty of philosophy being to reconcile mind and matter, you may begin with matter, and attempt to explain mind in terms of matter, or you may begin with mind, and attempt to deal with matter in terms of mind. But always, in the principle of consciousness, you are confronted with the " I know " and with " that which is known "—the subject and the object. The self which is conscious appears to determine the object of which it is conscious, and, equally, the object appears to determine the consciousness. How to explain the contradiction that the mind determines that which itself determines the mind?

Coleridge concludes, with Schelling, that the principle of consciousness can be neither simply the thing perceived, nor the self perceiving it. It must be both. The conscious self must include the subject and the object, the perceiver and the perceived, the knower and the known, the infinite and the finite (*i.e.* an infinite number of finites)—mind and matter. It is by the unifying faculty of the Imagination that these opposite forces are reconciled. The infinite spirit presents to itself finite objects. Subject in one aspect, object in another, it is both infinite and finite. "In the existence, in the reconciling, and the recurrence of this contradiction consists the process and mystery of production and life." "The intelligence . . . tends to *objectize* itself and . . . to know itself in the object."

His speculation takes him further. The reason does not, as in Kant, merely postulate an idea of God, as an hypothesis; it has an intuition, an immediate knowledge of God. And the Imagination does not merely take up the objects given in sense; it embraces them, penetrates them and reads them as symbols—symbols, not *standing for* something behind them, but as partaking of the nature of Infinite Mind. Thus in immediately apprehending Nature it mediately apprehends God. For " Nature is the art of God," just as things taken up from Nature become the art of man. "The true system of natural philosophy places the sole reality of things in an ***Absolute***, which is at once causa sui et effectus, πατὴρ ἀυτοπάτωρ, υἱὸς ἑαυτοῦ—in the absolute identity of subject and object, which it calls nature, and which in its highest power is nothing else than self-conscious will or intelligence. In this sense the position of Malbranche, that we see all things in God, is a strict philosophical truth."

It is the imagination, then (the "primary"), which—in every human consciousness—presents to the mind its own world as external to itself. And it is the imagination (the "secondary"), in a rarer and more active capacity—that of the artist—which represents and re-creates this external world in its fuller nature, namely—as that which is congenial to the spirit, and actually its own. Thus Coleridge, in his all too brief *résumé* :

> The IMAGINATION, then, I consider either as primary, or secondary. The primary IMAGINATION I hold to be the living Power and prime Agent of all human Perception, and as a repetition in the finite mind of the eternal act of creation in the infinite I AM. The secondary Imagination I consider as an echo of the former, co-existing with the conscious will, yet still as identical with the primary in the *kind* of its agency, and differing only in *degree*, and in the *mode* of its operation. It dissolves, diffuses, dissipates, in order to re-create ; or where this process is rendered impossible, yet still at all events it struggles to idealize and to unify. It is essentially *vital*, even as all objects (*as* objects) are essentially fixed and dead. .
>
> FANCY, on the contrary, has no other counters to play with, but fixities and definites. The Fancy is indeed no other than a mode of Memory emancipated from the order of time and space. . . .

Perhaps we may say that it is the characteristic of the artistic Imagination always to achieve the miraculous—

always to break down that seemingly insuperable barrier between mind and matter. "To make the external internal, the internal external, to make nature thought, and thought nature—this is the mystery of genius in the Fine Arts. Dare I add that the genius must act on the feeling, that body is but a striving to become mind—that it is mind in its essence!" It is by reason of something in common between Nature and his own soul that the artist is able to create the forms of nature according to his ideal. That limited nature which he sees with his eyes, hears with his ears, constitutes the finite objects of his consciousness. But all Nature in its infinite totality he seems to conceive, not as God, but as the objective thought of God. And I think Coleridge means that it is by virtue of the (unexplained) association of the Reason of man with the Reason of God that man's Imagination is able to discern the externalized thought of God in the forms of Nature. Thus Nature in a certain sense seems to be imposed on him; but, in proportion as his Imagination is an echo of God's, he recreates it as his own. "Believe me, you must master the essence, the *natura naturans*, which presupposes a bond between nature in the higher sense and the soul of man."

If that be so, it might be asked, why is the artist never content just to copy mere nature? Two answers instantly present themselves. Firstly, "What idle rivalry!"—The art of God is the totality of nature—nothing less—and its unity and beauty lies in its indivisible wholeness. Fragments stolen from nature would be nature disunified, broken, without character or beauty.

And, secondly, the mind, when the imagination is not active, presents to itself only dead, mechanical nature, bare sensation, memory, associated ideas, at best the creation of Fancy—nature, without the life that makes it what it is. Coleridge seems to mean that only by ceaseless creation can that which is created remain alive; that nature is the art of God because the divine Imagination is active in it; and that it is material for the art of man just so far as man's creative imagination is re-creating and ever re-creating it. Its very life, its character, depends upon being actively created. And so the Imagination cannot be content to "copy." Its function is to diffuse, dissolve and re-create; to make the external internal, fashioning new images in its own semblance, in its own effort to become divine.

And so in all artistic creation there will be "imitation," but not "copying." In all imitation there is "likeness and unlikeness, or sameness and difference."

> If there be likeness to nature without any check of difference, the result is disgusting, and the more complete the delusion, the more loathsome the effect. Why are such simulations of nature, as wax-work figures of men and women, so disagreeable? Because not finding the motion and life which we expected, we are shocked as by a falsehood, every circumstance of detail, which before induced us to be interested, making the distance from truth more palpable.

III

Coleridge, in that last passage, is beginning to pass from the difficult and disputable sphere of his metaphysic to the expression of his critical taste, which, while in accordance with his metaphysic, is really, as we have seen, prior to it, and in any case may stand without it. On this pragmatic plane he is concerned with judgments which may be considered and accepted by those who will not for a moment accept, or perhaps even consider, his more abstract speculations.

In this spirit he asks, what is the "ultimate end of criticism"? It is to "establish the principles of writing," not to "furnish rules how to pass judgment on what has been written by others."

We have seen that he would have us "judge in the same spirit in which the Artist produced, or ought to have produced." But that "ought to have produced" is essential. For him it is among the "principles" of poetry that it is *making*, not *shaping*—ποίησις, not μόρφωσις. If this principle be granted it follows that rules cannot be "given from without," for if they could the power of poetry to *make* would be denied, and the power of the Imagination would cease to be one of growth and production. It is idle to lay down rules for what the poetic product should be, for a single defiant act of creative genius is enough to prove them vain.

So we shall not declare what the poet may do. We can only say what he is, or what sort of activity gives a man the title of poet, and his work the title of poem. To define this activity is to lay down a first principle of poetry.

Starting, then, from the broadest possible conception of poetry, as the "regulative idea of all the Fine Arts," he ventures on a preliminary definition. It is "the excitement of emotion for the purpose of *immediate* pleasure, through the medium of beauty."

So Coleridge, like all the romantic poets and critics, stresses the necessity of feeling, or emotion, or Passion (by which, as he says elsewhere, he understands "an excited state of the feelings and faculties"). But, be it observed, it is not the passion or excitement in the mind of the poet that he is here (in the *Principles of Genial Criticism*) speaking of—though that is presupposed (as is clear from *Biographia*, chapter xviii.). The essential thing in poetry which he is here affirming is that it should arouse this emotion in others. So art, for Coleridge, does not exist to satisfy the creative impulse of the artist, but to *communicate* his state of mind to others.

And next, it is " for the purpose of *immediate* pleasure." Here "pleasure" is contrasted with "truth," which is the object of science. And it is "immediate" because it is derived from the experience solely in and for its own sake—it is what we should call a "disinterested" pleasure. It does not arouse pleasure by reason of some other satisfaction that might be implied—for instance, the satisfaction of an appetite, or the moral satisfaction that may arise from the contemplation of sound maxims, or from that spiritual health to gain which some persons undergo courses of literature as if it were a sort of massage. The pleasurable experience derived from a work of art is its own intrinsic pleasure, and none other. It may happen to be useful, moral, instructive, health-giving. But it is not for these results that it is pursued, or for any results other than the pleasure arising directly from itself.

Nor is it enough to set up pleasure as the purpose. It is pleasure arising " through the medium of beauty." And when these words are added, it appears that it is misleading to name *pleasure* as the *purpose* ; for " the Apollo Belvedere is not beautiful because it pleases, but it pleases us because it is beautiful." The satisfaction is of a specific kind, and is perhaps possible to all persons in a small degree, though Coleridge seems to hold that it can only be experienced to the full by men of much sensibility, whose faculties have been trained to appreciate the beautiful when they see it.

So his definition of art is not complete till he has given

us his definition of beauty. He seizes on the point which critics from the time of Aristotle onwards have not ceased to demand in a work of art: that it should have unity, the wholeness of a living organism. So Coleridge, with the mystical philosophy of Plotinus never far from his thoughts, finds that in unity lies the essence of the beautiful:

> The Beautiful, contemplated in its essentials, that is, in *kind* and not in *degree*, is that in which the *many*, still seen as many, becomes one. Take a familiar instance, one of a thousand. The frost on a window-pane has by accident crystallised into a striking resemblance of a tree or a sea-weed. With what pleasure we trace the parts, and their relation to each other, and to the whole!

And again:

> The sense of beauty subsists in simultaneous intuition of the relation of parts, each to each, and of all to a whole; exciting an immediate and absolute complacency, without intervenence, therefore, of any interest, sensual or intellectual.

Finally he links this on to his doctrine of the Imagination, when he concludes that:

> The Beautiful arises from the perceived harmony of an object, whether sight or sound, with the inborn and constitutive rules of the judgment and imagination: and it is always intuitive. As light to the eye, even such is beauty to the mind, which cannot but have complacency in whatever is perceived as pre-configured to its living faculties.

IV

I have already passed from the first Coleridge—the transcendental philosopher, the apologist of Romanticism—to the second, the genial and cosmopolitan critic passing dispassionate judgment upon art. On this second aspect of his work I must say something more in the next chapter. But it has already become apparent that these two sides of his genius are not separated into water-tight compartments; that at many points they meet and merge and are complementary the one to the other. The trouble about Coleridge's metaphysics, from the point of view of æsthetic criticism, is that he gives us more than is necessary—or perhaps healthy, in so far as we are thinking of art, not of God—to adopt as a practical starting-point or principle. To many of us it may be fascinating to pursue these speculations. But the weakness of all philosophical systems is that the conclusions they arrive at are always shown, by subsequent thought, to have been, if true, only provisionally true. From their nature they are always debatable, and subject to endless argument and opposition.

Now it is surely no paradox to say that in art we are upon surer ground than in philosophy. Both, in a certain sense, are progressive with the human race, assuming new forms from age to age. Nevertheless, there is a finality about a given work of art which there never is about a philosophical thesis. Poetry may reach a state near to perfection in relation to the society of its time, and retain a power of satisfying long after that society has passed away. Each work of art is unique within its kind, and may be unsurpassable. But the philosopher's thought is part of an endless chain, and is always surpassable. Plato's logical work—vast as its influence still is—is an infant product compared with the philosophy of to-day. But the tragedies of Sophocles and the sculpture from the Parthenon are as valid to-day as they were two thousand years ago. They have been succeeded, but never surpassed.

Philosophy may take us on a longer journey, but in art

we have the security of treading comparatively familiar ground. It deals always with circumstances of human life—including, no doubt, the baffling problems of the intellect with which human beings perplex themselves—but always with human life; whereas philosophy goes beyond circumstance, and claims all Being as its subject-matter. Art proclaims no truth which it can demonstrate; but perception demands no proof; its evidence is within itself. And as art moves within the sphere of the perceivable it rests upon a basis which, within its borders, is not so uncertain, so ever-shifting, as that upon which philosophy, unbounded, gains a precarious footing.

I need hardly say I am not seeking to disparage the efforts of those whose business is with the philosophy of art. Art, like all other things known to humanity, must be the subject-matter of its proper science. What I mean is this, that the experience of art is prior to all theory of art; and that the practical conviction of the fastidious critic should be the basis of his theory; the theory should not be built up so as to override and govern those convictions. If that happens, errors may be transferred from a domain where false or half-true conclusions are always possible, to a domain where error is never necessary. That is why there is always danger in some of those logical theories of art—such as Futurism, Abstract Art, and the like—because they tend to transfer any error which may be inherent in their logic into the properly non-logical, intuitive, more certain domain of art.

That is why, for practical guidance, we should seek for principles on what I have called a lower plane of truth. This is the way of most of the great poet-critics. When they generalize, it is in judgments always close to their direct experience and practical conviction. Coleridge soared far above this plane into the cloudier distances of metaphysics. But, as we have seen, he started with convictions arrived at on the lower and surer plane of certitude. And so his metaphysical researches, often questionable as they are, did not darken his poetic convictions, and sometimes helped him to a better understanding of truths which inhered in those convictions.

They led him, for example, to the truth that art can never be a mere slavish *imitation*, or copying, of nature, that it is always nature impressed with the die of the artist's temperament ; that a picture or statue which may be said to imitate reality, will be like a real object, but always with a difference.

This is one of the principles we cannot escape from. In all art, there is life, and not-life—less than life, and more than life. As we saw when we were discussing the primitive drawing made by a savage on the wall of his cave, it will be less than the reality it represents, but also something more. It must lack the flesh, the warmth, the actual throbbing movement which are so much in the reality, but none the less it has something that the draughtsman has added to it—if only the generalization of man's two - leggedness, or one - headedness, or his tendency to be clad—the idea of living man has been triumphantly re-created in dead material. But it is no matter whether we take the savage or the civilized artist, we find him always engaged on the same task, developing a technique (understanding of his tools—chisel, brush, pen—and handy rules for using them); a fuller knowledge of his medium (paint, stone, sounds, words, rhythms, metres); a greater knowledge of the *objects of representation* (men in action, men in the surroundings of nature, home, work or play) ; and a fuller knowledge of his own mind—his perceptions, will, intellect, understanding.

Coleridge, intent upon some aspects of this question, said little about the resistant quality of the *medium* in which the artist works ; and he said little about the artist's need of knowing human life as it is, the life familiar to men, the life which he is to represent, the life which, in a work of art, must be recognizable and intelligible if his meaning is to be communicated. The greater part of his attention was given to the part played by the imagination. We need not know the ultimate source of the imagination or the metaphysical meaning of personality to recognize these forces when we find them, and to know that they are active agents in all vital art. Plain observation of the lives of the greater artists goes to confirm Coleridge's view that the poet, the painter, the sculptor each holds it as his ideal to present nothing less than his whole awareness of life. He is limited, of course, by conditions of time and space. In practice he concentrates now on this aspect of life, now on that ; one mood of his is represented here, another there. But the more at any given moment, in a fine passage of poetry or a beautiful pose of the human figure, he succeeds in suggesting a background of wider life, the infinite totality of experience, the more he thrills us. All the greater passages in literature owe their sublimity to this multiplicity or intensification of emotions—to this broadening, or deepening, of the world of poetry.

If Coleridge is right in insisting that the authentic Imagination includes all the activities of the soul—the intellect, the will, the perceptive faculties, the emotions—it follows that the imagination is a power which the artist can only use when he is at his best—when he is in the fullest possession of himself—when he is not writing from caprice, or for argument's sake, or in accordance with convention. It appears to be his ideal to project the whole of himself upon the whole of life ; and his practical task, to get as near to this unattainable ideal as the limited divinity within him can compass.

Chapter Twenty-one

COLERIDGE AND GOETHE

"THOU seem'st to me like Saul, the son of Kish, who went out to seek his father's asses, and found a kingdom," says Frederick to Wilhelm Meister, at the end. Thus it may have seemed to be with Goethe himself, who, having started with the blind adventures of his youth, and having submitted himself to every experience that civilization seemed capable of offering—poetry, poetic controversy, politics, philosophy, theology, love, science—settled down at length in the serene confidence that he had mastered the art of life and held the key to at least the practical mystery—the handicraft—of art.

Coleridge never attained to that serenity. He had too much limited the practical side of his life and of his art—"mismanaging" his sensibility—ever to attain that happy balance of perception and judgment. But he had been through many of the same intellectual experiences. He had been born, with faculties all alert, into the same restless, inquisitive, romantic world. He had felt the same youthful disgust at the artifice of literature circumscribed by French standards. He and Goethe had studied the same authors at the same moment of the world's history, and both had been attracted by the doctrine of Frederick Schlegel, that literature is the "comprehensive essence of the intellectual life of a nation." And just as it happened that in a certain stage in his career Coleridge, reading Schelling for the first time, discovered that he and Schelling had arrived independently at the same conclusions about the Imagination, so, in the more practical judgment of art, Coleridge and Goethe in later life seem often to have reached the same goal.

In a very profitable chapter of the *Biographia* (chapter xv.), Coleridge turns to what he himself calls "practical criticism." Here he seeks to discover the traits of poetry which may be ascribed to pure poetic genius—the "qualities in a poem, which may be deemed promises and specific symptoms of poetic power." He thought that the promises of strength, in spite of immaturity, in the early work of a genius such as Shakespeare would be most likely to reveal qualities springing essentially from the "inspiration of a genial and productive nature." He chooses, therefore, not the greater works of Shakespeare, but early works—*Venus and Adonis*, and the *Lucrece*—with a view to tracking down the gifts that "may be cultivated and improved, but can never be learned" (for "poeta nascitur non fit").

(1) The first of the four qualities he examines, all important as it is, need not at this moment detain us—the "perfect sweetness of the versification." "The sense of musical delight, with the power of producing it," is either born in a man, or it never appears. It cannot be acquired.

(2) The second promise of genius is in "the choice of subjects very remote from the private interests and circumstances of the writer himself." He observes that in *Venus and Adonis* "you seem to be told nothing, but to see and hear everything." The reader's attention is all the more engaged because of "the utter *aloofness* of the poet's own feelings, from those of which he is at once the painter and the analyst."

Goethe makes exactly the same point. "The highest, the unique function of art," he says, "is to represent."

> Poetry of the highest type manifests itself as altogether objective; when once it withdraws itself from the external world to become subjective it begins to degenerate.
>
> So long as the poet gives utterance merely to his subjective feelings, he has no right to the title.

Side by side with which we may put the identical sentiment expressed by Coleridge:

> Where the subject is taken immediately from the author's personal sensations and experiences, the excellence of a particular poem . . . is often a fallacious pledge of genuine poetic power.

Here indeed is high authority—that of Coleridge, the romantic, and Goethe, the ex-romantic — to set up against what is alleged to be the besetting sin of the romantic writers. The answer is this. The criticism exposes a fault to which these writers were undoubtedly prone—some more than others. Their romantic creed gave them little protection against it. None the less we have seen that the weakness was not inherent in, or sanctioned by, the creed itself. Coleridge, their apologist, denounces it.

The point made by Coleridge and Goethe is twofold, and one aspect of it is the more emphasized by the Englishman. There should be detachment and disinterestedness, firstly (*a*) in the choice of subject-matter; and secondly (*b*) in the treatment of it.

(*a*) We are often told that every person has the material for one novel in his own life (the general criticism is quite as applicable to fiction as to poetry). This statement, in a sense, is true. A person with slender creative power may find in his own history the one and only experience which he has realized so vividly that he can re-create it and make it vivid for others. But if that is all that he can do it is a sign rather of the limit to his powers than of his powers. Moreover, if Coleridge is right, such a work may not spring from the true artistic impulse. The true artistic excitement arises from " the energetic fervor of his own spirit in so vividly exhibiting, what it had so accurately and profoundly contemplated." It is of the essence of artistic creation to be able to extend the range of human interest beyond those things which the individual has personally experienced. The whole world is there, before the true poet or novelist, to be exhibited in the light of his all-embracing vision. The artist is one who sees, understands, re-creates, and shows.

Here we have the reason why even so great a writer as Dostoievski, when he is drawing on his own vivid personal experiences, often creates painful impressions without the beauty that belongs to tragedy ; whilst such a one as Turgenev evokes the beautiful from all that he touches.

(*b*) But it is not only in the choice of subject-matter. It is also in the treatment. And here many of our English novelists, who have satisfied the major requirement, have fallen short in their method of presentment. Dickens himself, with all the world as his plaything, is never content to keep his intrusive personality behind the scenes. Nor is Meredith, nor Thackeray, nor George Eliot, nor Stevenson, nor Mr Wells (the last often defies the canon in regard to matter as well as treatment—and that is why, in his psychological novels, he so often repeats himself. On the other hand, whilst he is apt to look too exclusively within for his more important *persons*, he admirably externalizes the social panorama of his time.

And in this respect few writers, if any, have ever equalled him).

Jane Austen came near to the "utter *aloofness*" of which the critic speaks—perhaps as near as is necessary for complete success within a certain kind.

But there is another kind, which achieves a specific effect by the cunning of its detachment. Prosper Mérimée, perhaps, was the first who consciously wrote in this style. De Maupassant has been its most conspicuous exponent. Turgenev and Tchekhov cultivated it. Henry James, with a difference, made it his own—"with a difference," because the all-too-curious spectator made his presence tangible.

But here I am passing to a kind of literature where a special technique has been introduced to increase the effectiveness of a writer's creative power. Coleridge was speaking of the innate power alone. Technique may give it a special quality, or an added potency. But it is useless unless the original power for profoundly contemplating and vividly exhibiting is already there.

(3) For convenience of treatment I take the fourth characteristic named by Coleridge, and speak of it as the third. It is that which he defines as "DEPTH, and ENERGY of THOUGHT":

> No man was ever yet a great poet, without being at the same time a profound philosopher. For poetry is the blossom and the fragrancy of all human knowledge, human thoughts, human passions, emotions, language.

This is identical with the dictum of Wordsworth, who, as we have already noticed, said that "poems to which any value can be attached were never produced on any variety of subjects but by a man who, being possessed of more than usual organic sensibility, had also thought long and deeply." In neither case does this mean that the purpose of poetry is to expound intellectual views. It is rather that the habit of thought has entered into the very constitution of the poet's mind, and that his profounder intuitions are therefore pregnant with it. Coleridge puts the case thus :

> What then shall we say ? even this ; that Shakespeare, no mere child of nature ; no automaton of genius ; no passive vehicle of inspiration possessed by the spirit, not possessing it ; first studied patiently, meditated deeply, understood minutely, till knowledge, become habitual and intuitive, wedded itself to his habitual feelings.

Now Goethe held with absolute conviction that it is the business of the poet to present the individual. He must deal, intuitively always, with particular objective realities. None the less his view comes near to that of Coleridge. "The poet," he says, "must grasp the individual" ; adding: "And if this gives him a firm hold he will by means of it present the Universal." But, it may be said, this does not necessarily mean that he attains this universality as the result of conscious reflection ; if truth is thus exhibited it is the result of happy intuition. But Goethe does not leave the matter there. "One must *be* something," he says, "in order to *do* something. The success of a work of art depends upon the degree in which what it undertakes to represent is instinct with *idea*."

Goethe had not the same bent towards systematic speculative study as Coleridge. Though he did not prize ideas any less highly, he did not believe that the most fruitful ideas result from incessant philosophical inquiry. He agreed that philosophy is necessary as one part of that all-embracing experience which is essential to the equipment of a poet. But in his view experience, many-sided experience, in the "right nature," provides the best schooling for the mind as a whole. "All the thinking in the world," he says, in one mood recorded by Eckermann, "does not bring us to thought; we must be right by nature, so that good thoughts may come before us like free children of God, and cry, 'Here we are!'"

This view, in regard to the process by which the right thoughts come, is not very far from that of Coleridge. The latter would be disposed to say that you get at thought by thinking and feeling combined, and that thinking would embrace life; Goethe, that you get at thought by every kind of living, and that life will embrace thinking. For the practical necessities of art their view is the same; knowledge must be "wedded to the habitual feelings": good thoughts must "come before us like free children of God." For both, what a work of art undertakes to represent must be "instinct with idea."

(4) We turn, in the fourth place, to Coleridge's third characteristic of the born poet. Having observed that images, however beautiful, faithfully copied from nature, do not of themselves characterize the poet, he goes on:

> They become proofs of original genius only as far as they are modified by a predominant passion; or by associated thoughts or images awakened by that passion; or when they have the effect of reducing multitude to unity, or succession to an instant; or lastly, when a human and intellectual life is transferred to them from the poet's own spirit,
>
> "Which shoots its being through earth, sea and air."

Coleridge seems here to suggest two ideas, similar, but not identical. He is thinking, first, of the effect which is produced in poetry when in any particular passage the excitement of the poet's imagination is fully revealed in the language and imagery. It is the product of his imagination as it appears in this and that detail of his work.

More important is the second idea, which refers to the effort of the imagination in conceiving and producing the work as a whole. The words to be emphasized in the above passage are: "modified by a predominant passion" and "reducing multitude to unity." The unity revealed is not that bare "one-ness" required in the Aristotelian plot; it comes from the "predominant passion"; it occurs when the whole treatment—Coleridge surely means treatment, and not merely "Imagery"—"moulds and colors itself to the circumstances, passion, or character, present and foremost in the mind." The poet in this happy vein is not presenting us with mere passages borrowed from life; he is dealing with a single situation to which he may see a thousand events significantly contributing, a situation profoundly characterized by its own quality, seen under its own atmosphere, pregnant with its own "predominant passion." It is a single flash of light thrown upon a whole chapter of life, every incident in which is seen, under that light, in its proper perspective.

The poet, novelist, artist who treats life in this way does not start from a generalization about life, and proceed to give us particular examples which illustrate it. That is the way of some didactic modern novelists and dramatists who use their heads where they ought to use their imagination. The imaginative way is that in which Joseph Conrad conceived, as he has told us, the plot of *Lord Jim*—it first presented itself to him as the vision of a single dramatic situation, when he imagined the captain, looking over the side of his ship, tempted to desert his crew. Coleridge himself alludes to *Lear* and *Othello*, each of which has a single, simple, passionate *motive*—the tragedy of a doting father, the tragedy of a doting husband.

In the case, or cases, which Coleridge is speaking of, the poet is not content to give us a bare representation of life, but life in terms of himself. And not only is it that, but it is life crystallized in the shape of one pervading idea or interest which holds all together and constitutes its poetic unity. Its one-ness does not arise from the fact that all its particulars can be subsumed under a single proposition from which the mind started. It was individual at the beginning and all the time. It was first and last a living organism rooted in the imagination—a single image made up of many images, all the parts related to the whole as the limbs and trunk are to the human frame. One harmony, one perspective, one theme absorbs the whole subject-matter of the poem and the concentrated activity of the poet's spirit. In this lies its individual character, its unity, its beauty.

Now Goethe is perhaps a little more disposed to emphasize the stubbornness of the material in which an artist works. His mind turns more readily to questions of technique. He never forgets that the artist has to deal with the hard facts of life, and that life is reluctant to lend itself to the plans of the poet. "Fact must give the motive," he says, "the points that require expression the particular kernel." None the less, "to make a beautiful enlivened whole, *that* is the business of the poet." But he had no idea of creating this wholeness by anything so artificial as the "Three Unities." He pours scorn on the stupidity of that invention, and declares that "comprehensibility is the purpose, and the three unities are only so far good as they conduce to this end." But he knows that a great deal of contrivance and accommodation is necessary before the artist can become expressive:

> Certain conditions trammel the production of every work of art, no matter how great and practical a genius the artist may be who handles it. The material upon which he works may be entirely under his control, but he cannot change its nature. He can only present in a certain aspect, and limited by certain conditions, what is in his mind.

Those "conditions" cannot lightly be disposed of. The artist is not dealing with a fluid. He is dealing with something not altogether tractable, which it is idle to pretend he can fully understand. He is dealing with a part of life as his theme, and some material of life as his medium. He is always faced with the problem of producing likeness through the unlike, spirit through matter, life and motion through what is mechanical and inert. Still, it is "through his personality, his character, that a writer makes his mark." The material has to be subdued, and made to yield to his personality. "Individuality of expression is the beginning and end of all art." "Generally speaking, it may be said that a writer's style is a true expression of his inner self." For Goethe, as for Coleridge, it is always that inner self which is declaring its mastery in art, and revealing its energy for all the world to see as something altogether, triumphantly, "objective."

"The plot is the first thing," said Aristotle. We must have unity arising from a "predominant passion," said Coleridge. Goethe is as direct as the Greek. In one of his conversations with Eckermann he speaks of "the great importance of motives, which no one will understand."

"Our women have no notion of it. 'That poem is

beautiful,' they say, and by this they mean nothing but the feelings, the words, the verses. No one dreams that the true power of a poem consists in the situation—in the *motive*."

"*The true power of a poem consists in the situation—in the* MOTIVE." There we have the inner truth of the Aristotelian dogma translated into plain modern language, and it should be inscribed on a monument more lasting than bronze. Coleridge meant it, and fumbled with it. Goethe meant it, and said it clearly. The true power of a poem, a novel, or a play consists not in the characters, the thought, the description, or the fancy, but in the situation, or motive, which includes all of these, and is prior to all of them, in the sense that the whole is prior to the part. The same idea was recently expressed by Mr Arnold Bennett, when he said: "Every novel should have a main theme that can be stated in ten words."

Thanks to Eckermann, we have some delightful illustrations of the applicability of this truth even to the lightest of poems. Chancing upon a book of Serbian love-poems which pleased him, Goethe "in a few words characterized these poems according to their chief subjects." "I think you will be pleased with the valuable *motives*," he said.

Here are a few of them:

(1) Modesty of a Servian girl, who never raises her beautiful eyelashes.

(2) Conflict in the mind of a lover, who, as groomsman, is obliged to conduct his beloved to another.

(5) Complaint of a youth that a mother gives her daughter too much liberty.

(10) What trade shall my husband be?

(11) Joys of love lost by babbling.

"I felt," adds Eckermann, "as if I were reading the poems themselves."

The reader may be tempted to make the experiment for himself. He might try it with *Comus*, with *King Lear*, with *Alice in Wonderland.* What *motive* shall we write down for "Drink to me only with thine eyes," or "To Althea in prison"? Shall we venture the following for "It was a lover and his lass":

> Two lovers, enchanted by the prettiness of a spring morning, live in the moment like birds.

And so on, in the case of any poem you please, so long as it is a good poem, and has a *motive* to yield.

Chapter Twenty-two

THE METHOD OF SAINTE-BEUVE

DE Quincey, Hazlitt, Charles Lamb, Leigh Hunt —when we come to critics such as these we see how far the world had moved from the Augustan period. The whole direction of thought had changed. We are among a new order of critics, all of them more or less deeply influenced by the Romantic movement, men for whom literature had become an open country free to the explorer. We see them roaming through literature, basking in it, stopping to taste the fruits they fancy—appreciating, discriminating in an individual way, asserting the claim of personal taste and private judgment.

In the second quarter of the century, it is true, it became the fashion to admire the methods of the Germans. Carlyle helped to create this fashion, and insisted that "criticism has assumed a new form in Germany." "The question has now become," he wrote in 1827, "properly and ultimately a question on the essence and peculiar life of the poetry itself." The critic now asks "not only what was the poet, and how did he compose; but what and how was the poem, and why was it a poem and not rhymed eloquence, creation and not figured passion." But Carlyle scarcely pursued the German method beyond the point of admiring it as a prodigy. The spectacle of it thrilled him. That looser romanticism with which he enchanted Victorians appears in these winged words:

> Criticism stands like an interpreter between the inspired and the uninspired; between the prophet and those who

hear the melody of his words, and catch some glimpse of their material meaning, but understand not their deeper import. She pretends to open for us this deeper import.

I doubt if Carlyle had much new light to throw on the question of critical standards. With him, we are still in a world where the artist, being inspired, is a law unto himself, whose divinity needs nothing but a critic fit to proclaim him. We are tempted to ask whether this new-found freedom had ousted all standards. Had it conferred an infinite number of rights, and no obligations? How, amid the diversity of literary types, the irresponsibility, the freedom, the licence, was the critic to find any guiding light, any certain clue, any fixed star by which to find his way in an uncharted country?

Certainly, the "Legislators of Parnassus" had lost their legal authority. Never have the critics returned with rods of office in their hands to administer an inflexible law. But if they lost their official status, power still remained with them. They flourished, in other raiment, with different powers, but with undimmed lustre. Especially was this the case in France, where the classicist's love of authority remained even when the critic had submitted to the new ardours of romanticism. The little circle of writers who distinguished themselves in the Paris *Globe*, in the twenties, were propagandists and advocates. They believed in freedom in politics, in literature, and in art; and romanticism, for them, was "Protestantism in literature." The most famous member of this group, Sainte-Beuve, first came prominently before the public as friend of the romantic poet, Victor Hugo, and "trumpeter" of his poetic virtues.

It is natural, perhaps, that this period, if any, should have evolved a great critic of whom it has been thought possible to say that he had no "method," or, at least, no hard and fast principles. One writer has even said of him that "just because he had no hard and fast system of critical principles his fame as a critic is still undimmed." If this judgment should pass unchallenged, we might well conclude that the search for principles is fatuous. If a critic excels by dispensing with them, what need to go further?

But the real truth is, not that Sainte-Beuve is discarding method, but that he is asserting the need of new methods. Criticism could never again effectually pursue the outworn paths or adopt the old rules. Once let it be granted that the artist creates only in accordance with the laws of his own being, and that no law imposed from without can be counted upon to fit his case, then the critic must readjust his position. Is there any place for him in a State where it seems that anarchy has been proclaimed?

Yes. Sainte-Beuve found that there was room enough for the critic, but it was necessary that he should begin again, approaching from another angle. We may refrain from setting up laws imposed from without, but at least the writer must conform to the laws of his own being. From his personality he cannot escape; from that personality, all that he does must spring. Before we address ourselves to the arbitrary task of *judging* an author, there is a preliminary task—that of *understanding* him. This he held to be the first duty of a critic. In the performance of this duty, at least, there was a critical method that could be applied. For to understand a work, what is it but to understand the author? And to this end biography, scientifically used by the right kind of investigator, afforded the clue.

The forty years (1829 to 1869) during which Sainte-Beuve was writing his *Portraits* and causeries (*Lundis*), belong to the period when it was passionately believed in intellectual circles that science held the key to every riddle of the universe. From the science of natural history men were passing to the sciences of the social organism, of the mind, of religion, of ethics. It was becoming the habit of the time—and Sainte-Beuve was certainly affected by it—to think that there was no field of inquiry in which science might not ultimately yield the answers to all the problems. And so in this matter of the *understanding* of literature, Sainte-Beuve looked round for a *method* based upon that of the exact sciences.

He starts from the hypothesis that to understand a work it is necessary to understand its author. Therefore the first task that confronts the critic appears to him to be a biographical one. "Literature," he says, "literary production, is not for me distinct or at least separable from the rest of man and human organization; I can taste a work, but it is difficult for me to judge it independently of my knowledge of the man himself." *Tel arbre, tel fruit.* When we know the tree, we know the fruit. He admits the difficulty of discovering everything about the lives of the ancients, and this ignorance he thinks a handicap to appreciation. But at least we know the lives of the moderns. Let us, then, follow every clue that presents itself, examining our author's life, scrutinizing the turning-points in his intellectual career, meticulously pursuing every fact about his environment that may shed light on his character.

In the essays on Chateaubriand he elaborates this method of his, freely borrowing the language of science. Indeed he even speaks of "the future exact science of character." Though he admits that man can never be known quite like animals or plants, he nevertheless opines that a day will come when :

> . . . a new science will be established, when the great families of wit or genius (*familles d'esprits*) and their principal divisions will be determined and known.

But this new science which he looks for will require no ordinary men for its experts, but artists. For it would always be "so delicate and mobile that it could exist only for those who have a natural vocation and talent for observing" ; it would always be "an *art*, requiring a clever artist, just as medicine requires medical skill in the practitioner . . . and as poetry can only be touched by a poet." Sainte-Beuve's critic, then, is definitely a specialist, a man born just for that work, the work of criticism—a man endowed with "this kind of talent and facility for understanding the groups, the literary families." He must be "a good naturalist in this vast field of the mind."

Such, then, is this ideal critic, an artist who knows the science of his subject, a scientist who has the artist's eye. He will be unremitting in his search for all the relevant facts. He will look first for clues to the writer's character, in the race to which he belongs, and the country of which he is a native. He will inquire about his ancestors, and his contemporaries. He will be interested in his parents, and especially his mother. He will not neglect sisters, brothers, children, or education, studies, upbringing. He will fix his attention closely on the group with which he voluntarily associates himself as a young man. This period of youth and early friendship is the golden moment in which promise reveals itself, ideas germinate quickly, and mind gravitates to mind. Then it is that the *esprit vivant* of the young enthusiast catches fire from the glow of those about him. In the fellowship of the *group* ideas are actively exchanged, and mind vies with mind in equal intercourse—here the man of talent gets his send-off, and his opportunity for development, for expanding his intrinsic qualities. Thus it was with Sainte-Beuve himself in the poetic group of *La Muse française* (in 1824), the critical circle of the *Globe* in 1827, and *Le Cénacle* in 1828:

> I define the *group*, not as the accidental and artificial assemblage of clever men who agree on an end, but the natural and spontaneous association of young minds and young talents, not exactly similar and of the same family, but of the same *flight* and the same *Spring*, hatched under the same star, who feel themselves born, with varieties of taste and vocation, for a common work.

In the progressive effort to *understand* the personality of his author, the artist-scientist-critic will become especially watchful at this fateful moment of his investigation—the moment when he is expecting something significant to happen. This is what he must not fail to fix—the "first poetic or critical centre"—it is the "womb in which he takes his shape"—it is the "true date of his birth" ("*sa vraie date originelle*"). And we call to mind that Coleridge, too, when he "endeavoured to discover what the qualities in a poem are, which may be deemed promises and specific symptoms of poetic power," went back, in the case of Shakespeare, to his earliest work, to the *Venus and Adonis* and the *Lucrece*—"works which give at once strong promises of the strength, and yet obvious proofs of the immaturity, of his genius." Though Coleridge was seeking for a clue only in the manifest work of the poet, and Sainte-Beuve was looking at the circumstances under whose influence it came to birth, both fix on the same critical moment of youth when first spreading its wings for flight.

From this point the critic proceeds, noting how his author passes from his activity in the group to successive stages of his adult self, now going forward, now back, reaching at last his maturity, now the moment of falling off, now the sad time when some grow cold and dry, or hard and bitter, and the smile becomes a grimace. And throughout the inquiry he will not fail to learn all that he can about the author's religion, his friends, his attitude to nature, love, money. He will follow every clue that may help to lead to his *genre d'émotion*.

All of this is Sainte-Beuve's preliminary to the judging of an author, and his book.

Well—it sounds somewhat elaborate, a little cut-and-dried — more so, surely, when thus set forth, than the method he actually employed in his own essays. But it is only in the stating of it that it becomes too formal, too much a thing of rule-of-thumb. Certainly his practice was in the main biographical, personal ; certainly it was to *personality* that he looked for his clue in literature ; nothing that elucidated personality was irrelevant to him. Arrive at a *definition* of the man, he said ; you have then *defined* his work. Understand, and in the light of understanding, *define* ; that is the critic's job.

We must return to that in a moment. And we shall soon see that this cut-and-dried account of his own method was certainly not Sainte-Beuve's last word about himself. Literature might be a growing plant, or a forest of growing plants, in which the botanist, text-book in hand, might roam with observant eye. But not thus exclusively studied would it yield up, for him, all the varieties of its sweetness. Yet there was another critic, Taine, his contemporary, who adopted a similar method, and embraced it, far more literally, far more systematically, pushing it to its logical extreme—even to its logical absurdity.

Taine's contribution to literary science lay in his study of literature as the product of social forces. For him, the man of letters was the creature of the age in which he lives, the society into which he is born, and the fleeting circumstances, in a given time and place, which mould him. He enunciated his famous doctrine of the (1) *race*, (2) the *milieu*, (3) the *moment*. (1) His history of English literature is an account of what he takes to be typical works of typical men of the English race as they emerge at successive epochs. (2) The thoughts and writings of each of these men receive an impress from his *milieu*, the society and civilization in which he lives, the thoughts which are in the air he breathes. (3) Granted these two broadly determining conditions, it remains to study the *moment*—by which is meant, not so much the instant in time, as the *momentum*, the "impulse at a given stage of development," through which the writer's gathered store of potential force is released in its predestined direction.

Frederick Schlegel had already studied the evolution of literature in a spirit somewhat similar. But Taine gave to it a neat, an almost biological, exactness. And it was surely time that some use of his method should be applied to the study of literature, on the one hand, and to the study of history, on the other. For what is history without the distinctive thoughts of a period which are represented in the sum of its literature? And what is literature, without that living society which it so deeply penetrates? Homer is not only Homer. The *Iliad* and the *Odyssey* are vivid chapters in the history of the world. Sophocles, Euripides, Shakespeare are something more than themselves—they are their age, not, indeed, expressed in terms of its average common self, but of the finest, and therefore the most real, thing of which it was capable. If we would know the character of a given period in all its forms it would be enough, or nearly enough, if we knew all its literature, good and bad, permanent and ephemeral. And often we could pick out half-a-dozen authors, and say—In the works of those men you may see the trend of a decade, the direction of that generation's thought, the urge which in their instant of time was making humanity what it was about to be. If anyone should wish to understand the thoughts and manners of English people in the ten years following the war, let him examine the writings of half-a-dozen men in the ten years preceding it—Wells, Shaw, Bennett, Galsworthy, E. M. Forster, Max Beerbohm—and he has the clue in his hands.

Taine's method is of great importance for history and biography. But it is not enough, and Sainte-Beuve, though sympathetic, knew that it was not enough. The large, general, shaping forces which hurry men along the main road are not all; there is also distinguishable in each of them an essential, *individual* quality which makes him wholly mysterious, wholly incalculable, and different from everyone else; and precisely the presence of this individual, unique quality in a man's personality occasions that special personal delight which is the most captivating thing in literature.

The theory of the *age* and the *moment* does not explain why *no two* men are alike ; why one great man, original, unique, excels all others.

We cannot, after all, reduce the study of literature to an exact science, to a branch of sociology, or pathology, or even ethics. It may be true, as Taine says, that " man, like every other living thing, changes with the air that nourishes him " ; but, says Sainte-Beuve, " in these finenesses which you admire and seem to savour so well, you are wrong to see only a *result* and a *product* of circumstances. There are always, let us hope, *des âmes délicates*, fine spirits who will seek their proper ideal, their own chosen expression."

It may be, he says, that the human mind flows like a river, but there are distinctions of quality even in the drops of water ; there is an infinite variety in the forms of talent. And he demands, therefore, of the critic, that he should " give an account of them and tell us how and why they are of such and such an order and quality rather than another."

So, in the last resort, when we know all that we can know about the *milieu*, about the race, about the family, about heredity, there will still remain an elusive quality which is individual, distinctive, an element which the critic must track to its source in the only place where it can be found—in the author's personality. It is this which he must understand. It is this which it is his task to *define*. Sainte-Beuve would have his critic set himself, not hurriedly, but as the final task following long study, to drag to the light of day that essential element in character, which may be clearly revealed or may lie hidden, but in any case determines the author in all his moods, in all his phases, in all aspects of his creative work. Just as Goethe held that every work of art has a *motive* which can be summed up in a sentence, and just as Mr Arnold Bennett says " Every novel should have a main theme that can be stated in ten words," so Sainte-Beuve believes that the personality behind the art can be similarly defined, and the " characteristic name " affixed to it. Thus he professes himself satisfied with his own definition of Chateaubriand as " an epicurean with a catholic imagination." And thus, we may recall, Matthew Arnold was content to sum up Byron in two sentences borrowed from Goethe : this " splendid and puissant personality " was " the greatest talent of our century," of whom it must be further said, " the moment he begins to reflect, he is a child."

But if this business of definition, of affixing the " characteristic name " to an author, appears to be, for Sainte-Beuve, the last stage of the critic's task, we must not suppose him to mean that it can be isolated from the study preceding it. Nothing could be more mischievous than a glib generalization, or even a true generalization which lends itself to glib, uncomprehending repetition. We may generalize truly about a character, but to know the generalization is not to know the character. Theologians might agree that God is adequately defined as " Omnipotence and Omniscience," but to know only so much would not be to know God. Sainte-Beuve appears to mean, not that a label, a tag, has any virtue of its own, but that when we have intimately, exhaustively studied the work and character of an author, then all fits itself into its place for the penetrative mind, and words shape themselves to define what only at this stage we can know. Only when all the individual traits are already familiar is it possible to put a personality fairly to the question, to sum him up, to see the many aspects of him as one, in perspective.

That, I think, is what Sainte-Beuve is aiming at. For the final understanding of an author we shall gather into one view the whole of his work, and envisage it as a single task — his monument, his contribution to humanity, his personality exposed in literature. Thus the "characteristic name" may be like the well-found title to a book, or the motto of a university, or the emblem on the shield of a knight. In a word, at a glance, it may summon before us the distinctive personal force which gives character to a man's work.

There is one other question we must put to Sainte-Beuve before we leave him. Unlike so many of those whom we have been discussing, he is not a considerable poet, he is not what is known as a "creative" writer; he is preeminently "the critic"; he has loomed large before the world as one "born to judge." What view does he hold of the critic as related to the artist? Does he, so gifted a "judge," sharply distinguish himself and his kind from those who are born "to write"?

Well, Sainte-Beuve certainly recognized that there exists a certain kind of critic who lives the purely critical life, and is content to be a sort of monstrous negation of all other qualities in order that he may live in the authors whom he serves. Such a one he discovers in Bayle, whom he ironically dissects in *Du Génie Critique et de Bayle*— one whom Sainte-Beuve describes as having realized the critical ideal more fully than any other author. What is this ideal? It is shown as that of a man who should have no art of his own, no distinctive style, no special views which he wishes to propagate, no strong bent in religion, no passion towards life, no predilections disposing him to favour this or that opinion, this or that form of art. He should have no creative genius, no philosophic system. Distractions of this kind would limit his proper critical genius. He must be the same to all men. His characteristic quality will be an infinite curiosity, which will accompany him on his endless travels with all sorts of persons in all sorts of country. His part is to relax himself so that he may see and understand all things from the point of view of each author whom he pursues, laying himself open to the influence of that other's art, style and thought, and never obscuring these with his own. He must be tolerant, dispassionate, balanced, curious, aware that "everything is possible, and nothing certain." Such a one, supreme in the domain of criticism, was the "excellent Bayle," of whom Sainte-Beuve is convinced that he never wrote a verse in his youth, never dreamed of the green fields, and was never in love with a woman. These deficiencies, "this lack of talents, lack of passions, lack of higher gifts, made Bayle the most accomplished critic of his kind who ever existed."

Of his kind—of his *genre*. A *reductio ad absurdum*, is it not, of the "ideal critic"? Certainly it was not thus that Sainte-Beuve himself approached the study of literature. He at least had not mortified the flesh and the spirit by eschewing the seductions of verse in his youth, the lure of religion, or even the maddest pursuit of love. He, assuredly, never succeeded in divesting himself of strong personal points of view, nor were his essays, in their structure and writing, without an *art à soi*, a *style à soi*.

And much as he might talk about that new "science" with which the critic was to track down the artist's life and character, did he not himself insist that this very "science" would be so "delicate and mobile" that it would also be "an art which would require a clever artist"?

Indeed we may as well face without delay the implications which have already become apparent. How can the man whose soul is stripped of all those elements which are of the very stuff of art—the passions, preferences, impulses towards nature, or religion, the many strong opinions, the many marked sensibilities, which, experienced or at least comprehended by the artist, are woven into his work—how can such a man understand what the artist has written? If it be asserted that it is not necessary for the artist to experience what he portrays, that it is enough for him to have observed and understood, the argument is unaffected—we must still ask, How can the critic possibly criticize till he has come to the same understanding, through the capacity of his spirit to adopt the same sentient and sensitive attitude towards observed experience? What the artist feels or is aware of, the critic also must be able to feel or be aware of. What the one has been able to construct, the other must be able to reconstruct; and unless imagination and creation enter into the reconstruction it will not be a reconstruction—it will be something less than the original, or different; and to that extent the criticism will be inefficient.

Are we then to say that the critic is himself an artist? Surely, the answer is Yes. I am meaning by critic not the man whose sole work is the collection of facts about literature, not the expert in literary origins, the comparer of texts, the archæologist in the world of letters—but the man whose talent lies in the interpretation of works of art. Such a man must have the qualities of a literary artist in a high degree, otherwise he will neither understand the works of art which he studies, nor be able to communicate to others his own impressions and conclusions about them.

But, it will be objected, artist and critic are clearly distinct. The latter is not the originator. At best he is the follower along a path which the other has cut. I agree. The critic's job cannot, of course, be identified with that of the very artist whom he criticizes. It appears to be different in two ways.

Firstly, there is, as Sainte-Beuve recognizes, a scientific side to the critic's work. He is concerned with definite historic facts which he must not alter. His subject is a man whose real deeds and character he must not, from any artistic consideration, change or in the least degree modify. He is bound, not by the laws of the beautiful or the ideally true, but of the actual, however brutal, however distorting to his picture. He is required to pursue, not the universal truth of life, but historic fact, the actual successes and errors in the artist's thought, observation, expression and execution. His task, to this extent, is scientific, and circumscribed.

But the critic is also an artist. He must be able to reconstruct an author's thought. He must have the insight to see, not only what he achieved, but what he did not achieve—what he wished to do, but did not—or what he might perhaps have done if promise had been fulfilled, or his life had been rounded off to its harmonious completion. Such re-creative work is creative, just as the artist is said to create when he re-creates life. How then does this artistic work of the critic differ from the artistic work of the poet, the novelist, the dramatist?

Surely the answer is, that the difference lies not in the art, but in the subject-matter chosen. Every good writer is to some extent a specialist, and chooses his theme in accordance with his special interests. One fills his mind with the tragic emotions of princes; another, with the moods of the sea and the experiences of men who live in ships; another, with the simple feelings of men and women born to plough and sow and reap. Novelist, poet or rhymester will take us according to his special fancy to the life of a Court, of an English provincial town, or a Middle-Western American city; he may show us the beasts of an Indian jungle, or the terrors of the Canadian Wild; we may be led by him through the jingle of the *Bab Ballads* or the eccentricities of Wonderland. Each artist has his own province, and thither he takes us. That province may be the land of books.

When this last is the subject he chooses, and he submits also to the scientific conditions which I have named, the artist is a critic. His theme is literature. He is an artist whose subject is art. Shakespeare reconstructs the life of a Hamlet, an Othello, a Lear. The critic of Shakespeare reconstructs the mind of Shakespeare as he finds it revealed in his life and art. Books and authors, and their relation to life, are the critic's subject-matter, just as men and women, and their relation to life, are the usual subject-matter of other artists. And just as great understanding of men and women, and their living background, is needed in a novelist, so great understanding of books and authors, and their living background, is needed in a critic. The subject chosen is different; the demand on artistic capacity is the same.

Chapter Twenty-three

MATTHEW ARNOLD

I

"MR ARNOLD did not merely criticize books himself. He taught others how to criticize them. He laid down principles, if he did not always keep the principles he laid down. Nobody, after reading *Essays in Criticism*, has any excuse for not being a critic."

Thus, in 1902, wrote Herbert Paul, his irony shielding him, in quite the modern way, against the assaults of Victorian earnestness. But he is more than half serious. How could he not be, since the spell of Matthew Arnold, years after his death, still imposed on the English world his conception of the critic's office? Far away in a dim past was that age of Dryden when men repeated, "Aristotle has said so." Now the proper cry was, "Arnold has said so." After a brief period of discord and anarchy we find ourselves once again face to face with Authority. Once again we are asked to follow what Herbert Paul calls "principles" of criticism, laid down by an austere writer who "taught others how to criticize." For half-a-century Arnold's position in this country was comparable with that of the venerable Greek in respect of the wide influence he exercised, the mark he impressed upon criticism, and the blind faith with which he was trusted by his votaries.

And yet we have only to mention Aristotle, only to speak in terms of critical "principles," to see at once that Arnold's main task is of another order altogether. I am not alluding to the fact that the former knew none but the classics of Greece, the only literary models available to him, whilst Arnold, having the literature of many nations and ages before him, was limited only, of his own choice, to "the best that is known and thought in the world." Nor does the main difference lie in the fact that Arnold repudiated the idea that the critic should be an "abstract lawgiver." Both of these considerations are important. But there is a prior fact which arrests our attention.

In that body of Arnold's work, dealing with critical principles, which has most affected the public mind, and has passed into currency as his distinctive doctrine, he is dealing with a function of criticism that did not concern Aristotle at all. Aristotle shows us the critic in relation to art. Arnold shows us the critic in relation to the public. Aristotle dissects a work of art. Arnold dissects a critic. The one gives us the principles which govern the making of a poem; the other, the principles by which the best poems should be selected and made known. Aristotle's critic owes allegiance to the artist, but Arnold's critic has a duty to society. He is a propagandist tilling the soil so that "the best ideas" may prevail, making "an intellectual situation of which the creative power can profitably avail itself." To prepare a social atmosphere which will stimulate the artist—to make the best that has been written familiar to the public—this was the new task of criticism. It was to be a contribution to the problem of "perfection," or "how to live." It was on the way to becoming a branch of social reform. And perhaps it was for this very reason that his doctrines readily took root in England, appealing to the practical English mind which he had himself so sternly criticized. It came to pass that the apostle of "disinterestedness" appealed to the apostles of betterment.

Matthew Arnold discussed and defined more clearly than any other writer before him the relation of the critic of literature to the society in which he lives. That is the subject of *Culture and Anarchy*, and of some of the *Essays in Criticism.* Here lies his distinctive contribution to the study of critical principles.

But having stated this fact about him, and before proceeding to examine it further, I must hasten to add that he did not omit to consider criticism from the other side. There was a stage in his career when criticism as an examination of the principles of art filled his thoughts, and it is not a coincidence that this occurred early in his literary life, when he had recently been writing the best of his poems, and his deepest interests still lay in the making of poetry rather than in judging it for the benefit of others. He did not completely separate the critic from the poet till he was at some distance from the latter's point of view.

II

Let us first consider, then, what that younger Arnold, the poet-critic, had to say about the inner principles of poetry, seen from the artist's side—in the Preface to the Poems of 1853, for example, or in the lectures *On Translating Homer*. We shall not be so much struck by any originality in his judgments as by the fact that this man, already established as a poet, afterwards to be still more firmly established as a critic, joined his verdict to that of other pre-eminent critics. What do we find in common in Aristotle, Coleridge, and Goethe—what least common denominator is contained in their critical doctrines? The choice of an excellent action, unfolded by appropriate treatment, so that it may afford pleasure, this pleasure consisting in a total impression derived from the organic unity of the parts within the whole—this much, for Aristotle, Coleridge, Goethe, and in like manner for Arnold, was essential to a great poem. When Arnold subscribes to these older doctrines we may be sure it is not in the spirit of one glibly repeating truisms. He was not unacquainted with the modern view that the subject does not matter so long as it is faithfully treated by a powerful mind. He had contemporaries who were saying then, as men are still saying, that art consists solely in the expression of the impressions in the artist's mind. He himself speaks of the "false aims" prescribed by "the modern critic": "'A true allegory of the state of one's own mind in a representative history,' the Poet is told, 'is perhaps the highest thing that one can attempt in the way of poetry.'" "An allegory of the state of one's own mind!" he cries indignantly. "No, assuredly, it is not, it never can be so: no great poetical work has ever been produced with such an aim."

He enlists Schiller on his side. "All Art," says Schiller, "is dedicated to Joy. . . . The right Art is that alone, which creates the highest enjoyment." If you start from that axiom, it follows that a representation is not enough; it has to be one from which men can derive enjoyment. This is as true for tragedy as for comedy—and for this reason true tragedy never presents the merely painful, never shows "a continuous state of mental distress . . . unrelieved by incident, hope, or resistance; in which there is everything to be endured, nothing to be done." Such situations, painful in life, in literature are morbid. Tragedy resolves pain in the energy of human action.

For Arnold, then, as for Aristotle, the plot is the first thing. Vainly will the poet "imagine that he has everything in his own power ; that he can make an intrinsically inferior action equally delightful with a more excellent one by his treatment of it." His first task is to select an "excellent action." It was precisely because he was dissatisfied with the subject—not the treatment—of his *Empedocles*, whose situation seemed to him painful without being tragic, that he decided to exclude that poem from his new collection.

But what actions, he asks, are the most excellent? And he replies "those which most powerfully appeal to the great primary human affections ; to those elementary feelings which subsist permanently in the race, and which are independent of time." Side by side with this we may put a sentence which occurs in one of the lectures on Homer, where he defines the *grand style* as that which "arises in poetry when a noble nature, poetically gifted, treats with simplicity or with severity a serious subject." Have we here once again the "high seriousness," the σπουδαιότης, of Aristotle, the *gravitas sententiæ* of Dante, that "weight of meaning" for which grand words (*grandiosa*) were alone adequate? Or is Arnold taking us a little further? The greatness of a subject makes a difference—we agree. An "excellent action." Yes, it "doubles the impressiveness" of the poet. The permanent as opposed to the ephemeral—what less can we ask for in "verses fit to live"? That the simple themes of the old world can be used again and again, there is no doubt about it. Yet in all the passages in which this question is discussed Arnold makes us feel that he has turned a blind eye to literary experiences which were not available to Aristotle or Dante, with the result that he discovers a peculiar disqualification in the life of our own time, by which the actions belonging to it become unsuitable for great poetry. What special fitness, he asks, has the present age for supplying subjects by means of which poets can afford the highest pleasure to men? We live in an "era of progress," an age of "industrial development," an "age wanting in moral grandeur"—it is lacking in the elements which are needed for the exercise of great art.

Would Arnold dare to commit himself to such a limiting view were he alive to-day? Would he dare to pass over so disdainfully the poetry, drama, or fiction of such men as Ibsen, Walt Whitman, Flaubert, Thomas Hardy, Tchekhov, Verhaeren? Is there nothing in the works of such writers which can afford to men "the highest pleasure which they are capable of feeling"? How can this usually discerning critic, who says that art is a "criticism of life," venture to condemn so much life as unfit for the artist's criticism?

Perhaps we may detect here the source of a strange error which he appears to commit in that later essay on Count Leo Tolstoy. He says:

> The truth is we are not to take *Anna Karénine* as a work of art; we are to take it as a piece of life. A piece of life it is. The author has not invented and combined it, he has seen it; it has all happened before his inward eye, and it was in this wise that it happened. . . . The author saw it all happening so—saw it, and therefore relates it; and what his novel in this way loses in art it gains in reality.

It "gains in reality." The art positively loses wherein the novel gains! There must be some defect in a theory of art which would make the artist reject the very elements that make for success. Wherein lies this excellence arising from the presentation of "life," if that life itself has not proved excellent material for Tolstoy's art? If in his grand manipulation of realistic details Tolstoy has made us feel "This is a piece of life," and "This is excellent," who would care to join Arnold in denying that the success of the result is not a success in his art?

Simplicity and severity are good. But Arnold has given us no good reason for concluding that art demands the exclusion of the complex, or the shunning of an age of material progress. His faith in the guidance of pre-eminent models, inspiring as they may be, tended to hide from him the potential excellence of the new and untried, of the fresh material from which new art forms and adaptations of the old are for ever being evolved.

He is on safer ground when he confines himself to those principles which he shares with Aristotle, Coleridge and Goethe. They and he agree that the plot, or action, or motive is the first thing. They agree also that its unity, the "total impression"—not, as Arnold puts it, "occasional bursts of fine writing," or "a shower of isolated thoughts and images"—is what gives a poem its essential character. "What distinguishes the artist from the mere amateur," says Goethe, "is *Architectonicè* in the highest sense; that power of execution, which creates, forms and constitutes; not the profoundness of single thoughts, not the richness of imagery, not the abundance of illustration."

Poetry as a serious representation of an excellent action, having the object of creating the highest enjoyment—so much we may accept from Arnold. It includes the tragic, it excludes the morbid. It aims at the unity of a "total impression." Here, for the moment, we may leave the younger Arnold, in the best of company, and turn to consider later and more characteristic phases of his work.

III

We find him now in the capacity of the critic of criticism, or the critic who had a mission to the world to fulfil. Having given up the frequent writing of poetry he assumed another rôle, that of a teacher. Holding, as he did, that literature is a "criticism of life," he conceived it to be his duty as a critic of literature to bring it out into the open in the life of society. "A disinterested endeavour to learn and propagate the best that is known and thought in the world, and thus to establish a current of fresh and true ideas"—that is the keynote to his task. It is threefold in character. First, there is the critic's duty to learn and understand—he must "see things as they really are." Thus equipped, his second task is to hand on his idea to others, to convert the world, to "make the best ideas prevail." His work in this respect is that of a missionary. But, thirdly, he is also preparing an atmosphere favourable for the creative genius of the future—promoting "a current of ideas in the highest degree animating and nourishing to the creative power."

The function of Arnold's critic in the broadest sense of the term is to promote "culture"; his function as literary critic is to promote that part of culture which depends upon knowledge of letters. The greater contains the less. In *Culture and Anarchy* he discusses the duty of the critic as a man of culture concerned with all aspects of living. Like so many eminent Englishmen of his period he had a good deal of the missionary in his composition. He was evidently stung to the quick by the taunts of John Bright, Frederic Harrison, and *The Daily Telegraph*. Not that he was in any way shocked at being described as a Jeremiah; but an elegant Jeremiah, a spurious Jeremiah, a Jeremiah without a mission—that was unbearable to him. And so he was not content to defend the *curiosity* of Sainte-Beuve by declaring that it was a quality "praiseworthy and not blameworthy"—a quality of culture springing from "desire after the things of the mind simply for their own sakes and for the pleasure of seeing them as they are." For Arnold, this desire to know, "to see things as they really are," was not enough. Culture has for him also a moral aspect. It is a *study of perfection* which moves by the force, not only of the passion for knowledge, but also of "the moral and social passion for doing good."

Yes, Arnold has committed himself to that. He leaves us in no doubt about his view. The man of culture is as much concerned with making the truth prevail as in seeing and learning it. He aims at "getting acceptance for his ideas," in "carrying others along with him in his march towards perfection."

I am not trying to find fault with Matthew Arnold for identifying the culture of the critic with propagandism. I am only seeking to ascertain where he stands, and just what he means when he makes so much play with the word *disinterested*. Does he mean exactly what some of us mean to-day when we say that the artist must be "disinterested," and also the critic in appreciating the artist? I think it is clear that he does not. The "interests" from which he would have us be free are those which militate against intellectual and moral perfection. Our judgment, he tells us, should never be swayed by the prejudices of the "Barbarian," the aristocrat who has "spirit and politeness," but is "a little inaccessible to ideas and light." Still less must it be swayed by the blind impulses of the "Populace," which Arnold chooses to speak of in terms of *bawling*, *hustling*, *smashing* and *beer*. Most of all will it shun that falsification of ideas which marks the Philistines, the complacent middle classes who like fanaticism, business, money-making, deputations, comfort, tea-meetings, or "hearing Mr Odger speak." Culture will always seek to disentangle itself from untruths and half-truths, from values which are attached to the machinery of life rather than that spiritual life which machinery should subserve; it will distinguish means from end; and the end it will set before itself is that of perfection, spiritual growth, governed by "sweetness and light." It must shun provincialism, which may take the forms of excess, ignorance, or bathos, and endeavour to be "in contact with the main stream of human life." Exactly what he means by *Philistinism*, and by *disinterestedness*, is clearly stated in this passage from the essay on Heine:

> The enthusiast for the idea, for reason, values reason, the idea, in and for themselves; he values them, irrespectively of the practical conveniences which their triumph may obtain for him; and the man who regards the possession of these practical conveniences as something sufficient in itself, something which compensates for the absence or surrender of the idea, of reason, is, in his eyes, a Philistine.

There we have Arnold's account of Philistinism, and of the opposite quality of culture which determines the critic. The critic will be disinterested in the sense that he will pursue only the ends of cultural perfection, and will be uninfluenced by the coarser appeals of the Philistine.

In analysing the pernicious influences which beset the critic Arnold has made a great advance, and has rendered a service to criticism. He has put before him for his guidance a majestic ideal of intellectual and spiritual excellence, in accord with the best that has been known and thought in the world. But let us frankly face his position. He has urged that the critic should be free from ignoble interests; but in doing so he has asked for his subjection to certain other interests which may be the more subtly beguiling because they are noble. He has emancipated him from certain intellectually unworthy interests only to bind him all the more tightly to spiritual interests determined, however sweetly and reasonably, by "the moral and social passion for doing good."

This is not that disinterestedness which some of us to-day demand alike from the artist and the critic. Perhaps I may venture to quote words that I wrote in 1913,[1] when I said that art "not only calls forth activity, but *disinterested* activity—and by that I mean an activity of the kind which is especially called forth in the fine arts, and not that which science, or religion, or ethics might call forth without the aid of the arts. To preserve the analogy of golf, it may happen—and generally does happen—that the playing of golf makes the limbs more elastic and promotes general health. But to take an interest in golf is not the same thing as to take an interest in the health-producing results of golf. The true golfer is he who plays golf for its own sake and without any ulterior end, without thought of consequences, although consequences of some kind are inevitable. In the same way the activity called forth in all art, both in the artist at the time of creation and in the man who is appreciating it, is disinterested; he is, in proportion as he is an artist or an appreciator of art, concerned at the moment in nothing but the subject-matter of the artist, and the treatment; in making or receiving a certain effect. . . . When I say that the activity of the artist is disinterested, I do not mean that he may not be concerned with any conceivable theme under the sun, but that his business is to

[1] In *Personality in Literature.*

provide us with an experience, and that any end he may have beyond making that experience vivid and complete is an alien end, destroying his singleness of purpose, wholly disruptive of his art and destructive to its energy."

Now that, I admit, is the attitude which primarily concerns the artist, and it only concerns the critic when he is putting himself at the viewpoint of the artist. But it will scarcely be denied that the first business of the critic is to endeavour to put himself at that viewpoint, to see the work of art from within and without as nearly as possible as the artist saw it. Just as disinterestedness, with the meaning I have attached to the word, is an indispensable mark of genuine creative activity in the artist, so, in the case of the critic, it is a measure of his effort to associate himself with the artist. Now to this first and most essential part of a critic's task Arnold's "disinterestedness" has no reference. It is even a question whether it may not rather stand in the way, for it introduces preconceived schemes of perfection which may baulk his understanding, disturb his perceptions, and hinder fair criticism — schemes of excellence, be it noted, which do not exclude somewhat arbitrary moral values. We shall see in a moment that Arnold's own power of appreciation was occasionally disturbed by precisely this influence, leading him to over-praise in some cases, to under-praise in others. The disinterestedness of the critic, in the sense which I have indicated, is not what Arnold demands.

But I admit the duty of the critic no more ends with dumb appreciation than the duty of the artist ends with the dumb internal expression of his impressions. Certainly he must go out into the world to break a lance on behalf of the authors whom he esteems, or to smash reputations which have undeservedly been won. It is here that his social activities begin. It is here that he will need to set his face against "ulterior, political, practical considerations about ideas," and set himself to "communicate fresh knowledge" in the light of "the best that is known and thought in the world," and to "create a current of true and fresh ideas."

We have noticed at an earlier stage of this inquiry how the secular arts in the Middle Ages were driven underground—beneath the surface of the governing cultivated life of their era—through the absence of any such current of ideas as Arnold speaks of. The absence of any effective recognition and criticism of the art of poetry — the intolerant attitude of a society whose civilization was based on ecclesiastical ideas—deterred, during long periods of European history, the development of progressive poetic forms which only a civilized literary society can hand on from generation to generation. Now an age of literary activity, as we have seen, is necessarily also a keenly critical age—it is one in which ideas are bandied about, in which thought about the arts becomes infectious. The poets themselves, it has been apparent, are always among the critics, talking at least about their technique, and occasionally unfolding a theory of the processes by which they work. And sometimes it is only when the most fruitful effort of an age is spent that formal criticism steps in and stereotypes ideas that the creative artists initiated.

Arnold is of opinion that the process can be reversed—that it is not so much the rush of ideas from artist to artist that produces the great period of poetic activity, but that the potential poet is waiting, sterile, till the intellectual material has been made ready for him by the professional critic. The critic is in the position of John the Baptist, preparing the way for one whose shoe he is not worthy to unloose. "The elements with which the creative power works are ideas; the best ideas on every matter which literature touches, current at the time." Who provides these elements, these nourishing ideas, this food for the Shakespeares and Wordsworths of the future? We feel some slight over-emphasis of the majesty of his own calling when Matthew Arnold replies, "The critic." It is he who "discovers" the ideas, he who propagates them, and nothing remains for the literary genius but to walk in and undertake the grand work of "synthesis and exposition."

Well, no doubt the powerful critic plays his part in fertilizing the soil and in watering the young plant. And if it be true, as I have suggested, that the critic himself is an artist whose chosen subject-matter lies in the life of literature, then he, too, must play his part in the tossing to and fro of ideas between artist and artist. But Arnold has advanced no reason for believing that his is more than one of the many voices which fill the air and set the echoes ringing, stirring the creative impulse of the potential poets in our midst. This art impulse does not necessarily spring from formally correct ideas—it is started by notions of any and every kind hurtling from side to side. It is not released only by the force of culture, though culture will keep it in the strait and narrow path.

Arnold claims too much for the critic. But in putting his claims high he has done him no disservice. Which of us would not pay homage to the critic of whom it could be truly said: He freed himself from the cogs of life's machinery, he pursued knowledge for its own sake, he loved ideas for their sweetness and light, he sought unremittingly to make the best ideas prevail and to apply them to life, he communicated to the world the fresh knowledge he had found, and he avoided the errors of provincialism, endeavouring always to set himself at the centre of the current of world thought?

IV

So much, then, for the duty of the critic to the public. But what of his duty to literature? By what means does he discover the best? Arnold, as a critic of criticism, endeavours to answer this question.

He does not claim, or wish, to probe to the "metaphysic depths," like Coleridge. Indeed, he thinks that in doing so we should "darken the question," obscure the sweetness and light. He prefers an empirical test, one which can be applied after long experience with beautiful poems and ideas—taste or "tact" being in the last resort the indispensable guide. "Critics give themselves great labour," he says in *The Study of Poetry*, "to draw out what in the abstract constitutes the characteristics of a high quality of poetry. It is much better simply to have recourse to concrete examples;—to take specimens of poetry of the high, the very highest quality, and to say: The characters of a high quality of poetry are what is expressed *there*." He bids us shun the false valuations of the "historic estimate" and the "personal estimate" and attain to a "real estimate" by learning to feel and enjoy the best work of the real classic, and appreciate the wide difference between it and all lesser work. If we ask how we are to know this best when we see it, he answers that it is enough, in general, to acclaim it—it is there, and there. But if that is not enough, he adds that the high qualities lie both in the matter and substance of the poetry, and in the manner and style, and these have "a mark, an accent, of high beauty, worth and power"; the substance and matter will possess, in an eminent degree, "truth and seriousness," and this character is "inseparable from the superiority of diction and movement" which marks the style and manner.

Longinus, it is worth recalling, laid down a few tests by which we may be sure that literature has the true accent of the sublime. There are passages, he said, in which we may recognize "the beauty and truth of the sublime" because they "always please and please all (fastidious) readers"; and because they make "the utmost demand on the attention," force themselves upon us "importunately, irresistibly," and "take so strong a hold on the memory that they cannot be forgotten"; and because they are such that the answer would be favourable should we ask, How would Homer or Demosthenes have been affected? We may be sure that Arnold would have subscribed to all these conditions when he said that the most useful method of discovering the worth of poetry was "to have always in one's mind lines and expressions of the great masters, and to apply them as a touchstone to other poetry."

Admirable indeed are most of the lines which he has marked for men of all the ages to admire, and carry in their minds as touchstones. Unforgettable is

καὶ σέ, γέρον, τὸ πρὶν μὲν ἀκούομεν ὄλβιον εἶναι

and

> If thou didst ever hold me in thy heart,
> Absent thee from felicity awhile . . .

And he presents us with a series of passages from Homer, Dante, Shakespeare and Milton, all of which, but one, would hold their own in any anthology of immortal verse—though it is surely deficient in that it gives us no lines from Virgil. But I admit to experiencing some sense of shock when, amid these supreme, silencing lines, we come upon these from Milton :

> And courage never to submit or yield
> And what is else not to be overcome.

The sentiment is excellent. The moral is a noble one. It recalls all the admirable ethical qualities which Milton gives to his heroic Satan. But in regard to the "style and manner," the "diction and movement," from which "the matter and substance of the best poetry" are "inseparable," what are we to say of these indifferent lines with their redundant phrases? Milton morally exalted—poetically, in his weakest vein. Does not the choice of this passage reveal just the danger to which Arnold exposed himself when he set up an ideal of perfection too much associated with the problem of "how to live"? I have already suggested that Arnold's powers of appreciation might be twisted by his preconceived schemes of moral excellence. The choice of this passage is a case in point. When thus deferring to his sense of moral values might he not more happily have recalled those lines from Virgil where a similar moral sentiment is expressed in language of unmistakable excellence :

> Felix, qui potuit rerum cognoscere causas,
> Atque metus omnes et inexorabile fatum
> Subjecit pedibus strepitumque Acherontis avari [1]

[1] Happy he who hath power to discern the causes of things, and hath trampled upon all fears—fears of inexorable fate and the din of the greedy river of Hell.

lines which are worthy to be included among the nobles of his collection.

If I am right in thinking that in this example Arnold has tripped, we must attribute the error to some defect of judgment and tact, upon which in the last resort his choice of models depends. And we have seen that he has handicapped his own judgment by making it the servant of preconceived standards of excellence which are as much moral as æsthetic. This bias in Arnold's artistic make-up from time to time conflicts with a purely disinterested judgment. We see it in the choice of these lines from Milton. We see it, in his otherwise admirable estimate of Burns, when he oversteps the mark through his dislike of "Scotch drink, Scotch religion, and Scotch manners." We see it in his harsh treatment of Keats in regard to Fanny Brawne.

Arnold would probably agree that his method of comparing passage with passage is not a sufficient test for determining the value of a work as a whole; we have seen that he himself insisted that we must judge a poem by the "total-impression." But there is no reason why we should not extend his comparative method, not resting content with detached judgments from isolated passages, but comparing the whole impression we have in our mind of one work with the whole impression that has been stamped upon our minds by a masterpiece. The comparative method is an invaluable aid to appreciation in approaching any kind of art. This is just as true of fiction as of poetry, of painting as of literature. And it is helpful not merely thus to compare the masterpiece and the lesser work, but the good with the not so good, the sincere with the not quite sincere, the clever with the too clever by half.

It is profitable to put passages by Charles Doughty side by side with passages from, say, Miss Sackville West's poem, *The Land*, or to contrast whole poems by Mr Humbert Wolfe with whole poems by Mr Sacheverell Sitwell. And similarly in painting. It is profitable to pass from a display of pictures by one artist in the Leicester Galleries to a display by another artist in the next room; and to walk round to the National Gallery to complete the impression.

Arnold has provided us with an excellent example of how to use the comparative method, and he has enabled us to see that it may be fruitful in the highest degree when employed by a critic of exceptional "tact." Some of us may feel that in his famous distinction between the *historic*, the *personal* and the *real* estimates of literature he has a little underrated the significance of the personal. It is true, we may easily be carried away by "our personal affinities, likings and circumstances" to attach greater importance to a work than a more detached critic would allow it. But it should be remembered, the fact that a piece of literature means much to us personally may indicate that we have found the utmost that is really in it. We are always in danger of getting less than the utmost from any work of art. Is it not, after all, one of the aims of the alert reader to put himself *en rapport* with the author and his subject, and so gain a sense of intimate personal relationship? It is arguable that no judgment about a book has become a real judgment until it has become a personal one. Surely it was for this very reason that Sainte-Beuve was at pains to know all that could be known about the life and circumstances of a man of letters. He did not expect to be able to define a work until he had formed a personal estimate of its author.

Some have felt that Arnold is too austere, too exacting. Few of us, however, are in danger of erring on that side. But we may ask whether it is fair to demand that all hills should be Alps. Is there not an excellence in some minor poetry worth while on its own account? May we not miss its qualities if we too insistently disparage it by contrast with the greatest? "The mass of current literature," he said, "is so much better disregarded." That is true enough. But apart from permanent values, contemporary literature may have a use for us precisely because it is contemporary—because it is written for us, because it faces our problems, because we can discern whatever subtleties it possesses as men in a different age may be unable to do. If we too far disregard current literature we shall be out of touch with the quickening forces of our time, which have special meaning for us, and about which it behoves us to make up our minds. And it is just in regard to this current literature that a true critical faculty is most needed. The established classic will take care of himself. But the critic has a duty to perform to the young writers of promise and to obscure contemporaries who have never won their meed of praise; and another duty to those too prominent ones who have climbed, trespassing, on to pedestals.

Arnold did a service to criticism by his sheer inexorableness. There was no compromise in his war to the end against deception, insincerity, charlatanism. "In poetry, which is thought and art in one, it is the glory, the eternal honour, that charlatanism shall find no entrance; that this noble sphere be kept inviolate and inviolable." In defending its honour we can never afford to neglect his bidding to keep in mind those universal and shining examples which have been handed down to us from the past through many languages, filling our minds with that right reason which rejects excess, which puts new half-truths to the test of higher truths, and distinguishes the alive, the vital, the sincere from the shoddy, the showy, the merely clever.

Chapter Twenty-four

ART AND MORALITY

IF even the prophet of "sweetness and light" was not quite immune from influences which he deplored, what shall we say of John Ruskin—that arch-missionary in an age of missionaries? Arnold made but a slight concession to the ethical demands of the mid-Victorian age. Ruskin gave in full measure all that it asked for, in a theory of art which was to satisfy the humaner conventions of middle-class morality.

We saw how Sir Philip Sidney, faced with that attitude of stern suspicion towards poetry which the Puritans of his time inherited from the early Christian Church, was constrained to pacify them, and to argue that poetry was not the evil thing it was supposed to be, but on the contrary was consistent with correct religion. Ruskin had no need to pacify the Puritans of his time. He was of their way of thinking. The full respectability of the arts having long since been established, they were quite ready to go half-way to meet him, and he all the way to meet them. As for them, had they not Wordsworth always with them, and Tennyson? The moral thunderings of Carlyle were reassuring; and all the most popular fiction-writers of the time were on the side of the angels. There were difficulties to get over in the atheism of Shelley. The private life of Byron was scandalous and disconcerting. But Ruskin taught them how to discriminate. In so far as literature fell short of Victorian standards of morality, to that extent it was simply bad art. All art that was art was of divine origin. It was the "witness of the glory of God." Beauty was "dependent on a pure, right, and open state of the heart," and was accessible only to the Blessed who are "pure in heart, for they shall see God."

Ruskin may be compared with Plato, in that "art and morality" was a problem for both of them, and both were on the side of the moralist. (There was this considerable difference, however, that whilst Plato subjected the moral notions current in his time to the most searching scrutiny, no dissenting minister could have accepted the Victorian code, on its angelic side, more simply and whole-heartedly than Ruskin.) For both of them moral considerations dominated all considerations, and were never irrelevant. Yet they came to opposite conclusions. The view current in Plato's day was that the arts, existing as much to instruct as to please, satisfactorily fulfilled this mission. Plato challenged the view. He concluded that from their very nature they conflicted with morality, and therefore he banished them from his State. But Ruskin found that from their very nature they coincided with morality, and he gave them his blessing. Plato condemned the arts because they were immoral; Ruskin praised them because they were superbly moral. The one drove them from the city because they were founded in the delusions of sense, the other welcomed them because they sprang from the divine Intelligence operating through the Imagination of man.

The Beautiful, for Ruskin, was simply described as "a gift of God," [1] and this description he applied both to the desire of it, and the thing desired. All the fine arts must be "didactic to the people, and that as their chief end." [2] The function of the artist was to teach nobility. In Part III. of *Modern Painters* he had begun by laying down that: "Art, properly so called, is no re-

[1] *Modern Painters*, III. 1, 2.
[2] *Aratra Pentelici*, Lecture IV.

creation; it cannot be learned at spare moments, nor pursued when we have nothing better to do. It is no handiwork for drawing-room tables, no relief of the *ennui* of boudoirs; it must be understood and taken seriously, or not at all."

That is excellently said; and unexceptionable also is his statement that the results of the arts are "desirable or admirable in themselves and for their own sake," and that they have no "taint in them of subserviency to life." He had already made it clear that by "subserviency to life" he meant to that part of life which is served by such things as "houses and lands, and food and raiment." It is only in this meaner sense of Utility that art is Useless. In the higher sense it is supremely Useful, in that it enables man to fulfil his real function, which is to be "the witness of the glory of God, and to advance that glory by his reasonable obedience and resultant happiness." Pre-eminently Useful to us, in the pure sense of the word, is "whatever sets the glory of God more brightly before us."

The feeling of the Beautiful, according to Ruskin, does not depend on the senses, nor on the intellect, but on the heart, and is due to the sense of reverence, gratitude and joyfulness that arises from recognition of the handiwork of God in the objects of Nature. The same divine power operating in the artist inspires him to blend or fuse his mental impressions into beautiful pictures or poems. His account of the sources of art, and in particular of the artistic Imagination, is a somewhat crude adaptation of the theory of Coleridge. The latter, we recall, said, of the "secondary Imagination," that it "dissolves, diffuses, dissipates, in order to re-create; or where this process is rendered impossible, yet still at all events it struggles to idealize and to unify. It is essentially *vital*, even as all objects (as objects) are essentially fixed and dead." To some of us, the God in Ruskin's doctrine will seem too much a "god of the machine," miraculously at hand to solve all difficulties which arise. But he says many telling things which do not stand on his theological dogmas in the long chapters in which he amplifies the romantic theory of the Imagination.

He speaks of three functions of the Imagination: "It combines, and by combination creates new forms." (Imagination Associative.) "Again, it treats, or regards, both the simple images and its own combinations in peculiar ways." (Imagination Contemplative.) "And, thirdly, it penetrates, analyses, and reaches truths by no other faculty discoverable." (Imagination Penetrative.)

Imagination, in the first sense, is not to be confused with composition, which consists in the mere grouping of certain ideas or images—an art that can be taught. It is a "prophetic action of mind" which out of an infinite mass selects certain ideas "which are *separately* wrong, which together shall be right, and of whose unity, therefore, the idea must be formed at the instant they are seized." The artist sees his picture from the first moment. He is able to correct an imperfection by the addition of another imperfection, and create in the whole a thing of beauty. The Imagination Penetrative by intuition and intensity of gaze reaches "a more essential truth than is seen on the surface of things." The Imagination Contemplative enables the mind to pass beyond the simple ideas set before it, imparting to them quite another spiritual significance, "striking them as it were with the die of an image belonging to other matter."

I must pass over the many suggestive things that Ruskin says, arising out of, but not wholly dependent on, his theory of the sources of Imagination. In this chapter I am concerned with his doctrine that the artist is the servant of God whose mission it is to go forth into the highways and hedges and compel men to come in. He is a teacher. He is by nature a pre-eminently "moral" man. His function is to make men better.

Ruskin finds himself confronted with a difficulty from which he seeks to escape too easily. He has said that Beauty addresses itself to "the moral part of us," and this brings him face to face with two objections, which he thus states :

"How does it happen that it is ever found in the works of impious men, and how is it possible for such to desire or conceive it ?

"On the other hand, how does it happen that men in high state of moral culture are often insensible to the influence of material beauty ; and insist feebly upon it as an instrument of soul culture ?"

The answer to these questions is important to him, because he says (in Part III. of *Modern Painters*, Section I, chapter xv.) that the end and aim of his labour is "the proving that no supreme power of art can be attained by impious men ; and that the neglect of art, as an interpreter of divine things, has been of evil consequence to the Christian world."

He seeks to get over the difficulty by distinguishing between two kinds of experience which may arise in the enjoyment of art. One is the "mere animal consciousness of the pleasantness," which he calls Æsthesis ; the other is "the exulting, reverent, and grateful perception of it," which he calls Theoria. The latter alone accompanies the "full comprehension and contemplation of the Beautiful as a gift of God." Now he admits that the first, or inferior sense, is necessary to the appreciation of beauty; that it is given, " like the hearing ear of music, to some more than others"; and that it may be given in large measure to "men of impious or unreflecting spirit," who may cultivate the perceptions of beauty "on principles merely æsthetic, and so lose their hallowing power." In the works of such men there is "a taint and stain, and jarring discord, darker and louder exactly in proportion to the moral deficiency."

There are sentiments in this passage which may compel us to respond to Ruskin's argument. But the following objection instantly arises. Ruskin admits that this element of "æsthetic" perception is indispensable in the activity of art; he admits also that it may be present in the impious no less than the pious; from which it follows that this element cannot be judged by moral standards. Here then is something indispensable in the functional activity of the artist which cannot be put to a moral test.

Plato fully admitted this insuperable difficulty. For him no less than Ruskin it could not but arise out of a dualistic theory, in which a world of Ideas was above and apart from a world of sense. But he was consistent and logical. Finding that the arts were inextricably mixed up in this delusive world of sense, he cut them root and branch out of his ideal State. Ruskin no less admits that the arts are involved in this "inferior" part of man's nature, but seeks to make the best of both worlds by shutting his eyes to the consequence of his own premises. There can be no excellence in art without the inferior "æsthetic" excellence; yet no excellence is to count but that which derives from the separate sphere of the spiritual. The position is untenable.

But passing over this difficulty, let us pursue the argument on his own "Theoretic" ground. We are to assume that the excellence of a work is in the last resort to be judged according to the goodness of the artist made manifest in it. That being so, will our judgment of it vary according to the ethical school to which we belong? Shall we praise *goodness* according to the Epicureans, or *goodness* according to the Stoics? *Goodness*, according to Dr Martineau, or *goodness* according to Harriet Beecher Stowe? *Goodness* according to Dean Inge, or the Bishop of London? Will the artistic judgment of an Anglo-Catholic be quite different from the artistic judgment of an Evangelical, and that of a Jew from a Christian? Are we really to subject art to these difficult and disputable tests of moral excellence?

But perhaps Ruskin would sweep aside these questions as derogatory, and say that he is speaking of the broad human virtues which all men recognize, and of the evident vices which all condemn. If this is his position, he seems to mean that a work of art should be pronounced excellent precisely in so far as it glorifies the most commonplace of the virtues.

I hope I shall not be found guilty of wantonly overlooking, in the pursuit of the argument, what there is of truth in Ruskin's position. I readily admit that moral considerations cannot fail to enter into the subject-matter of every artist who is handling life and character. A moral issue may characterize the theme which has been chosen — as it does in the *Œdipus* dramas, in *Hamlet*, in *Macbeth*, and in most of the great tragedies of the world. Characters will often be lovable or the reverse according to the manner in which their moral attributes have been sympathetically treated. Morality being one of the principal issues in life belongs to the very fibre and texture of all art. It cannot be otherwise, for life is its subject-matter.

This life, of course, is life as the artist sees it. His powers of seeing determine the quality of the work. All that belongs to his personality—not excluding his moral character—must determine the work which he produces, so that when we pass judgment on it we are passing judgment on everything in his mental and moral make-up which he drew upon in the effort of creation. Moral attributes cannot be irrelevant.

Mr John Galsworthy once said that no man can be declared great in the fullest sense who is lacking in goodness. Few would care to challenge the truth of this. Napoleon Bonaparte afforded an example. But it was not only to men of action that the saying applied. Did not the essential malice and meanness of Swift's character deprive his writing of the highest quality? Some might observe that the moral obliquity of Oscar Wilde corresponds to the purely superficial cleverness and the absence of feeling which mark his literary compositions. Others would point out that the tone and quality of Byron's work are as adversely affected by the slipshodness of his character as they are favourably affected by his high spirit and physical courage. Who is there does not feel that the fond allusion to "gentle Shakespeare" names but one of the likeable qualities which he cannot have been without?

But we are on dangerous ground when we begin to draw particular conclusions of this kind. I would not care to press the force of any one of the above obvious illustrations, for there are so many conflicting elements in the character of every individual that it is hard indeed to say which, at any given moment, is uppermost, or to be sure, even when one is known to have been uppermost, just how it has influenced the subtler perceptions.

Still, we seem to have been conceding much to Ruskin's view, and to have admitted that ethical considerations, both as regards the character of the artist, and the characterization within the theme, must be given more weight than at first we appeared willing to allow. Must we still maintain that Ruskin was wrong?

The answer is, emphatically, Yes. I maintain that Ruskin has misstated the problem; that he has given a false answer; and in so doing has put before us a fundamentally false conception of the character and function of art.

Let me quote in full that passage from *Aratra Pentelici*:

> 1. Not only sculpture, but all the other fine arts, must be for the people.
> 2. They must be didactic to the people, and that as their chief end. The structural arts, didactic in their manner; the graphic arts, in their matter also.
> 3. And chiefly the great representative and imaginative arts—that is to say, the drama and sculpture—are to teach what is noble in past history, and lovely in existing human and organic life.
> 4. And the test of right manner of execution in these arts, is that they strike, in the most emphatic manner, the rank of popular minds to which they are addressed.
> 5. And the test of utmost fineness in execution in these arts, is that they make themselves be forgotten in what they represent; and so fulfil the words of their greatest Master,
>
> "THE BEST, IN THIS KIND, ARE BUT SHADOWS."

There Ruskin has at least done us the service of being clear. He does not say that the arts *are* instructive; that they incidentally teach; that, being noble, they cannot fail to do us good. He says something quite different—that their proper character is to be teaching agencies—to instruct is their function. Nothing else matters in comparison with the necessity that they should be "didactic to the people." They are to attain this end by a subtle form of deception—a noble deception, doubtless (ψεῦδος γενναῖον)—but still a deception, making themselves be "forgotten in what they represent"—catching our attention, tricking our fancy, arousing our pleasure in objects and images, in order that we may be decoyed into learning moral lessons which the artist was hiding up his sleeve. It is no use to affirm in one breath that the arts exist for their own sakes, and that they exist for the sake of something else.

If Ruskin had been content to say that the artist is bound to deal with moral questions, or that a beautiful work cannot fail to have an ennobling effect, or even that only such works as have an ennobling effect are in the fullest sense beautiful, then we should not be disposed to quarrel with him. But he declares that it is the function, the characteristic of art as art, to convey moral truths; and to say this is surely to ignore its real essence, and to obliterate the difference which distinguishes it from science and rhetoric.

It is the business of the scientist to *learn*, *know*, and *prove*. It is the business of the rhetorician to *persuade*; of the moralist, to *teach*. It is the business of the artist to *show*. "Life *ought to be* like that," says the moralist. "Life *looks* like that," says the artist. Having had his intuition, and being satisfied with it, what other duty can he own but that of expressing it as perfectly as he can and communicating it to others? Having seen his vision, and being in love with it, can he betray his art by handing it on in any other form but that in which he sees it? True, we may condemn him for the satisfaction he feels in this or that, and may dislike him if he is in love with unworthy objects. In that case we may ask him to refrain, but we cannot in the name of art ask him to express his intuition in any but an artistic way—namely, exactly as he sees it.

The function of the moralist is to exhort. That of the artist is to exhibit. The aim of the one is to influence action. The aim of the other is to awaken perception. The satisfaction of the moralist in an action always has reference to an End beyond that action. The satisfaction of the artist in the work of art is complete in itself, and knows no perfection beyond its own perfection. Art cannot be determined by the needs of action, but only by the imperative demands of vision. You can only see an image as it is, and if you attempt to falsify your vision in order to present an object "didactic to the people" you have been treacherous to your art.

My plea is for a clear distinction between two properly different modes of activity. It is no justification, as I hope will appear later, for another form of cant, known as "Art for Art's sake."

Chapter Twenty-five

WALTER PATER

I

WHEN we distinguish between art and morals we do not mean that the life of art is in its nature different from other kinds of life; that it is made up of ideas peculiarly its own which dwell aloof in some starry world reserved for poets, painters, or musicians. Art is the more itself in proportion as it is quick with real life, or imparts to ordinary life its choice but not alien spirit. It is in the *mode* of its activity that it is distinct. The actions of the moralist are considered excellent as the means to an end. The activity of art is its own end.

"To treat life in the spirit of art, is to make life a thing in which means and end are identified," writes Walter Pater in his essay on Wordsworth; and he adds: "to encourage such treatment, the true moral significance of art and poetry." The work of the great poets is "not to teach lessons, or enforce rules, or even to stimulate us to noble ends; but to withdraw the thoughts for a little while from the mere machinery of life, to fix them, with appropriate emotions, on the spectacle of those great facts in man's existence which no machinery affects." In contrast with Ruskin, Pater almost reverses the order of values. Art is no longer the servant, but is to be the master; the highest morality will be to enable as much as possible of life to be lived in the spirit of the artist.

For Pater the problem of literature is the manner in which it represents an approach to life; and the whole task of criticism is to approach literature in the same way. Literature and the arts for him are not merely a part of life; they seem to become the whole of life in so far as it is lived in the finer way of the spirit, and in so far as it is objectively expressed. When Plato was seeking to discover the principles of Justice, he looked for them "writ large" in the life of the State. When Walter Pater is searching for the principles of art, he looks for them, writ large, in the spiritual life of the artist—the greater whole out of which each poem, or novel, or painting, or sculpture, or symphony is brought to birth. The story of *Marius the Epicurean* is the story of this rarefied experience presented as a continuous evolution, the soul-experience of a man who with scrupulous thoroughness lives the artist's life. If Marius were just a man, if he were indeed a flesh-and-blood person whom we were to meet every day in life, or even in ordinary fiction, we might feel his lack of full-bloodedness, an uncanny monkishness in his complete indifference to the workaday affairs of the world. He is a thing of light and of shadow, and disembodied thought—disconcerting indeed to the common man.

Yet, as we read, we do not miss this common humanity in him. We do not have to suppose that any Marius lived just, or only, the life that Pater has so sparingly given his hero. How indeed could *experience* be so rich, so varied, so coloured, while it was so "attentively" studied, for Marius, if it had been at all times so "sicklied o'er with the pale cast of thought"? But Pater has aimed only at unfolding the spiritualized side of him. The life he is presenting is emblematic. It is his purpose to trace that finer thread of pure gold in the artist's life, which, as seen in Marius, may be conceived as the stuff of which art is made. The work of Wordsworth suggests for Pater "an absolute duality between higher and lower moods," and this means that much of his poetry gives expression to a commoner side of him which was not poetic at all, though doubtless necessary to him in order that he should be a man. (The poet, after all, must be a man before he can be a poet.) Well, that common side, which exists in all real, tolerable men, is not shown in Marius. That is because Pater, here, is not concerned with all humanity, but humanity only when it is listening to the music of the spheres—humanity at its highest point of sensibility and apprehensiveness, realizing the fullest potentiality of its own character—humanity when it is in the mood either to create fine art, or to appreciate it to the utmost.

"Marius," in the main, is a study of that course of life in which experience is consciously pursued for its own sake. How marvellous an evidence it is of the artistic genius of Pater that he should have been able so to treat the abstract principles of art—terribly dead intellectual matter for most of us—as to make them live almost like persons, just as he himself observes that the philosopher Plato talked of and loved abstract Ideas as if they were persons. Pater, if anyone, may serve to persuade us that we are right in saying that criticism may be an art whose subject is literature or the thoughts of artists. The thoughts of Marius stand forth for us to be looked at like curious stones in a collection, tangible, bright, without ceasing to be *thoughts*. They are the thoughts as of one resting in a boat on a river, alive to all sounds and impressions, whose ear is quick to hear the faint, distant plashing of an unseen oar on still waters.

We must stay with Pater for a moment in company with

this strange, interesting Marius, who may stand for us as a type of the man who is, above all things, "attentive" to life, seeking that in it which will enrich the spirit, and resolved to get from the experiences of religion, speculation, or literature just so much as each can contribute to his careful art of living. We observe with what youthful earnestness the mind of the boy Marius is open to the ceremonial influence of the ancient, but now artificial, Roman religion. We see him in contact with the austerity, the discipline, of the Stoics; and again, attracted by the mystical teachings of those who professed to expound Platonism. But he does not fall a prey to that "enervating mysticism." From its fascinating influence he is delivered by his virility, by his "hatred of what was theatrical," and by "the feeling, increasing with his advançe to manhood, of a poetic beauty in mere clearness of thought, the actually æsthetic charm of a cold austerity of mind; as if the kinship of that to the clearness of physical light were something more than a figure of speech." He begins to conceive of himself as the "passive spectator of the world around him," and at the age of eighteen, turning from poetry to the "literature of thought," he began to seclude himself from others "in a severe intellectual meditation, that salt of poetry, without which all the more serious charm is lacking to the imaginative world." It was at this age that he felt he must "determine his bearings, as by compass, in the world of thought," bent on going into affairs and ascertaining his outlook, without disguises. And so from Epicurus he passes back to old Heraclitus, and through the doctrine of "perpetual flux" learns to correct the "false impression of permanence or fixity in things," and to feel scorn for a "careless, half-conscious, 'use-and-wont' reception of our experience," guiding himself by "loyalty to cool and candid reason, which makes strict attentiveness of mind a kind of religious duty and service."

Attentiveness. How Pater holds to that word! And how much it signifies in his account of the artist-critic's life!

From Heraclitus it was an easy step to the Protagorean doctrine of "man as the measure of all things," which had value for Marius as giving him something to rely on, "the exclusive certainty to himself of his own impressions." And thence again to Aristippus of Cyrene, whose theory that "things are but shadows" became no languid nihilism, as it might have been, and "generated neither frivolity nor sourness, but induced, rather, an impression, just serious enough, of the call upon men's attention of the crisis in which they find themselves." It became a stimulus to activity and an "inextinguishable thirst after experience," as understood by this "happily constituted Greek," who turned its hard, bare truths "into precepts of grace, and delicate wisdom, and a delicate sense of honour." The Cyrenaic doctrine gave him the "initiation" to which he aspired, and left him equipped, when he was sent back to experience, to the world of things seen and heard and felt, with "a wonderful machinery of observation, and free from the tyranny of mere theories."

We shall not forget that *Marius the Epicurean*, though not quite a novel, is an imaginary portrait, and that the subject of it (living in a grown-up period of the world's history which Pater conceived to be rather like our own) is not explicitly put before us as the type to which every true artistic temperament may be referred. And yet, the more we read Pater's critical writings, the more I think we shall find that the artist *par excellence* whom he asks us to admire is the artist who reveals the temper of Marius;

and in like manner he himself, as a critic, endeavours to approach literature in just the same contemplative, fastidious, curious spirit in which Marius approached life. Art and the appreciation of it are not for him easily reducible to closely fixed principles; they are rather a matter of *temper*, a temper better illustrated through the personality of such a one as Marius then described in philosophic terms. He requires a mind that should be "free from the tyranny of mere theories," and yet full of thought; free as a cluster of leaves to rustle in response to every movement of beauty, and yet disciplined, austere. The lighter side of Epicureanism—*carpe diem* —pluck the moment—"Gather ye rose-buds while ye may"—this was not enough; there are the "crises" in which men find themselves, the interesting turning-points in this and that series of events, which should be taken seriously in proportion as they will repay the attention of a thoughtful, sensitive and disciplined mind. The dull inexpressiveness of "use-and-wont" is pushed away to a back place in life; mere convention is given only the small value it deserves; the convictions which others value are sacrificed if they stand in the way of "that clear-eyed intellectual consistency, which is like spotless bodily cleanliness, or scrupulous personal honour." Marius, with some touch of the Stoic still lingering in his nature, but pre-eminently Epicurean, with all the graciousness of the Master of Cyrene, his openness of mind, his contemplative habit, his desire to make the most, for the enrichment always of the spirit, of all that experience can give, expresses the attitude which Walter Pater would have us bring to literature. His critical mind will be one which began, in the process of initiation, by weaning itself from dogmas, from stereotyped ways of thinking, making itself receptive to new opinions, new modes of expression. The attitude is that of the careful searcher, the explorer, the fastidious mind ever responsive to beauty wherever and in whatever form it appears, and tactful in discerning the *comeliness*, the *blitheness*, the *graciousness* (words dear to Pater) that it may carry with it.

A critic approaching literature in this manner was not likely to begin by enunciating general principles. "Critical efforts to limit art *a priori* . . . are always liable to be discredited by the facts of artistic production." We should no more expect Pater, at the outset, to lay down a code of æsthetic rules than Marius to arrive for the first time in Rome with a preconceived idea of the perfect capital of an Empire. His way is experimental, tentative, bringing the trained sensibility of a keenly alert mind into contact with an author's work, the object in the first place being to find out what the work is like, and then what there is distinctive about it, and, finally, what in it expresses the peculiar, the unique power that is characteristic of the author and represents him at his best. Thus, in the poetry of Wordsworth he finds qualities that belong to the real Wordsworth, and inferior qualities that are a sort of "alien element" in him. What he is searching for is his "peculiar savour," his "special power."

> Those who wish to understand his influence, and experience his peculiar savour, must bear with patience the presence of an alien element in Wordsworth's work, which never coalesced with what is really delightful in it, nor underwent his special power.

And again, as in Marius, we hear of the need for an "initiation," a *disciplina arcani*, to which the critic must submit himself, following patiently the devious and often unsatisfactory paths of Wordsworth's poetry, if we are to reach the secret of his "special and privileged state of mind." It is because of the constant manifestation in him of these "higher and lower moods" that he thinks the reading of Wordsworth "an excellent sort of training towards the things of art and poetry" begetting a "habit of reading between the lines" and "a faith in the effect of concentration." Those who can bear to undergo his influence in this way "become able constantly to distinguish in art, speech, feeling, manners, that which is organic, animated, expressive, from that which is only conventional, derivative, inexpressive."

The "expressive" thing, then, that which really expresses the essential personality of an author—the peculiar quality of power and meaning which is the gist of him, distinguishing him from everything else that ever was—this is what Walter Pater as a critic is looking for. It manifests itself in thought or sentiment, and in style—and in these two together as inseparably *one*. And when, after long pursuit of the difficult way, he comes at last to the "crisis," and finds it worthy of attention, he does not, after all, shrink from enunciating some principles which his laborious method has led him to.

II

It is characteristic of him that he should discuss his principles of criticism in an essay on "Style." It is a part of his apparent diffidence that he should seek to get at qualities of "soul" through its outer qualities of physical form—not that he asks us to recognize the man "by the Athenian garments he hath on," but by the shape and gestures of the body through which the soul declares itself.

And so, in discussing diction, style, form, he is discussing a central problem of the literary art.

About these three words there are a few observations which should be made before we examine Pater's essay on "Style." In the ordinary usage of the second and third we are apt to give them too narrow a meaning; and this usage, though not without its convenience, leads often to confusion of thought and absurdity in criticism. *Diction*, of course, simply means *wording* or *phrasing*, and implies *choice of words*; and so is an element in style (Aristotle uses the same word λέξις to denote both *diction* and *style*). *Style* is simply manner of writing (which includes choice of words), and is commonly contrasted with *matter*, meaning thought. We sometimes hear people say that the *style*, or *manner*, is good, but the *matter* is bad. This is a confusing, though unavoidable, way of talking, for the word *matter* is used with a different meaning from that which we generally attach to it. It properly means any material out of which something is made before it has been handled for a special purpose. Thus wool is the matter or material out of which cloth is made, and cloth the matter out of which coats are made. Sounds, properly speaking, are the matter out of which words are made, and words are the matter out of which we make speech. Thus we might suppose that when we contrast *style* with *matter* we mean by the last the medium—the stone which a sculptor chisels, the paint and canvas which a painter employs, or the words which are written by the poet. But we do not. Nor do we mean the concrete objects which these works may be supposed to represent. (In music there are no such corresponding objects in the natural world, and because this confusion of representation does not arise in music, it has been arbitrarily described as the most perfect of the arts.)

Those who distinguish *style* or *manner* from *matter* indicate, by *matter*, the thought, the ideas, which the artist intends to express.

Often the word *style* has been used to cover no more ground than the word *composition*, which, in writing, means simply putting together words, sentences, paragraphs in a certain order. Composition, just as much as style, depends upon the mind. It is the mechanical side of writing, and, when good, arises from mechanical correctness in the ordering of our ideas. The moment we cease to be content with "use-and-wont," or mere rules, and give ever so little play to personality, or originative impulse, then the order of words in which we express ourselves becomes a matter of style rather than composition.

Aristotle said "the perfection of style is to be clear without being mean." The eighteenth-century prose-writers talked much about "elegance," "dignity," "sublimity" and the like; and they, like the Greek rhetoricians, were disposed to tell us more about the rules and technical devices by which to attain those qualities than about the faculties with which we discern them. But clearly the decision about the words we use and the way we use them rests in the last resort upon perception, sensitiveness to language and to its correspondence with ideas—upon *tact* or *taste*.

And yet people still often speak about taste as applied to style as if it were simply taste in choosing words, in putting them together in sentences and paragraphs—as if words and sentences were something hanging in the void, beautiful as mere sounds, appropriate without being appropriate *to anything*, right merely as language without regard to rightness of expression! All of which, of course, is absurd. Even the Jabberwock rhymes of Lewis Carroll or the Mulla

Mulgar verses of Mr De la Mare owe their quality to the fact that they rightly express that particular sort of fancy or topsy-turvydom with which each poet is making play.

Style, then, means the way in which we use words for the purposes of expression—expressiveness being the gist of the whole matter. It implies the degree of perfection or imperfection with which a writer expresses his meaning. Language must be confused if the thought behind it is confused, and it cannot be clear unless the thought is clear. Ornament is an excrescence unless it belongs properly to the idea—all else is verbiage and nonsense. We speak of a " trick of style " when words are used to impress the reader, though no striking idea is really conveyed by them—in which case it is not style at all—it is merely an insulting noise. On the other hand, true style may obviously be as subtle as the subtlety of the writer's perception, solemn, ornamental, severe, odd, or gay according to his temper. It will be slipshod, conventional, characterless if the writer's mind is moving carelessly along the grooves of "use-and-wont" ; and it may be so even when the ideas are sound, ideas arrived at, perhaps, in a happier mood, but now, in a less happy mood, imperfectly expressed, in language which deprives them of their life and lustre. Style cannot be more than a reflection of the author's personality, though it may be much less. It is good, or expressive, when the language he uses conveys his personality with some exactness, or that part of his personality which is actively engaged in the task he has in hand.

Style, though always external, is not to be thought of as merely external. It should be, as De Quincey said, an *incarnation* of thought ; as Ben Jonson said, " in all speech, words and sense are as the body and soul."

Diction—style—form. Perhaps we may say that all form in literature includes style in the same manner that all style includes diction. It implies the totality of all the elements that go to make a work of art. It is the shape that the whole takes when every part has fallen into its place according to the design which the artist had in his mind throughout. Form, therefore, is the expression of a thought-organism. It is the objective order that has been imposed on matter by the mind. And we may understand by it either the shape that our ideas take when the creative effort is complete, or the corresponding shape given to the medium through which the artist works.

III

If, in the foregoing section, I may seem to have been travelling over too familiar ground, my excuse is that I wished to show that even the most elementary consideration of style brings us, before we have done with it, to the central problems of the literary art; and we find ourselves arrived at the point where Pater, in his essay on "Style," begins. Writing as a kind of "good round-hand"—he is not interested in that. In this essay on "Style" he finds the occasion suitable "to point out certain qualities of all literature as a fine art, which, if they apply to the literature of fact, apply still more to the literature of the imaginative sense of fact, while they apply indifferently to verse and prose, so far as either is really imaginative."

Once again, then, we are faced with that distinction which we have had to keep before ourselves at all stages in this inquiry—that between De Quincey's "literature of knowledge" and "literature of power"—the didactic and the æsthetic—science and art—literature where "the imagination may be thought to be always an intruder," and that where it is supreme. Walter Pater puts it as well as it can be put:

> Just in proportion as the writer's aim, consciously or unconsciously, comes to be the transcribing, not of the world, not of mere fact, but of his sense of it, he becomes an artist, his work *fine* art; and good art (as I hope ultimately to show) in proportion to the truth of his presentment of that sense.

Not fact, then, but his "sense of fact"—that is what the artist is seeking to present. For him, no photographic "imitation" of reality, but a transcription of his vision of it.

But truth—that also comes into it. "There can be no merit, no craft at all, without that." But truth in what sense? Truth in regard to reality? Truth, in correspondence with some higher judgment of value? Pater at this stage is disregardful of those issues. He is speaking only of truth in the presentment of the sense of fact—accuracy of transcription. "All beauty is in the long run only *fineness* of truth, or what we call expression, the finer accommodation of speech to that vision within."

This "truth," we see, lies in the expression, and is not predicated of the vision itself. The quality of the vision, its worth-whileness on its own account, he does not here discuss, still less its relationship to any wider field of reality—though we have seen that elsewhere he distinguishes between "higher and lower moods" in Wordsworth. This high quality, here, he appears to take for granted; the Epicurean in him, for the moment at least, is content with that; and we may wonder whether, as with Marius, the old Heraclitian refrain, "All things flow, and nothing abides," lies at the back of his mind, or the words of

Protagoras, "Man is the measure of all things," or the sad "Things are but shadows," which the Cyrenaic accepted so cheerfully. The life upon which he seems to be concentrating his mind in this essay on "Style" is that of the clear, shapely words which form themselves into a body for the soul, as if the soul possessed no other capacity but that of being put into the perfect words that were meant for it. What makes the "vision within" worthy of expression? Is one vision no worthier than another? These are questions which he here disregards. Granted this "sense of fact," then the whole effort of art is concentrated on giving to it the perfect outward form.

From the point of view of style that is, after all, the only problem; and we may well be satisfied that we have from Pater a number of principles—if that is not too considerable a word—by which the quality of the best writing can be judged.

First, then, there is no place in Pater's hierarchy of art for the mere "popular author"; nor can we picture any vast Middle-Western audience which his man of letters will be at pains to address. Just as Longinus, we recall, limited the right to judge to those who have submitted themselves to the discipline of letters, declaring that "the judgment of literature is the long-delayed reward of much endeavour," so Walter Pater:

> The literary artist is of necessity a scholar, and in what he proposes to do will have in mind, first of all, the scholar and the scholarly conscience—the male conscience in this matter, as we must think it, under a system of education which still to so large an extent limits real scholarship to men. In his self-criticism, he supposes always that sort of reader who will go (full of eyes) warily, considerately, though without consideration for him, over the ground which the female conscience traverses so lightly, so amiably.

He will give to words exactly that sort of *attention* which Marius studied to bestow on the facts of experience, disciplining himself to find in each just so much value as it is fitted to hold. He will tolerate no short-cuts, no hackneyed illustration, no "affectation of learning designed for the unlearned." His scrupulousness and self-restraint in choosing words for their exact and their finer meaning will have "for the susceptible reader the effect of a challenge for minute consideration ; the attention of the writer, in every minutest detail, being a pledge that it is worth the reader's while to be attentive too."

The literary artist thus understood will be one who has "winnowed and searched through his vocabulary," making for himself an instrument that can faithfully express his spirit, seeking to restore to words in general their "finer edge," dreading all "surplusage," shunning the facile, the otiose, the purely ornamental ; and "he will never depart from the strictly pedestrian process, unless he gains a ponderable something thereby." He will be a "lover of words . . . opposing the constant degradation of language by those who use it carelessly."

So much for the medium of the literary art, the word-material upon which it works. Care in the use of this material matters so much because it enters everywhere into the structure, and is necessary to the carrying out of "that architectural conception of work, which foresees the end in the beginning and never loses sight of it . . . a condition of literary art, which . . . I shall call the necessity of *mind* in style."

Mind, then, being one indispensable element, revealing itself in design, in structure, in careful adjustment, at every point, of words to sense, and of the part to the whole, the other necessary element in style he distinguishes as *soul.*

By this he means the element of personality which communicates itself to language not by taking thought, but by attracting it into " the peculiar spirit " the writer is made of. " By soul, he reaches us, somewhat capriciously perhaps, one and not another, through vagrant sympathy and a kind of immediate contact." It is through this quality that we " seem to know a person in a book."

His distinction of these two elements in style serves to indicate that even art has its science, and does not despise the knowledge won by study, which helps it over the technical difficulties of expressing in words what is given in intuition. It is the artist in the architect who conceives his idea of a cathedral ; he hands it over to the scientist in him to study the strains and stresses ; the scientist hands it back to the artist, who begins again ; and so on, between the two, till the plan is finished, and the building begins to arise.

I must not dwell on that fine passage in which Pater describes Flaubert as " the martyr of literary style," seeking with anguish " the one word for the one thing, the one thought, amid the multitude of words, terms, that might just do." His doctrine of " that finest and most intimate form of truth "—truth as expression—does not merely repeat the old saying, " The style is the man," but, as he intends it, asserts that the style is the real man —" the man, not in his unreasoned and really uncharacteristic caprices, involuntary or affected, but in absolutely sincere apprehension of what is most real to him."

There we have an example of the word *sincerity* used, not as Matthew Arnold used it, but in that sense which I have already indicated, by which is understood the single-mindedness of the artist in the task he has set himself. And in this distinction between what is " most real " in the man from his "uncharacteristic caprices" we have once again the recognition of "higher and lower moods" —an admission of quality residing in the vision itself.

This brings us back to a question I raised just now, which seems to occur to Pater only as a sort of afterthought, and with some slight misgiving as to the trend of his argument. At an early stage in the essay he had said that the attempt to transcribe the writer's "sense of fact" was the mark of "fine art"; and he had gone on to say that this became "good art" in proportion to the truth of his presentment of that sense; and now, as if in a postscript, he hints that it has yet to become "great art" by virtue of some dignity in the subject.

Up to now, he has said nothing about the subject. He has treated it as if it were a matter of indifference—as if the content of the vision were of no significance, so long as the expression of it, whatever it might be, were perfect. All that he has said about style and its function in art is convincing upon one condition—that *what the artist had to say* was worth the saying—a condition which may seem obvious enough, for we can hardly suppose him to mean that the perfect expression of the purely trivial is the serious business of art. The question is only worth raising because other critics, following thus far in his footsteps, have landed themselves inextricably in this absurdity. And he, too, might seem to lend his countenance to such a view when he says that *all* beauty is only "fineness of truth, or what we call expression"; and again, *all* art "does but consist in the removal of surplusage."

He does not leave us there, but the fact that he only withdraws us from this difficult position in a kind of postscript serves to show his leaning; he, in Epicurean mood, is disposed to regard experience rather as form which life takes than as life which undergoes form ; the emphasis for him is upon words, choiceness of words, their arrangement and structure, as if in thus giving a body to the soul they exercise some esoteric power, residing in them by their own right, by which a work of art gains whatever it has of richness and flavour. When he is writing thus we sometimes miss the sense of any strong current of human life flowing behind or through this shapely style which he has granted to his artist, just as we felt that Marius himself was abstractly searching for an experience which, had we ever got close to it, might have proved vague or empty. Marius seemed to be trembling with apprehensiveness of life. That is enough, for an abstract account of him. But if he had touched this life, grasped it, actually handled it, would it have dissolved in dust ? Pater has described the exquisite possibilities of artistic expression, and there are moments when we are left with the uneasy feeling that it might be no less exquisite, as expression, even if the thing expressed were nonsense.

Pater has corrected this misapprehension, enabling us to see that it was all a matter of emphasis, of the manner of approach. Suppose we consider matter and form in art as concave and convex—distinguishable, though not to be separated—we observe that he is disposed to look mainly at the one side. But in proportion as manner of expression becomes more important to a critic, and the matter expressed less important, he will inevitably incline to an aristocratic view of art. The raw material of life, with its boisterous emotions and its infinite variety of sensations, is the common property of all, from the most ignorant to the most highly cultivated. But nicety of expression is for the few who are trained in language, who "have the science of their instrument." Pater, inclining thus to the aristocratic view in literature, takes too little account of those rough diamonds in the world of letters who triumphed because they had so much to say, though no doubt their triumph would have been greater had they said it better. What slovenly writing there is in Dickens! What utter disregard for the "finer edge of words"! Yet we cannot deny his creative power, his possessive and possessing "sense of fact," which with amazing disregard for the decencies of language (a disregard which was, of course, a defect of sensibility) he contrived, clumsily but powerfully, to exhibit amid the chaos of his novels. "All art does but consist in the removal of surplusage!" Suppose we put Dickens aside. We must still ask: What about Shakespeare? Is there not surplusage in every page? And Victor Hugo, and Dostoievski, and Browning? We might go on to name most of the Romantics and half the great Realists. This surplusage, this excess, this inexactness, this failure in fineness and in balance—all are, as Pater indicates, strictly defects in art, depriving the writer of power; they are defects to which our English writers are especially prone. But after all, as Ben Jonson said, "That is worse which proceeds out of want, than that which riots out of plenty." By putting all the emphasis on rightness of language, whilst appearing to underrate the stuff of life on which everything depends, is there not some risk of playing into the hands of the Philistines, by confusing style with *preciousness*?

Pater was far too much of an artist to fall deeply into an error which only critics who are not artists fall into, or philosophers who have not acquainted themselves with the artistic experience, or would-be artists who subsist on shadows of experience. The real artist's "sense of fact" is rooted in life itself. Great art, said Pater, however grudgingly, in that last paragraph, "has something of the soul of humanity in it." But his way of writing did much to fortify the self-esteem of those theorists and poseurs who made so much play with the doctrine of "Art for Art's sake."

IV

That doctrine had its origin in France, was transplanted to England by Whistler, and was carefully tended by Oscar Wilde and members of the *Yellow Book* group. Ruskin was the gadfly who stung Whistler and his friends into the extravagant over-statement of a case which Pater was qualified to put with sanity and with reserves. That "sense of fact" which the latter never, in the last resort, divorced from life or from the "soul of humanity," became, for members of this clique, an ideal, self-subsistent world of impression which was the exclusive property of the man blessed with the artistic temperament. Whistler was provoked and disgusted when he heard Ruskin declaring that "art must be didactic to the people." He rightly replied that art is not didactic at all; it cannot deny its own nature by taking over the functions of the preacher. And what have "the people" got to do with it? This apparent desire to degrade art into a branch of demagogy made Whistler see red, and, if I may strain the figure, we may suppose that Oscar Wilde saw at least pale pink. The common man, with his crude desires and his boorish interests, was not worth a moment's consideration by the artist, who was preoccupied with other affairs, which he alone was competent to apprehend. Moreover, the artist had no interest in vulgar representation. What he saw with his own finer perceptions, the impressions which formed themselves in his mind after long pursuit of his own vision, had validity for himself alone. He wrote, painted, and modelled in accordance with his own ideal, and only those who cared to pursue his lonely way and adjust themselves to his vision were qualified to share his satisfaction.

The elements of truth enunciated by these combative or posturing men are clear enough. The pleasure or satisfaction in art is its only end ; it cannot serve two masters. Whatever the "subject" that an artist treats, his fidelity is to what he sees, when he has endeavoured to see to the best of his powers. Ruskin, too, admitted the truth of this, and wisely warned the Impressionist against violating the sacredness of his own Impression. "If," he said, "he supposes that, once quitting hold of his first thought, he may by Philosophy compose something prettier than he saw, and mightier than he felt, it is all over with him."

There was much profit in a warm advocacy of the disinterestedness of art. But there were two respects in which these champions of æstheticism went astray. They overlooked the fact that all art, whether it be realistic or impressionistic, romantic or classical, symbolical, allegorical, expressionist, imagist, futurist, vorticist, or abstract, *has its roots somewhere in reality.* It always seeks objective expression, and must always have a subject whose nature it is to be objectified.

That is the first error. And the second is similar. They believed that the æsthetic faculties which the artist employs are special and peculiar, and different in kind as well as in degree from those which are employed in other activities. There, modern psychology as well as common sense is against them. This view implies a further fallacy, that it is no part of the artist's aim to *communicate* his vision—he writes or paints to please only himself, and is utterly indifferent to the approval or disapproval of others. The evidence of the great artist-critics of all times is conclusively against a doctrine so satisfying to the self-esteem of unrecognized genius.

Pater, withdrawing himself in the course of his argument, seems to become aware of the possible degradation of it. No, he says, he does not intend "a relegation of style to the subjectivity, the mere caprice, of the individual, which must soon transform it into mannerism." He retires from his extreme position almost as if in momentary panic. He even goes too far, in suddenly granting humanitarian as well as humane characteristics to "great art"; and then, regaining his habitual calm, concludes that it "finds its logical, its architectural place, in the great structure of human life."

Chapter Twenty-six

EXPRESSIONISM

I

IN his careful book upon *Contemporary Criticism* Mr Orlo Williams speaks of the need for "tidying up" our judgments about the literature of the immediate past and the actual present. He speaks of this as a "colossal labour" which awaits some critic of massive intellect and wide knowledge who will have "disinterested energy powerful enough to force order upon this confusion." It is indeed a tangled skein which such a labourer would have to unravel. What a variety of literary forms, techniques, interests, purposes, temperaments, he would have to consider! What cross-currents flowing from the other arts, and from philosophy, science, and politics!

Before the last century was out the confusion was already bewildering enough. There were psychological, romantic, realistic and naturalistic novels; a babel of doctrines, moralistic, æsthetic, impressionist, symbolist, mystical, materialistic, idealistic; conflicts of ideas between thinkers of the Darwin and Haeckel school and the transcendental idealists of the T. H. Green school, with side-influences powerfully thrown into the mêlée from Ibsen, Nietzsche, Walt Whitman and Samuel Butler! The confusion becomes greater in the first dozen years of the new century, with its intense earnestness, its reforming zeal, its palpitating soul laid bare in books which combined neo-romantic ardour with realistic methods. It exhorted us in "intellectual drama." It harrowed us with "slices out of life." It inflamed us with self-conscious exhibitions of the passions. From that pre-war maëlstrom we have emerged into our present so different age—light, debonair, ingenious, experimental, inquisitive, slightly ironic and flippant. And still we are busy ringing the changes on terms which indicate theories, schools, coteries—Post-Impressionist, Cubist, Futurist, Vorticist, Expressionist, Imagist, Modern British Art, Abstract Art . . .

Supposing Mr Williams' encyclopædic critic should really attempt, and succeed in, his colossal task of "tidying up" all this confusion—supposing he classified all the tendencies and forms, and arranged in due order the types which were admired thirty, twenty, ten, and two years ago—what consequences can we imagine for to-day? Some added clearness for the clear-minded, certainly, but also confusion thrice confounded for those who seek to regulate their art by the newest theories. For if there is any one outstanding characteristic of our age it is admiration of novelty, and disdain for the established, the canonical, the recognized and, therefore, the outworn. Consider the modern dislike for anything that can be called Victorian. The Victorian is fixed, put in its place, "tidied up"—anything that savours of it is to be eschewed. Consider, again, how any style of painting that repeatedly commends itself to the Royal Academy is regarded (I do not say without reason) by younger painters as obsolete and expressionless, and they ransack their brains to discover contrary theories of expression which they can apply in new forms of art. If this organizing critic could really arrange all the literary activities of recent years, hanging them neatly, as it were, on the walls of his own literary Academy, at the same time persuading the great public, which is always the conventional public, to pay heed to him, what a hurrying and scurrying there would be among all the clever young persons (affectionately spoken of as *les jeunes*, or even *mes jeunes*) to accomplish something utterly different, rendering everything that happened up to yesterday out of date—or rather—as if that were much worse !—" dated ! "

Such efforts on the road of adventure are always enlivening, though from the nature of the case most of them must be trivial. They are straws showing how the wind blows—and it appears to have been blowing in the same direction for quite a long time. (Like everything else, the pursuit of the new may become a besetting habit.) The effort to get away from the conventional, the ordained, the habitual, has been a characteristic common to the three principal periods which have made up the last forty years of English and American literature. It started as a vigorous, healthy movement—in protest against use-and-wont and in praise of what is individual and originative. The world, no doubt, was ripe for such an assertion of individuality, for it was heard now from this direction, now from that, till the echoes of it were ringing in the ears of the reading public. Now it came from that " chanter of personality," Walt Whitman ; now from Ibsen, who exposed Peer Gynt to the charge that never in all his life had he " been himself" ; now from Nietzsche, praising the superman for his Will to Power. Shaw and Galsworthy in their criticisms of society expanded a similar doctrine ; Wells embraced it as offering a way of release for the too long stifled passions ; D. H. Lawrence found himself in a world set free for lovers ; Miss Romer Wilson conceived a heaven on earth in which perfectly free individuals came into being over the corpse of a dead " Society " ; and James Joyce, his mind freed from conventions, sought expression in images released from time and space, and language released from the narrow rules of grammar.

The demand for freedom from outworn intellectual and moral rules led, of course, to demands for freedom from all rules. The claims of personality are always apt to degenerate into claims for caprice. Lack of respect for what is merely "established" tends to excessive respect for mere novelty. As in morality, so in literature and art. We have seen how the æsthetes who discussed "Art for Art's sake" believed that each of them held a little candle locked up in the chamber of his soul, and by the light of it saw within himself the only reality that mattered. He did not write or paint for the many-headed public which could not penetrate to that dim shrine. After them came artists of many kinds, who under one theory or another asserted the supreme necessity that the artist should express the vision that was personal to him, never "representing" reality, but either restating it in terms of his vision, or not stating it at all, but expressing a condition of his mind through a formal structure, which, in some unexplained way, corresponded to it.

There are several schools of writers and painters whose theories echo the Protagorean doctrine, "Man is the measure of all things." "That is my world—take it or leave it," is the attitude, perfectly reasonable when it is qualified in certain ways, but with traps for the unwary, who do not qualify it. We saw that Pater for a moment came very near to falling into it, but turned back abruptly. Others have not paused to see where it was leading them, and, in particular, various groups of writers, painters, play-producers and even dancers, who call themselves Expressionists, have found confidence in what they supposed to be the doctrines of Signor Benedetto Croce. They felt, it appears, that his philosophy exactly fitted the needs of a completely emancipated art. Signor Pirandello, who has succeeded in imparting so much interest to the fantastic world of appearance which is the only reality to him—things "being" just what they "seem," neither more nor less—is a disciple of Croce, and professed, I believe, to be writing in accordance with the æsthetic principles of that philosopher. He is certainly put forward by his admirers as the greatest example of an "Expressionist" playwright; and by some strange confusion it seems to be held that an author who writes in an "Expressionist" way is one who always writes about Expressionism—which is scarcely more sensible than to say that a nervous writer is one who writes books about nerves. Such confusion of thought appears likewise to have influenced Mr W. J. Turner, when he wrote *The Man who ate the Popomack*, and Miss Susan Glaspell in *The Verge*.

There are painters of the same order of thought who believe that any too definite contact with reality, as seen through the eyes of habit, may contaminate their individual art and destroy their power of vision. They hold that children should not be taught to draw, because lessons would plant other people's ideas in their minds, hinder their originative impulses, and destroy the power of expression which should develop from within. Some even hesitate to teach their children how to write, lest such instruction should produce a kind of "round hand" in their characters, as expressionless as the "round hand" which Pater deprecates in style. There exist many schools, chiefly for young women, based upon theories of physical and mental culture, which seek to lure their pupils with dance, music and poetry to educate themselves through constant practice in self-expression. A literary and dramatic society associated with one of these schools, which was conducted by a distinguished dancer, a distinguished painter, and a distinguished musician, had a rule pledging its members to aim always at self-expression "without the least regard for the feelings of the audience."

So Pirandello wrote "Expressionist" plays, in which it is claimed by his friends that he exemplifies the principles of Benedetto Croce. The claim is absurd, because in all the æsthetic theory of Croce there is not a line which advocates, justifies, or even, I believe, so much as mentions any special kind of art described as "Expressionist." Of the many artists who deliberately set out to produce "Expressionist" works, or to produce any work in a special "Expressionist" way, there is not one who can find any justification for his method in Croce himself. The absurdity of attaching the label to a special kind of art lies in the fact that Expressionism, as the Italian philosopher uses the term, is not the characteristic of one form of art, but of *all art*—Sophocles, Shakespeare, and even Tennyson are just as Expressionist as Pirandello. If any artist could be a disciple of Croce—and how could an artist, *qua* artist, be a disciple of a philosopher? — he would not produce Expressionist art; he would simply produce art.

II

Let us then turn to what Croce himself has said, again trespassing for a moment on philosophic ground; for it happens that he has cast a kind of spell on the minds of talented artists, so that they have misunderstood his argument where it is sound, and appropriated it where it is faulty.

For Croce there are not two kinds of reality, one

existing independently outside the mind, and another within it. For him nothing whatever exists that is external to mind, though the mind, of course, for its own purposes, can conceive something as external.

Knowledge is of two forms: it is either intuitive, or logical; obtained through the imagination, or through the intellect; productive of images, or of concepts. The one is knowledge of individual things; the other, of the relations between them. By the intellect we may judge that "man is a thinking animal"; by the imagination we merely grasp the image of an animal characterized by the capacity for thinking.

Croce contrasts intuition with impression, sensation, the bare matter of experience; it is something more than mechanism, naturality, passivity. It is the active expression of impressions. "Every true intuition or representation is, also, expression. That which does not objectify itself in expression is not intuition or representation, but sensation and naturality. The spirit does not obtain intuitions otherwise than by making, forming, expressing."[1] The painter, for example, does not obtain an intuition when he merely feels something or catches a glimpse of it; but only when he sees it fully—that is to say, when he has expressed it in all its completeness in his own mind. The æsthetic fact consists in the creation, within the mind, of a form. The content of that form is sensation; intuition is an expressive activity of the spirit which gives it form. This activity Croce conceives as a sort of liberator, which "subjugates and dominates the tumult of the feelings and of the passions," so that a man frees himself from his impressions by giving to them objective expression.

[1] *Æsthetic: as Science of Expression and General Linguistic.* Translated by Douglas Ainslie.

In Croce's philosophy art is nothing but intuition, or the expression (within the mind) of impressions. The mind is always forming, or half-forming, intuitions, and either passing on from them to intellectual concepts or sinking back to bare sensation. The intuition becomes art when the spirit persists in it, intent only upon the activity of perfect expression, by which the impressions are elaborated to receive the die of the imagination. It is interesting to observe that there is nothing in common between Croce and those critics who contrast the experiences which we have in life with the experiences which are used in art. There is no difference in *kind* for Croce between this life and that life ; there is only a difference in *quantity*. Any impression—that is to say, any bit of life—may be material for the artist, who fulfils his proper function when he sees it clearly ; and clearly seeing is for Croce synonymous with clearly expressing. The artist is the man who vividly sees ; the vividness of his seeing is nothing else than vividness of expression. It does not matter what kind of life it may be. There is no superior excellence in this block of subject-matter or that. The excellence lies in the vision of it—in giving formal expression to impressions through the full activity of the imaginative power.

> When critics rebel against the theme or the content as being unworthy of art and blameworthy, in respect to works which they claim to be artistically perfect ; if these expressions really are perfect, there is nothing to be done but to advise the critics to leave the artist in peace, for they cannot get inspiration save from what has made an impression upon them. . . . So long as ugliness and turpitude exist in nature and impose themselves on the artist, it is not possible to prevent the expression of these things also.

I would ask the reader to pay heed to this passage, for we must return to it. Sufficient for the moment to observe that it is hard to see how a "critic" can pass any judgment on a theme which exists only in the artist's head, or can have anything to say about an "expression" which is not outwardly expressed. For at this stage—the only stage that counts for Croce in the æsthetic or creative process—everything is taking place *within the artist's mind*; the æsthetic expression is wholly inward; the impressions objectified are objectified only *for him*, and not in any physical form by which a critic can become aware of them.

It is true there does come a stage, according to Croce, at which the artist *may* (not *must*) externalize his expression; but this externalization, he insists, has nothing whatever to do with the proper activity of art. The artist is only an artist during the moments of free inspiration in which he "finds himself big with his theme, he knows not how." This inward expression becomes "beautiful" when it unfolds itself successfully.

The pleasure of art is the thrill which accompanies the self-liberation of successful expression. We call a thing ugly when we wish to designate "embarrassed activity, the product of which is a failure." Beauty is "successful expression, or better, expression and nothing more, because expression, when it is not successful, is not expression."

When Croce says that "the æsthetic fact is altogether completed in the expressive elaboration of the impressions," he is speaking of an activity that is wholly within the mind of the artist, and has nothing to do with the uttering or writing of words, or the fixing of lines and colours on canvas. "If," he goes on:

> If after this we should open our mouths and *will* to open them, to speak, or our throats to sing, and declare in a loud voice and with extended throat what we have completely said or sung to ourselves; or if we should stretch out and

> *will* to stretch out our hands to touch the notes of the piano, or to take up the brushes and the chisel, making thus in detail those movements which we have already done rapidly, and doing so in such a way as to leave more or less durable traces; this is all an addition, a fact which obeys quite different laws from the first. . . . This second movement is a production of things, a *practical* fact, or a fact of will. . . . The work of art (the æsthetic work) is always internal; and that which is called *external* is no longer a work of art.

What, then, are these actually spoken or written words, these painted pictures, these carved statues, if they are no proper part of the æsthetic act? They are merely "aids to memory," "physical stimulants" which enable the artist to reproduce his intuitions. The fact of their production implies a "vigilant will, which persists in not allowing certain visions, intuitions, or representations to be lost"; and when we elliptically call these physical objects "beautiful," we mean that they help us to regain the state of mind in which we had beautiful intuitions.

Croce has some difficulty in explaining how any other than the artist—that is to say, how an appreciator of his work—is able to gain a beautiful intuition by regarding the physically beautiful object. For he has insisted that art is intuition, and intuition is individuality, and individuality is never repeated. He has to postulate, if I understand him, an absoluteness of the imagination, such that the same images serve to stimulate the production of the same intuitions in different minds. Without this, he says, "spiritual life would tremble to its base." But, if I have rightly read him, how can this absoluteness of the imagination in all men be reconciled with his doctrine that an intuition is individual, unique, and never to be repeated? How can the critic, stimulated by a physical object, re-create a unique intuition as the artist expressed it? "In order to judge Dante we must raise ourselves to his level," he says. He might have added, "We must become Dante."

Not that he altogether disregards the difficulty. He admits that the physical objects may not suffice to stimulate the critic to the full æsthetic reproduction. He agrees that the latter must have the knowledge, the trained imagination, and the taste which will enable him to put himself at the viewpoint of the artist; and that historical research will help him to reconstruct the conditions under which he originally felt and expressed himself.

Croce has given us an admirably clear exposition of the truth that art is always a form of self-expression. And it needed to be shown that the ideas which enter into art are not different from the ideas that we have in all the activities of life; the same clear perceptions and searching intuitions are those which may illumine our minds whenever we are keenly sensitive to and aware of the vividness of experience. Again, he is right in explaining that art is not mere sensation. Sensations, or experience, as suffered, are life, and do not become art until the artist has to some extent detached himself from them, and devoted all his energy to seeing them and re-creating them in the fine light of contemplation. This energy of seeing, creating, expressing, has its own delight. It is all the more intense when the pain inherent in the subject of tragedy is converted into unembarrassed contemplation, just as drinking is more delightful when there is thirst.

But confusion arises because when he speaks about "art" he means something different from what all the rest of the world means. For him it is something that goes on in the mind before the artist begins to use pen, or brush, or chisel, and it is complete irrespective of the use of these implements. When others speak of composition or expression they mean composition or expression in a physical medium; for him the physical medium has, properly, nothing to do with it. What others call a "work of art," and a "thing of beauty," is for him not art, and not beautiful—it is only a physical stimulant to induce a beautiful intuition in the beholder.

The confusion is not only between his use of the term and ours. He himself occasionally falls a victim to it. Consider that passage in which he speaks of "critics" who "rebel against the theme or the content as being unworthy of art." If the theme belongs only to the spiritual intuition, the critic could know nothing about it, and could not rebel. Obviously, so far as a man's inner spiritual life is concerned, no one has a right to complain if it is ugliness or turpitude which has made an impression on him. No one in that case has the power to criticize the subject-matter of his intuitions, or to blame him in any way if his inspiration has been of this kind or that. Art, considered as a purely internal construction of experience, is beyond criticism, and is subject to no principles but those of his own nature.

Croce has introduced confusion by this reference to the critic, and has thereby misled his would-be disciples. The passage has been used by those who affirm that any and every subject is equally fit for artistic treatment; that there is no subject so squalid or mean but that the clear expression of it will become art. The same passage may be used to justify any form of eccentricity in art. "Such or such," says an artist, "is an impression which I have had. I challenge anyone to deny it. I have expressed that impression. There is the result." And the result, it would appear, no matter what it might be, being a perfect expression of an impression, must be good art, and the critic is asked to mind his business. Any caprice, any perversity, any ugliness, any abortion of a depraved or maddened mind would be, if this were really Croce's meaning, justifiable provided it were a clear intuition, a faithful expression of an impression.

But Croce meant nothing of the kind, and the allusion to the critic was only a slip on his part. On the contrary, though he cannot give powers to the critic to judge what he calls a work of art, he gives not only the critic, but even the censor of morals, the utmost powers to approve or condemn the objectified work of art, that outward physical form which is all he can be sure of, though it plays so slight a part in Croce's *Æsthetic.* When he does condescend to consider this externalized work of art, he gives no countenance to the view that the maker of it is free ; for the latter, in turning to this practical task, has put aside his artistry, and has lost the freedom of the artist. Indeed, Croce goes much farther in the opposite direction than most of us would go. We do not, he says, externalize all our impressions. "We select from the crowd of intuitions." For this purpose he would agree with Arnold that the choice of subject is of supreme importance. But for quite another reason. The artist, in making an external object, is leaving his proper sphere, and is entering the practical social world where economics, morality, propaganda begin to matter. His selection will be governed by "the economic conditions of life and of its moral direction." There will be justification for considering what is interesting, what is moral, what is educational, what is popular. In this inferior domain he has no claim to the liberty of the artist ; his work is now the affair of morality.

In other words, the artist may see what he likes, but he must not say what he likes. He is as free as the wind when his art is not what we mean by art ; but when he begins to create, as we understand creation, his liberty is gone, and it is right that he should submit to the censor, or be clapped into prison by Mussolini.

III

The main structure which Croce has erected topples to the ground because he has overlooked the evidence. He is writing about art, and he has forgotten to consult the artists. If he had consulted them they would have told him that the whole business of art is to *communicate* something to the world, and that that something will be beautiful. Croce has almost forgotten communication, as he has almost forgotten beauty.

At all times in the history of civilization the great literary artists and critics have described works of art in terms of their effects upon men. They have declared that the business of the artist was to please, or instruct, or exalt. In the course of this book, as we have passed from age to age, and artist to artist, we have watched this recurrent conviction that the creative writer was submitting his work for the judgment of the world. Some said that the writer wrote spontaneously, others that he wrote with pain and toil ; some that he followed principles of art, others that the spirit drove him. But none have denied for a moment that he was one who had something to deliver to the world —it might be a message—it might be a monument—but he gave it forth for men to judge.

Who, we may ask, is this philosopher Croce, that he should determine *a priori* the nature of the artists, and should judge their intentions without asking them what their intentions are? Who is he, that he should deny that they are concerned with the doing of something which most of them have affirmed to be the object of their endeavour? Against him is the recorded experience of the artists. Surely a philosopher's business is not to dogmatize as to what the artist's experience is, but to explain it as he finds it. The artist about whom he is philosophizing exists nowhere but in his own mind, or among the most complacent of those who have misused the expression "Art for Art's sake," and have constantly belied themselves by their hankering after recognition.

I do not dispute that there is a sense in which the expression "Art for Art's sake" is perfectly justifiable. It is well that the poet or painter should be wholly absorbed in his subject. It is well that he should write or paint according to his inner vision, intent on that alone, expressing his own ideal to his own satisfaction, and in his own way, allowing nothing to move him from his course. The path that he pursues will be the private way of the spirit. He will be guided by his own light. He can show reality in no manner but as he knows it.

How could it be otherwise? That which he has to give to the world is himself, his vision, and how could he communicate that to others except by faithful devotion to the ideal of "being himself"? He cannot compromise with himself, for if he did he would cheat the world out of just that which he seeks to give—his real, his undamaged spirit. Walt Whitman was a "chanter of personality," and gave his whole personality, undiluted, to the world. Ibsen said, "Be thyself," because oneself is the most that a man can be, and the most that an artist can offer.

But, it may be objected, Croce does make some provision for communication.

Some provision, yes, in a rather grudging manner. But he does not admit that it is any part of the artist's proper job to create a vehicle of communication. His artist, as artist, is interested in nothing but his intuition, and it is only when he puts away his æsthetic nature, and submits to his non-æsthetic, practical will, that he deigns to externalize his vision. Croce denies to the artist, as artist, what others have thought to be an essential element in the creative impulse, the desire to communicate his intuition to the world. Croce's poet speaks no language. At the most, his speech is a soliloquy.

Art, as I understand the term, implies language, and intelligible language. Whether it be in the medium of words or paint or marble or musical sounds does not matter. The outward reality of this language is the only common ground, the link, between the creator and the appreciator. Why is it, as Dante says, that "poetry and the language proper for it are an elaborate and painful toil"? Why is it that so many artists have found their medium tough, stubborn, resistant, calling forth so much of the mastery of a creative mind to overcome and fashion it? Because idea has to find incarnation in matter; the dead medium has to receive the form of living spirit. The gold on which Hephæstus wrought had to become black earth under his fashioning hands, and "that," said Homer, "was a very miracle of his craft."

If indeed it were the case that an artist puts away his artistry when he constructs the external form, by what virtue could it call up for others the intuition which it is intended to stimulate? If the artist has ceased to be an artist when he fashions it, there is none left to work the "miracle" of its creation. Deprive it of this miracle, and it can be no more than an empty sign, an inexpressive hieroglyph, a riddle to which there is no solution.

Miss Powell[1] has put her finger on a difficulty which seems to me insuperable in Croce's account of æsthetic communication. In his theory, she points out, the artist's intuition is elaborated out of his own experience ; but the appreciator is required to elaborate just the same intuition out of something quite different—namely, the physical work of art.

Does not this bundle of difficulties arise out of another omission on Croce's part—a fundamental omission ? He seems to have left out—*life.* I do not quite know what these "impressions" are that wander about so vaguely, so meaninglessly, so unexplained in the mind, which Croce postulates. I do not know what these inert mechanical things are doing till his artist pounces upon them, and by synthesizing them creates out of them an elaborate work of art. The place that they fill so wanly in Croce's theory is that which common sense fills with life itself. Whatever philosophic language we may use or discard, it is this reality from which the artist starts, the reality that we all objectify as life. It presents itself to us with all the fortuitousness of fact, fragments of experience that come upon us in the illogical time-sequence of a day's events—waking, a bath, breakfast, a catastrophe discussed in the newspaper, reflections about catastrophe, a telephone bell, letters written, a caller, more reflections, more ill-assorted atoms of experience. That is how life happens—impression following impression—and that is all it seems to be for Croce till the mind begins its conjuring-tricks. But this life

[1] *The Romantic Theory of Poetry : an Examination in the Light of Croce's "Æsthetic."*

as it accidentally happens is not life as we constantly envisage it even for the purposes of every day; still less is it life as we try and reconstruct it when we would "see it steadily and see it whole." The orderly mind puts it together, sorts it, restores it, and pictures it in some perspective. But the order it has created is not left hanging in the void of the mind. It is an order predicated of reality —of that world of reality from which the impressions come; and our construction must stand the test of all other impressions which impose themselves upon us, and if it does not we know that we have judged wrong.

What is the difference between a photograph, which is not a work of art, and a portrait, which is? Just this, that the photograph arrests that fragment in the life of a face which is conveyed at one and only one instant of time; the successful portrait conveys the character of the face which we discern by watching it through a succession of instants. The one gives the face between the moments of life—that is, not alive; the other gives us the living face.

Real life, of course, is changing from instant to instant, and art does not attempt to reproduce this motion as motion; rather, it fixes the character revealed in motion. There, Croce is with us. For him, too, art is characterization. But the difficulty I find in his theory is that he appears to give no adequate place to that insistent, persistent, inevitable, resolute thing which is life as it comes to us, as it is thrust upon us, which gives to us that which demands to be characterized in a certain way, and in no other way.

We say that "art is a criticism of life," and when we say that, we mean life has a determinatedness of its own, and that is why it is possible to determine it. We must suppose something intelligible before we seek to understand. The philosopher tries to determine it by philosophy,

He says, for example, "Man is a clothes-wearing biped." The artist determines it by showing us a picture of a biped thus distinguished. But though the artist proceeds by the intuitive, and not the conceptual, method his intuition presupposes always one universal judgment behind it—"Life is like that." There is one affirmation, and one affirmation only, that the poet, or the painter, or the sculptor makes all the time. It may be indicated by a gesture of the arm. "There! That is what life looks like when it is seen by the seeing eye." All the other affirmations are, as Croce says, only characteristics of the intuition, thought-elements in the picture which go to make it what it is, and contribute to its character.

The artist starts from life itself. How, then, is he to express himself, so that he may be understood by others who are sharing the common life of all humanity? Only in terms of something known within the compass of that life, in a material medium. That is why Pater's stylist has to winnow and search for the right words, that is why Winckelmann's sculptor must wrestle with his resistant material—because he is trying to get back into the world of sensible reality, of life, what he originally extracted from that same world. The externals of life gave him the impulse. The externals of life can alone give him the language with which to express what he has seen. All art, assuredly, is expression; but it is the expression of life, as the artist sees it, in a language which other men can understand.

And I said that Croce had forgotten, or almost forgotten, beauty. It is axiomatic, is it not, that a work of art is beautiful? Not, let me repeat, that beauty is an embellishment, an added quality; it penetrates the vision of reality to the very core, and it belongs to whatever joy or satisfaction we derive from it. Croce, as we have seen, differs from Arnold, Goethe, Coleridge, Dante, Aristotle and countless others, when he appears to say that the artist, as artist, is indifferent to the quality of his subject, and is bound to express anything and everything that has made an impression on him. (Here, I have necessarily overlooked that distinction between the internal and external expression.)

We may be pardoned if we prefer to accept the evidence of that august majority. If I am right in saying that the artist in producing his work thereby affirms "Reality is like that," the affirmation carries with it the rider: "It is worth while to look at it"—"it is interesting"—"I would not call it to your attention if I did not hope it is pleasing or beautiful." Amongst the multitude of intuitions of which the creative artist is aware, it is not till he lights upon one which gives him a sense of æsthetic worth-whileness that he will put forth his full creative effort. When at last he feels himself impelled, with Faust, to hail the "moment flying,"

> Ah, still delay, thou art so fair!

then, and not till then, he will be anxious to wrestle with the medium of expression and labour to share his vision with the world.

Chapter Twenty-seven

SOME CONCLUSIONS

I

"IF thought," says Mrs Virginia Woolf, in that book[1] which everyone was reading a little time ago, "is like the keyboard of a piano, divided into so many notes, or like the alphabet is ranged in twenty-six letters all in order, then" a very competent mind had "no sort of difficulty in running over those letters one by one, firmly and accurately, until it had reached, say, the letter Q." She then speaks of an order of mind still higher, that of "the gifted, the inspired who, miraculously, lump all the letters together in one flash—the way of genius."

There Mrs Woolf does two things. She shows us in the simplest possible way the distinction that I have been labouring so long, between the discursive, didactic process, and the immediate process of art. Also, instead of *stating* a truth, she has preferred to *show* it through the person of Mr Ramsay, and provides me with just the illustration I wanted of the artistic method. If I ask, Does she or does she not, in that passage, exhibit a truth? the answer can only be Yes. When I further ask, Does she present it in the imaginative or the strictly logical way? the only possible reply is, The imaginative way. The example, I think, is relevant to anything that may be said about truth in art, or art in science.

In the one case and in the other, be it noted, the alphabet is the same. There is no difference in the letters. There is not one world for art, and another for truth. It is all one world, though the artist, the scientist and the teacher have

[1] *To the Lighthouse.* Hogarth Press.

different ways of approaching it. Each of them has his place in literature, which, in the broadest sense, as Schlegel said, " is the comprehensive essence of the intellectual life of a nation." Written words contain all the letters, and are used by all the writers ; and in this general sense literature is the whole mind-life of the successive generations of men, most energetic, perhaps, when it springs from ideas bandied to and fro among contemporaries, but in the retrospect presenting peaks which dominate the whole vista down the life of the ages, high enough to be always visible, powerful enough to be always impressive. There is no kind of mental energy which it excludes. It is science, and it is art. It is learning, and poetry. It is religion, philosophy, history, politics, morality, physics, and all the written arts. It is mankind conscious of itself in every way—" the whole of man's intellectual life "—and we cannot think away one of the parts without altering the whole.

Literature, as regarded by a Schlegel or a Taine, is a social product. It is circulated, or stored, for the use of all who desire to help themselves from the sum-total of finished thought-work available in men's writing. All the parts of it are food for the mind, and collectively constitute world culture. When Coleridge said that " no man was ever yet a great poet, without being at the same time a profound philosopher," he was not confusing two different faculties of the mind ; but he was affirming the importance of the one to the other. The poet, he said, was one who had " first studied patiently, meditated deeply, understood minutely, till knowledge, become habitual and intuitive, wedded itself to his habitual feelings."

The kinds of literature are divisible only at our own risk. We distinguish between intellect, intuitions, feeling, and will, but we cannot separate them. We cannot deprive a work of art of its thoughts. We cannot strip the scientist of his flashing intuitions. The moralist enlists poetry and music on his side. Before we attempt to distinguish this kind of literature from that, it is well to begin by acknowledging the one-ness of the mind and all the literature that springs from it ; otherwise we may find it hard to account for the fact that a philosophic dialogue may be beautifully constructed, that a history may combine the characteristics of science and art, and that a poem may be pregnant with thought. Having first recognized this higher unity, it is then time to distinguish the subordinate unity of art as a whole, and of each kind of art.

II

There must have been long practice in the arts before any such distinction was definitely formulated. But in the *Iliad* and the *Odyssey* we can see that it is already recognized, and ripe for some kind of formulation. In those days of the early minstrels three characteristics of poetry or art are already mentioned. In the *Iliad*, describing the design on the shield of Achilles, Homer tells us that the marvel of it lay in the *illusion*—in wrought gold appeared the semblance of a black plough-land. Again, in the *Odyssey* we are told that the minstrel was honoured because he had the power to *make men glad.* And this very power of stirring the minds of men to gladness was held to indicate that the poem, in some mystic way, was also *true.* Here are three vaguely discerned elements—illusion, pleasure, truth. The beauty in a work of art seemed to spring from qualities such that it created pleasure, through illusion, in some way dependent on truth.

In a somewhat later period, when the field of "literature" was widened to include physics, philosophy and history, the issue became less simple. Poetry, as we understand it, was not clearly distinguished from other kinds of literature. To one of the Muses, Urania, astronomy was given as her province, and another, Clio, became the divinity of history. The ceremonies of religion, drama and poetry were intermixed. When drama developed under the influences of the Dionysiac festival, and Homer was regarded with religious no less than æsthetic veneration, the conception of the poet as a teacher tended to obscure his more essential function—to "make men glad."

But further reflection again cleared the issue. Plato is already on the track when he concentrates on imitation. He at least restored art to the sphere of illusion. It is neither the pure concept of Being, nor yet the actual world of appearance, that the poet and painter present, but a semblance of reality. Aristotle took what was relevant from Plato, and dropped his errors. He, too, concentrates on imitation, or representation—poetry is still illusion, representing reality through a chosen medium. The delight in it—and he takes it for granted that poetry exists to afford delight—depends on the pleasure which men take in recognizing likeness. They see a portrait and declare with joy, "Ah, that is he!" (ὅτι οὗτος ἐκεῖνος).

There, in a sentence, Aristotle has put his finger on something which, in the light of later criticism, we see to be very near the root of the matter. "Ah, that is he!"—such are the words of the spectator in looking at a portrait. They presuppose on the part of the artist the declaration: "That is how the subject looked like to me"; and the further declaration, as we shall see in a moment: "That is what I judge reality to be like." The point first to be insisted on is that the "imitative" artist presents something which is to be looked at, if not with the physical eye, at least with the mind's eye. He is presenting something which is to give pleasure, something beautiful, something communicable, immediately, intuitively, to whoever has the mastery of the medium employed. His work, whatever it is, must admit of being *visualized* by the mind, in the sense that it must admit of being taken in at one view, as a picture is, though its parts may be separated, not in space but in time. The thoughts that enter into it will attach themselves to the image, qualifying it, colouring it, enriching it, but always as subordinate elements in a whole which has to be envisaged.

But in accepting the word *imitate*, Aristotle was confining his attention too exclusively to certain kinds of art. In drama and in epic poetry, as in most novels, it is easy to think of the artist as one who imitates the actions or passions of men. But if Aristotle had given more attention to lyrical poetry he would surely have seen that the poet often is not imitating any object directly copied from life. What shall we say of the following :

> It is not growing like a tree
> In bulk, doth make Man better be ;
> Or standing long an oak, three hundred year,
> To fall a log at last, dry, bald, and sere :
> A lily of a day
> Is fairer far in May
> Although it fall and die that night—
> It was the plant and flower of Light.
> In small proportions we just beauties see ;
> And in short measures life may perfect be.

The only part of this poem which comes near to being a pure imitation of objects or events in nature is in the lines (5 to 8) in the middle. The first four lines state a universal proposition, but the intellect yields to the succession of images derived from nature. The last two lines are didactic statements, in which the representational element entirely disappears. In the whole poem the writer has presented a complex structure in which certain images are predominant, and some general reflections are intermingled with them. These complex thought-elements are projected in a form which holds them together in a unity, so that the intuition readily grasps all in one effort of the imagination. The last two lines, perhaps, stick out rather awkwardly ; they are not fully in the picture ; the didactic obtrudes, and our pleasure ceases.

Aristotle has created difficulties by seeking the unity which is necessary to a poem in the *objects*, or *incidents* imitated. But the unity we require does not reside in the incidents, regarded as external, but in the treatment. The sole need for artistic unity lies in the necessity that all should be comprehended in one view ; all the attributes must so cling together in the theme that it can be taken in immediately under the gaze of the imagination.

The words *imitate* and *represent*, then, are not quite satisfactory if we wish to indicate an element that is never absent in a work of art. The word that we need is *exhibit*. It includes imitation, for we may exhibit a likeness of reality ; but it includes more. Not all kinds of poetry fall under the category of imitation. But the poet may *exhibit* a complex structure in which feeling, thought and maxim may be merged in an intuition, the whole being apprehended imaginatively ; and he holds it up for us, he exhibits it, not to reason with us, not to persuade, but merely to make us *see* what he has constructed imaginatively, as a poet. The artist does not always imitate, but he always exhibits or shows.

This in no way conflicts with that other dictum, that all art is expression. The artist always knows that the thing which he is making and showing is self-expression ; but the listener or spectator can only *infer* that, whereas he knows by the evidences of his senses that it is something exhibited. Exhibition, then, is the fundamental fact in the æsthetic process. The scientist *tells* us ; the moralist or rhetorician seeks to *persuade* us ; the artist *shows* us. There we have the distinction between literature which is fine art and all other literature whatsoever.

Showing, of course, implies seeing ; and seeing implies a spectacle ; and that again implies the light in which it is seen ; and in the whole process unity is an essential, for without it nothing can be intuitively grasped in a single view. One or other of these elements belonging to the "show" (which may be seen with the mind's eye) has been insisted upon by the poets and the greater critics in all the ages. Aristotle said that the plot must be of such a length that it can be embraced by the memory, just as a picture is taken in all at once by the eye. For Longinus "beautiful words are the true and peculiar light of the mind," and he compared the genius of Demosthenes with a "flash of lightning." Such sense as there is in the long-taught doctrine of the three Unities springs from the same source. When Burke and others insist on the "synthetic" power of the Imagination, they mean that the artist combines many things to bring them within the range of a single act of vision. "Grasp the Individual," said Goethe, for it is only through the Individual that the Universal can be presented or shown. "As light to the eye, even such is Beauty to the mind," said Coleridge. "The Beautiful . . . is that in which the *many*, still seen as many, becomes one."

Showing, or exhibiting, then, is the essence of art. Its excellences, I think it will appear, are truth and beauty. The effect is enjoyment.

III

The artist, as an artist, is not suffering life. He is looking at it, regarding it, contemplating it. That, I think, is part of what Mr T. S. Eliot means when he says, in *The Sacred Wood*, that "Poetry is not a turning loose of emotion but an escape from emotion." In looking at life with the purely contemplative gaze of the Imagination, the poet is not enduring the emotions he looks upon ; the thrill that he has is the thrill of the spectacle—of the recognition that that is what reality looks like when a searching gaze is turned upon it. This does not in the least mean that the poet has no emotions when he is making poetry, but only that they are not the same as the emotions which he is exhibiting ; his may be the rapture of recognizing that his picture is a picture of life, and that he is making it well. His joy is the joy that arises from discerning the truth—a truth intuitively grasped, not logically stated.

I suggest that it is time to get rid of the misleading current notion that art is not concerned with real life. I find that even Mr E. M. Forster, in his *Aspects of the Novel*, lends countenance to this idea, and suggests that the reality of a character in a novel depends upon the laws of art, and not the laws of life. "The barrier of art," he says, divides us from Fielding's *Amelia* or Jane Austen's *Emma*. "They are real not because they are like ourselves . . . but because they are convincing."

But how will they ever be convincing unless they are like ourselves ? The fact that the novelist knows more about his characters, as Mr Forster tells us, than we can know about living individuals, is only another way of saying that the artist knows more about life than anyone can know without regarding life with the artist's eye. He gives us a semblance of reality which is more characteristic of life than anything which we discover in the duller glances of every day. The necessity of art for the spirit lies in just this, that it rescues us from the inattentiveness and obtuseness of so-called real life, from that diminished state of half-awareness in which daily impressions fly past us carelessly regarded, dulled by use-and-wont—a matter of sleeping and waking, knives and forks, bus fares and gossip —in which we lose the vividness of experience and miss the characteristics of the life that passes and passes. Art is concentration on those characteristics, those more deeply regarded aspects, which might so easily pass unobserved. It clutches at anything which promises some permanence among what is always fleeting. It loves *rhythm* and *pattern* because theirs is a recurrence which may go on for ever and ever. Above all, it is observant. It is what Pater calls *attentive* to life. It welcomes the brilliant perception, ὅτι οὗτος ἐκεῖνος. "Ah, that is he!" "That is what life is like"—a judgment arrived at when you see it "steadily and see it whole."

The popular criticism, "It is true to life," arises from a perfectly sound instinct. When an artist paints a portrait of a man he does not, of course, paint a man—his picture is not true in the sense that he has manufactured a breathing animal. But if he has done his work well he has given us a picture that has characterized the man—he has given us more of his personality than could possibly appear in any single instant of his living appearance. A novel may present to us a broad tract of social life. The individuals in it never existed, and never performed those actions. But by seeing them in the novel we may have a better insight into the character of that real tract of life than we could have gained by any partial observation of a few actual men. And here I may enlist Mr Forster on my side. "For human intercourse," he says, "is seen to be haunted by a spectre. We cannot understand each other, except in a rough-and-ready way. . . . But in the novel we can know people perfectly, and . . . can find here a compensation for their dimness in life. In this direction fiction is truer than history, because it goes beyond the evidence."

The poet or novelist is not content to "hold the mirror up to nature," for the simple reason that the mirror is not truthful enough ; it reflects no more than the accidents of life, whilst the artist is interested in characteristics. His business, as Arnold said, is a criticism of life. Life crowds in upon his consciousness, and he sees it in this curious way and that, vividly, ironically, tragically, tenderly, comically —according to his *genre d'émotion*—and it is thus he will refashion it for others to look at, in the medium of his choice.

But it is only his personal view, someone will say. Of course. It is a panorama of the world—or, perhaps, no more than a scene in a dell on the hillside—viewed from one point, the point where his personality stands. If he has faithfully given us the view from that point, it will contain as much truth as we can expect in a relative world. To give us the whole truth he would have to present to us all the views from all the points, the totality of possible experience that could enter into an infinite consciousness. We are content if his consciousness pierces, exposes, or enlarges experience ever so little—experience in this case *as looked at*, be it remembered, not suffered.

This truth that we require in a work of art is not that of "Reason in her most exalted mood." It is not that "grandeur of Inspiration" in the divine frenzy of which Blake revealed the eternal verities at the dictation of spirits. It does not transcend reality. It is not some unerring faculty of a "God in us" which enables us, with Ruskin, to penetrate the surface of things to "a more essential truth" behind them. Whether such powers exist, I have no means of telling—nor do I see that to possess them would be more wonderful than to have that power which we know to be ours—that of seeing life *as form*, fusing with the mind's eye the atoms of experience into images and shapes which become individuals, groups of individuals, groups moving hither and thither in the order of space and time, according to some strange law which we read into their being. We demand of the artist that the images which he fashions should be "like life"—an intelligible rendering of those half-finished images which we are all creating at every moment of our waking existence—it is for him to finish them, to make them clearer, to put them in their wider setting, and to that extent make all life less obscure. This kind of truth he is able to attain in proportion as his Imagination, or what Dryden calls the Fancy, is stronger and finer than other men's. "It is Fancy that gives the life touches."

IV

It is in this sense that truth is one of the excellences of Fine Art. And the other, I said, is beauty. By this I do not mean a Platonic Absolute mysteriously withdrawn from the sensible world, an Essence in which sensible things may participate. Nor do I mean by it an embellishment which can be added to a work of art. Some people speak of *adding* beauty to a poem or a novel as if it were an ingredient which could be put in or left out at will. It is not an ingredient. It is the quality of a work of art by which it attains its end—that of creating enjoyment. Granted that a writer has pursued the proper æsthetic method—that of exhibiting something for our inspection—and granted that he has done it in such a way as to carry the conviction of truth, the consequent enjoyment which we feel is an enjoyment of what we call the beautiful. I say "consequent" enjoyment, for it is just when these two elements are present—the intuition that is to be expressed, and the conviction of the relevance of that intuition to the realities of life—that the moment arrives which I spoke of in the last chapter—the moment when the artist is assured of the "worth-whileness" of his intuition, and is ready to hail it ere it flies :

> Ah, still delay, thou art so fair !

There are many who speak as if beauty belongs specially to the "artistry," the skill and knowledge of his craft by which an artist produces a certain effect. It is true, without perfection of technique the effect cannot be attained—without it, there will be no adequacy of expression, no showing of what the artist meant to show. But "artistry" in this sense is only one of the means to success in art ; it cannot enter into a definition of beauty. Again, when Winckelmann and others name some attributes of beauty, and say that certain lines in a profile are indispensable in a beautiful face, they are naming some possible conditions of beauty, but not those without which a thing cannot be thought of as beautiful. Even when Coleridge says Beauty is "that in which the *many* still seen as many, becomes one," he is naming what is essential only in the sense that it is a necessary condition of what is essential—namely, that the object of an intuition should be grasped in one view—that it should be show-able, and see-able. The success of the exhibition is measurable by the "immediate and absolute complacency" it excites.

That gift which the Homeric minstrel had of "making men glad" is indispensable to his art. That gladness which he brings to us is the sign that he has sung truly and sung well, and loses none of its sweetness even when the tale is one of woe and the listener is moved to tears at the recital. The beauty of it is something that we can only measure by the degree and quality of the pleasure caused in a mind attuned to the language. The poets and critics have used different words to denote that pleasure. For Aristotle it was just plain *pleasure*—a sound, colourless word, that can stand for many different kinds of enjoyment. Coleridge often uses the word *complacency*. "All Art is dedicated to *Joy*," said Schiller. "The right Art is that alone, which creates the highest enjoyment." For Dryden it is *delight* which is "the chief, if not the only, end of poesy"; but the delight of a "serious play" is "to affect the soul, and excite the passions, and above all to move admiration." Longinus sets his demands higher still—the work of genius aims at nothing less than *ecstasy*—at "lifting the reader out of himself"—in a flash it "reveals all the author's power."

Pleasure, delight, gladness, complacency, joy, rapture—such are some of the terms which the critics have used to denote the feeling inseparable from the appreciation, not of the beautiful *in* art, but simply of art—for it is its nature to be beautiful. The significations of these terms can be infinitely varied, for as no two poems are the same, the qualities of their beauty will be different, and so also the effects they produce in the reader's mind. In the last resort the quality and degree of the æsthetic experience evoked by a work is the measure of its excellence.

The poet, as we have seen, may cause tears by the sadness of the tale he tells. But he must never so tell it that his listeners suffer the experience of grievous life—he is seeking to show something to the reader, not to assault him—the experience he seeks to afford is that which comes from recognizing a true likeness of life. The truth in his picture is not, of course, absolute. It consists in his presenting what he believes to be, and men accept as, a more adequate rendering of life than they attain when their perceptions are less alert. The more poignant the tragedy and the more intense the feeling awakened, the more vivid the reader's joy, for his excitement is not the troubled excitement of actual life—no decision hangs in the balance, no practical consequences are to follow for him. There is no call upon his will, either to act, or solve problems. For art has no end beyond itself. In a tragedy he can be exalted by all the intensity which the spectacle of the warring passions can arouse, without the pain of their experience. By making us live in a world where we look upon and understand experience, the sublime artist may, as Longinus says, lift us out of ourselves, and make us oblivious of all that is actual. He takes us out of our own personal world, raises us into the vaster world of all humanity, and may hold us rapt in contemplation of the spectacle.

We have seen, then, that the artist's function is to attract our active attention to the object or the action which he is *showing* to us—that he will carry us with him always as spectators of his show, never as sufferers participating in it. The end is æsthetic contemplation—there must be no call upon our practical will, whose activity would at once shatter the æsthetic illusion. For this reason the artist can only succeed by convincing us at every stage. The moment a dramatist or novelist offends against probability, he challenges us to interfere, to alter the plot, to force the situation in another direction; and this disturbing introduction of opposition drives away complacency, and the charm is gone. In the same way if he outrages our sense of poetic justice by presupposing moral sympathies which are repugnant to us, again our acquiescence in the picture gives place to unrest or irritation calling for our intervention; and this belongs to the suffering of life, not the enjoyable activity of art.

That, perhaps, is why Matthew Arnold said that tragedy never shows "a continuous state of mental unrest." And that is why Aristotle said that tragedy will not tolerate the brutal spectacle of a virtuous man brought through no fault of his own from prosperity to adversity; and we can feel no complacence in regarding the situation of a bad man passing from adversity to prosperity, or the long-drawn-out sufferings of a villain on his way to the scaffold.

There is a passage in a letter by Joseph Conrad which sets forth admirably the way in which our enjoyment may be spoilt by a disturbing influence of this kind. It occurs in a long letter to his very intimate friend Edward Garnett,[1] in which he criticizes closely, and as some will think, too severely, his play *The Breaking Point*. It is only fair to say that there was no critic whose judgment Conrad valued so much, that he spoke later with unbounded admiration of his play *The Feud*, and that even in this case, where he was writing with the privileged frankness of intimacy, he recognized the author's "amazing talent for the stage."

"I know a little what writing is," says Conrad. "We

[1] *Letters from Joseph Conrad.* Edited by Edward Garnett.

come to our work attuned by long meditation, prepared, in a way, for what is to come from under our pen, by the processes of our imagination and of our intelligence and temperamentally disposed (since it is our own work) to accept its necessity — its truth." Then he proceeds to analyse the play, and to point out the feeling of helplessness and hopelessness which, he thinks, oppresses the reader as the agony is prolonged. "The poignancy of things human lies in the alternative. Grace as conceived and presented by you may be true but her position is no longer poignant. . . . You have every right to invite us to behold this woman perish. But the impression is that she is done for already and what we are to see is the mangling of her body. The play thus misses poignancy and becomes harrowing. It is so terribly harrowing that we want to take refuge in incredulity."

At this point, in the objections he raises, Conrad begins to behave like some audience which is restive because it cannot follow the story with conviction and feels strongly moved to get up and correct the actors. It is irritated—it is impelled to assert its own view of the truth—it longs to interfere with the action. "We ask ourselves on purpose to ease our feelings : what sort of lover is that who (under these circumstances) can't persuade her. It's inconceivable that the girl should have given herself to him and then suddenly should have become so insensible to his words, to his anguish, to his person. It isn't fate. It seems more like a spell, a mysterious spell which holds them both. And one goes on asking, what—who—cast it on them."

Here, positively, it is as if one saw an audience worked up into the frame of mind when it might begin to break up the theatre or otherwise violently assert itself—a condition of mind clearly incompatible with the complacence, the conviction, which is necessary to the appreciation of tragedy, and all the more so when a breathless situation tense with feeling makes the utmost demand upon the spectators.

V

The fact that this or that happens to have happened in real life does not weigh at all with the literary artist. Poetry is more philosophical than history, and things that have never happened may seem more true than mere facts, because they may be more like all the things that are always happening. In life, impressions crowd upon us in the chance sequence of space and time, just as in a London street hundreds of strangers pass almost unregarded, nothing to us, nothing to one another—though all might fit into some scheme if we knew enough about them, or even if we regarded them more carefully. The impressions which the artist presents are bound one to another by inner necessity. Each is enriched by the presence and pressure of all the rest; all assume their place in a group, elements in one situation which commands our attention. In Coleridge's account of the Imagination it might seem that the perfect, the ideal poet—could such a being exist—would be one possessed of a boundless imagination, who would grasp in one act of infinite vision all experience, and all the possibilities of experience, the universe lying before his eyes like an open map. The actual poet, with his finite imagination, must no less hold together in one view that lesser group of objects which interact and enrich each other in his vision. Always it must be the "*many*, seen as one," bound together not by accident, but inner necessity.

And that is why the *theme*, or *motive*, or what is crudely called *plot*, must be more important than anything else. "What is the novel *about*?" asks Mr Percy Lubbock in his clever study of *The Craft of Fiction*—a book which I had not read when in another chapter I quoted Mr Arnold Bennett's words: "Every novel should have a main theme that can be stated in ten words." It was several years ago that Mr Lubbock wrote: "What was the novelist's intention, in a phrase? . . . If it cannot be put into a phrase it is no subject for a novel; and the size or complexity of a subject is in no way limited by that assertion. It may be the simplest anecdote or the most elaborate concatenation of events, it may be a solitary figure or the widest network of relationships; it is anyhow expressible in ten words that reveal its unity."

In *ten words*. That precise brevity is attractive. I am fortified in the knowledge that a living literary artist and a living literary critic will support me in agreeing with Aristotle, Dante, Coleridge, Goethe, Matthew Arnold, and others whose opinions are at least not negligible. "The true power of a poem consists in the situation,—in the *motive*," said Goethe. "Our women have no notion of it." They will look for the beauty of it in "the feelings, the words, the verses," anywhere but there, where its power governs the whole, in the motive, theme—in that "predominant passion," as Coleridge called it, which permeates and *is* the situation. In like manner "our women" to-day, and some of the men, will look for the power of a novel, not in its theme, but in its characters, and they even prefer to affirm that the novel is not a form of art rather than admit that the characters hold anything but the first place. Of course, in so far as a novel is not a form of art, there is no more to be said about it in an æsthetic discussion. Cut fiction out of art, and he or she who practises it may follow his or her own path wherever it may lead. But if the aim is, not to instruct or persuade, or shock, but only to give pleasure, then there is no choice but to judge it as a good or bad example of the art of literature.

Aristotle, probably, is the main cause of the modern indignation aroused by the mention of the word "plot," because, when he said that it was "the first thing," he was content to define it as "the arrangement of incidents." So thin a conception of "plot" cannot possibly satisfy the modern novelist, or even the modern playwright. But the "motive," the "theme," is all that really needs to be understood for the stability of his argument—"an excellent action," in the broadest possible sense of the latter word. Nothing can possibly be "exhibited" so that the mind's eye can take it in in one view without the unity of theme which gives its character to the whole. It is *the character* of a book that constitutes its quality as a work of art, not its *characters* detached from it. The characters set to perform in a certain situation will always be part of the theme ; the theme could not exist without them ; the perfection of their portrayal is necessary to the perfection of the book. But there is only one sense in which characters can be "the first thing," and that is when a character *is* the theme. Miss Dorothy Richardson comes near to giving us a situation of this kind in *The Tunnel*, and still more in *Interim*. It is a defect in such a "character study" that it tends to be static, to lack the movement and development which belong to life ; and indeed it is only possible to give the character life—as Miss Richardson does—by setting it, if not against certain incidents, at least against certain environments and internal movements—and these last, though they manifest the character, are the framework of the theme.

The theme or motive is the first thing in a poem, play, or novel simply because it *is* the poem, play, or novel. It is, as Mr Lubbock says, "what it is *about*." And it is just because a great many writers have a very hazy idea of what their books are about, what they want to do with the characters, what aspect of the world they want to unfold, that they are content to say nothing matters but the characters. But something does matter beside the characters. They only live fully in art when they become part of a significant situation, which they, by being what they are, help to create. It is only so that the reader can find pleasure in contemplating what they are, think, feel, or do—the elements in a situation which so fit into their place that the mind can envisage them, and apprehend the *form*. Theme, motive, significant action is nothing, after all, but the correlative of form.

All art, externally considered, is form. It is never life lived—for that is life, not art—it is the semblance of life set up for our contemplation. The artist contemplates reality. However strenuous his own living may be, when his activity becomes æsthetic it is contemplative or regardant purely. That is why Goethe said, "So long as the poet gives utterance merely to his subjective feelings, he has no right to the title," and Coleridge deprecated the choice of a subject "taken immediately from the author's personal sensations and experiences." As Croce insists, it is not from emotion or suffering that the artist writes ; it is by shaking off such personal contacts and regarding our impressions with the Godlike eye of intuitive understanding, that he creates. To be an artist is not to feel all, but to understand all ; he is not limited to an understanding of what he has experienced. We may picture him with his curious eye regarding all the world, taking it to pieces and putting it together again for our amusement. They are writers of more limited imagination who confine themselves mainly to the treatment of what they have personally experienced ; and if they put into it no more than what they have felt themselves, their work will have no place in art.

VI

Some conditions which must be satisfied, if a work is to afford æsthetic pleasure, we have been able to glance at. But in this chapter I have hardly touched the more practical problem—the problem of How to write—How to set about it—How to accomplish the task of showing the thing that has been seen. On this I shall have not much to say beyond pointing to the advice of the greater writers. We have seen the danger of offering any " short way we should take not to err." If exact rules could be provided for the composition of a poem, genius might be dispensed with. On the other hand, it is not so certain that " the remedy of fruitfulness is easy." The defects of a little writer are of no importance, but the defects of a genius may be a tragic loss to the world. To the man with an abundant creative power it is never profitable to believe that poetry is spontaneous utterance. To such a one, spontaneous utterance may be fatally easy, and for him, as for any other man, hard work is always hard. " The best speech is that which is suited to the best thoughts." " Poetry and the language proper for it are an elaborate and painful toil." Such was the labour with which the poet Dante wrote. And Virgil, too, as Jonson reminds us, " brought forth his verses like a bear, and after formed them with licking." Shelley told us that "when composition begins, inspiration is already on the decline." If that is so, it is all the more reason why the poet should restore by his labour so much of the fire and brilliance as he can save from the fading embers of his intuition.

And because it is true that "words and sense are as the body and soul," the writer who is wrestling with his words, so long as he does not let them tyrannize over him, is also wrestling with the ideas that he has to express. There are not many geniuses like Blake, who claimed that his poems were dictated to him, and who *saw* as a vision what he afterwards painted as a picture. For the philosopher Croce the real work of art exists in the mind of the artist, and demands no externalization. We know that *Kubla Khan* and some poems by Blake were composed and finished before transcription began. But the evidence overwhelmingly shows that the majority of works of art were not thus composed, and it is improbable that they could have been. Even in such a case as *Kubla Khan*, the intuition of which this poem consisted inevitably took shape in words and metre, and the external medium of words and metre belonged to them as inevitably as if they were written down.

Given the theme, the remainder of the problem of creation is how to externalize it, how to make incidents, characters and thoughts fit into the place which the theme demands. At no stage of the operation does intuition cease ; the imagination governs it all—ideas and words, thoughts and sentences, theme and architectural structure—though it never despises the adventitious aids which come from a scientific knowledge of the tools. Walter Pater has shown us how much fastidiousness, how much scrupulous care, how much attentiveness to the fine edge of words is needed for truth of expression. It is only by strict conscientiousness that the style fully becomes "the man"; and it is nothing other than this man's "sense of fact" whose *adequacy to fact* the world is invited to judge.

The "necessity of being intelligible"—if the artist neglects that, he has no right to complain if he himself is neglected. We have a right to assume that the picture which is put before us for judgment was made to be looked at, that the poem was made to be read. We admit that the writer will be deeply preoccupied with his subject, for the very thing he has to communicate is life seen in terms of himself—his own undistracted vision. But communication is the end. The problem of art is to make objective that which has been subjective—to make life in terms of one man into an image of life expressed in terms of all men. Therefore the artist must be master of his medium, just as a pianist must know all about his instrument. He ought to know, for example, as Lessing has shown, that there are some effects which can be produced in painting which cannot by similar methods be produced in literature. The fact that the medium of painting consists of co-existent elements in space, whilst literature is always a sequence of words in time, imposes one set of conditions on the painter, another on the writer. Action, as Lessing rightly says, which presents such difficulties to the painter, can always be coped with by the writer. Conversely, detailed description of a scene, which can be taken in all at once in a picture, presents difficulties to the writer. He dares not cheat the imagination with a catalogue of characteristics, and will resort to movement, metaphor, personification, comparison, allusion and other *literary* devices by which words appeal to the imagination and enable it to grasp a scene. He will never "paint" a scene, for he is a writer; he will create it by the means within his power, his end always being to charm us into acceptance.

Suppose I am asked to consider a sunset. "Look," someone may say, "at its massed clouds; its serene glory of colour; its supremacy in the sky. How do you account for its beauty?"

The answer is, I do not account for it. I do not say what beauty is. And if the questioner should try to help me out by admitting that he has pointed to a beauty of nature, and I was speaking only of beauty in art, I should think the escape too easy. For the beauty of the sunset and the beauty of literature are not different in kind. If I seem to have said more than that there are certain conditions which must be satisfied before the beauty of art is achieved, then willingly I modify the position, and agree that the conditions, so far from being exhausted, seem to be inexhaustible. When Odysseus said that the god of his grace had given to minstrels the gift of wondrous song, he was not wrong in thus imputing to art an element of miracle. Something new is created. Something familiar is made strange. The alien becomes intimate. We may be content if we can recognize some conditions which are always satisfied before the miracle is wrought, some aim which the artist is always impelled to follow. The metaphysicians and the psychologists may tell us much more. But their danger, as they spin their fine-drawn web, is that the real thing, the beauty and power of art, may slip away between their fingers.

Chapter Twenty-eight

THE NOVEL

WE started by trying to get away from the books that are not books, the literature that is not fine art; and here at the close we find ourselves under the necessity of emphasizing the fellowship of all literature, of all the intellectual and imaginative effort that the world has committed to writing. Not that the distinction has gone—not that the way of the writer who teaches and the way of the artist who moves are the same—the contrast remains. But in fact we find the didactic and the æsthetic overlapping; at times confused; always interacting.

Only what is individual can be grasped by the imagination—but the individuality lies in the whole intuition, rather than in the elements of which it is composed. Individual facts may be the subject of writers who are not artists at all—diarists, for example, or would-be novelists who set down at random any experiences they remember, or annalists, whose proper business is the recording of things that have happened. But the moment an historian begins to arrange the facts in a certain way, throwing some into prominence, subduing the value of others, introducing order and perspective, then his "sense of fact" has intervened, an element of artistry has given character to his work. The great historian is always in some degree an artist. The vividness of Thucydides, the architecture of Gibbon, the cumulative dramatic force of Mommsen spring from the imagination of writers who know how to handle and present their material. Their works have a dual character. They must be judged by the canons of science when the weight of the evidence, the justice of the generalizations, the truth of the conclusions are the issues to be considered. But the visualizing of the theme, the construction of the narrative, the point of view and the style reveal the imagination at work, and belong to literature as an art.

Even philosophy reveals this duality of character. The philosophic mind engaged in wrestling with its argument works in the logical way; but there comes a point when the philosopher detaches himself from his concepts, when all his argument is drawn up before his mind like the picture of an army in battle array; he begins to see it all in an intuition, the very concepts grouping themselves before him as images; and in proportion as he succeeds in seeing his subject like this, he may be able to present even a logical argument in the beautifully ordered, the artistic form, of a Platonic dialogue. If on the other hand he lacks this intuitive power, or the artistic knowledge needed for just expression, he will present his argument clumsily, probably obscurely, like Kant in the *Critique of Pure Reason.*

So, too, with the essayist. The essayist who is writing a thesis on a definite subject, with a case, perhaps, to prove, or a set of facts to make known, may be considered in the same manner as the historian. His main business is didactic; but there will be artistry, good or bad, in his envisagement and handling of his subject. There is another kind of essay—that, for example, of Charles Lamb—in which the writer has no desire to inform, no idea of persuasion, no intention of stimulating the reader to any practical action. In such a case its character is entirely æsthetic; the thought is like the thought in a lyrical poem—it is merely a trait of the writer's intuition, an element in an image which mirrors his feeling about the world. It is put before us for no other end than the pleasure we may derive from reading it.

If, then, there is so much necessary overlapping of the didactic and the æsthetic in literature, how are we to draw the line, and say, "This is a pure work of art—that is not"?

Sometimes, indeed, we cannot. But where that is the case, where this is doubt, we may be certain that the satisfying effect of a work of art will be missing. The controlling motive which moved the author to write is decisive, if he knows what he is at. The writer whose object is to record or establish a truth, to promote a cause, or to stir us to action, has before him a clearly defined didactic object, and the art with which he may present his subject is subsidiary. The other, the artist, has no end whatever beyond the pleasure arising from the contemplation of his theme. The fable changes its character when it is the vehicle for an Æsopian moral. Mr Shaw distracts attention from his play whenever he makes it evident that he is reforming the world. This may be well enough for the world, but it is bad for the play. The teacher, the preacher, the lecturer will gladly employ all that they can borrow from art, to mitigate the severity of their studies with some distraction of pleasure. But pure art neither needs nor tolerates distraction from another sphere. It commands its own pleasure. It must be absolute master in its own house. And what need has the artist of the teacher's methods, when he can take what he likes from his matter, and use it in his own imaginative way?

Where, then, are we to place the novel? For the novel, we are told, is anything and everything. No limits are prescribed for it. "A fiction in prose of a certain extent" is the definition which Mr E. M. Forster,[1] following M. Abel Chevalley, is content to accept. " Principles and systems," he says, " may suit other forms of art, but they cannot be applicable here "—but, remembering that he is delivering a series of lectures on the subject, he adds : " or if applied their results must be subjected to re-examination." From the earliest days in the history of the novel, its authors have claimed the right to do as they please. " As I am, in reality, the founder of a new province of writing," wrote Fielding in *Tom Jones*, " so I am at liberty to make what laws I please therein." It was as if, seeing how other provinces of literature had been annexed by the critic and subjected to the harshest restrictions, the pioneers of the novel were determined to safeguard their rights and liberties against any future encroachment of critical tyranny. Certainly fiction writers have not been afraid to use this liberty. The novel has been made a vehicle for the teaching of history, the advocacy of causes, the showing up of abuses, and initiation in the secrets of sex. " It would almost appear as though any man with anything to say on any theme said it in fiction," writes Mr Philip Guedalla in an essay in *The Sunday Times*.[2] Any threat to the right of the novel to be and do anything is resented by bellicose literary democrats who guard it jealously, and fire at sight if they spy anything in the nature of a critic who " talks art." It may be that there is uneasiness—too flattering to the critic—lest with his measuring instruments he should tie the novel down to a specified form, destroy its elasticity, and deprive a thousand authors of their jobs. So strong is the prejudice that even the most discriminating persons resent the idea that the novel should be discussed in terms

[1] *Aspects of the Novel*, Arnold.
[2] 27th May 1928.

of art. Even Mrs Virginia Woolf, herself a most gifted exponent of the fine art of fiction, writes thus in *The Nation*:

> A novel in particular has roused a thousand ordinary human feelings in its progress. To drag in art in such a connection seems priggish and cold-hearted. . . . There is not a critic alive now who will say that a novel is a work of art and that as such he will judge it.

Mrs Woolf ought to know the audacity of critics better than that. She is a critic as well as a novelist. But, after all, is it so audacious? I can well understand a natural reluctance to drag in high considerations of "Art" in the lighter discussions about books, just as there are occasions when it would be bad form to talk about God. I also know that there are suburban and provincial circles where the mention of Art at any time, and of God at any time except in church, would be almost shocking. But Mrs Woolf does not belong to those circles. It is also a fact that when she wrote those sentences she had recently been writing her novel *To the Lighthouse*, a book which pre-eminently lends itself to minute analysis in respect of its carefully considered and very successful craftsmanship. We might be tempted to suppose that this author, who has herself made use of all that the most deliberate attention to technique can yield, with the proper object of giving the utmost scope to her imagination, is disarming criticism like the ancient orator who declared that he was a plain person ungifted in the art of speaking. But I prefer to believe that for the moment she was led away, as we have seen that Matthew Arnold was led away when he wrote: "We are not to take *Anna Karénine* as a work of art; we are to take it as a piece of life. . . . The author saw it all happening so. . . . What his novel in this way loses in art it gains in reality."

As if the "reality" of a book—by which it gains—could be separated from its art !

In spite of Mrs Woolf's terrible threat, there are critics who still live to say that a novel is a work of art, just as there are many novelists, of whom she is one, who openly pursue it with none but an artistic end. Even Mr Guedalla, in the article I have just alluded to, where he is sceptical of the future of the novel, fearlessly alludes to its "art-form." And even Mr E. M. Forster, who also says that "its humanity or the grossness of its material" hinders the novel from "as much artistic development as the drama," still speaks of it as a "form of art." Sir Walter Raleigh, who was alive not very long ago, throughout his book on *The English Novel* speaks of the fine art of fiction, and traces the gradual emergence of its "finely ordered artistic structure." And Mr Percy Lubbock has not yet been made to retract his declaration in *The Craft of Fiction* that "an art it must be, since a literal transcript of life is plainly impossible. The laws of art, therefore, apply to this object of our scrutiny, this novel, and it is the better, other things being equal, for obeying them." Mr Lubbock is alive.

Honest people will agree that few things are more disagreeable than the cant of culture. But to be ashamed of what is indispensable to culture is to make simplicity an impediment. The "high-brow" attitude is unpleasant, but its opposite, deliberately sought, becomes an affectation. Neither need arise in this connection if people would not insist on thinking of art as something *added* to literature, instead of being simply that which makes good literature what it is. In the same way people speak of adding beauty to a work, as if it were an embellishment which could be added or subtracted in patches, instead of being a quality of the whole. The novel is an art because it exhibits something which the artist believes to be like life, or true of life (not excluding necessarily the marvellous or the fantastic); and because he puts together these elements, in an intelligible external form, for no other purpose than to enable us to see what he has seen and to derive pleasure from it. We are bound to say that it is inartistic if in any way it misses this end. We are bound to say, in some cases, that the writer is artistically at fault—if, for example, he has some *arrière pensée* in his mind—if his real aim is not to please, but to turn us, say, into Liberals or Conservatives or Labour men. That would be a case of what we call artistic insincerity. Another example of insincerity occurs when an author is not true to his own imaginative vision, when he writes what he does not know, from ignorance, or what he does not mean, from negligence or deliberate intent to satisfy a convention, or to please an ignorant audience. The last is a form of insincerity, a betrayal of his real "sense of fact," of which even Shakespeare was by no means always guiltless.[1] A work of the first kind may be good propaganda, and may be praised as such; but truth requires that we should point out the simple fact, that artistically it is defective—it will not give us the pleasure of literature, though it may stimulate to political action. In the second case, the insincerity is not only a defect of art; it is a form of deception due to some such motive as fear, need of money, or love of praise from the many.

The novel, being what it is seen to be, cannot but fall under the general principles which govern every art. And it matters not in the least that its kinds are infinite, and its forms as multitudinous as those of life itself. Could the

[1] In the opening scenes of *Hamlet*, for example, he gives the audience what his producers demanded, and what they believed the public wanted, in an atmosphere of crude portent and vulgar terror. A similar criticism might be applied to the opening scenes of *King Lear*.

forms of fiction be more various than those of poetry, or offer more possibilities? The novel, because it is of so many kinds, and has so wide a range, is no more to be excluded from the privileges and the responsibilities of art than is poetry.

It is impossible not to agree with Quintilian that that is best which is done in the best way possible; a river flows with most force when it is unimpeded by superfluous rocks. Mr Lubbock, in writing his discriminating book on the craft of fiction, inevitably speaks to the same effect. "The best form is that which makes the most of its subject—there is no other definition of the meaning of form in fiction." "The well-made book is the book in which the subject and the form coincide and are indistinguishable—the book in which the matter is all used up in the form, in which the form expresses all the matter." That is admirably put. It presupposes that the subject (I will not call it the plot) —the subject, the theme, the motive—is already there. Mr Lubbock is explicit. "The power that recognizes the fruitful idea and seizes it is a thing apart. For this reason we judge the novelist's eye for a subject to be his cardinal gift, and we have nothing to say . . . till his subject is announced. . . . A subject, one and whole and irreducible—a novel cannot begin to take shape till it has this for its support."

Thereupon Mr Lubbock embarks on an illuminating analysis of Tolstoy's *War and Peace*. He realizes to the full the massive genius with which Tolstoy ranged so powerfully over great expanses of space and time yet dealt so finely with the living detail of individual scenes. It is just because Tolstoy seemed to have the power to do anything that it is worth Mr Lubbock's while to show where he has wasted this power. His objection is to its "loose, unstructural form." What is the book about? Its theme appears to be "Youth and age, the flow and the ebb of the recurrent tide." But we pass on. The motive changes. "War and peace, the drama of that ancient alternation, is now the subject." We find him, apparently unconsciously, "writing two novels at once." And in the midst of all he is "capable of thrusting into his book interminable chapters of comment and explanation, chapters in the manner of a controversial pamphlet." Here, in one of the most powerful novels of the world, produced by a writer whose creative fertility is unsurpassed, are grave defects on which Mr Lubbock has put his finger with perfect justice; by reason of them Tolstoy, great as is his achievement, has achieved much less than he might have done. If, through defects in his art, Tolstoy with all his genius has thus fallen short, how would those defects have appeared in a writer of much less natural power?

Thus, in his opening chapters, Mr Lubbock attacks the very heart of the problem of fiction as a fine art. The remainder of his book he devotes to a single aspect of the "craft." His aim is always to discover whether the way chosen by the novelist is "that by which the most is made of the story to be told." ("The most was never made of any story except by a choice and disciplined method.") But in discussing this question of method he confines himself to an issue which is important, but not by any means the whole issue, and his close tracing of it depends on a critical ingenuity pressed to a rather fine point. The question is that of "the relation in which the narrator stands to the story." He may use the simplest "pictorial" method, in which the narrator tells his story as he sees it. Or a person in the book may be made to tell it, the author being to this extent dramatized. Or he may employ the properly "dramatic" method, by which the author, entirely detaching himself from the story, lets the action speak for itself. Or he may use a variation of this method, by putting before us the inner movements of a person's mind, "reporting" his conscious experience, the narrator being still detached from the process. Or yet again, the author's mind may appear to be collaborating with the mind of one of his persons, "looking over his shoulder," as it were, "seeing things from the same angle, but seeing more."

Mr Lubbock illustrates the use of these various methods of narration by examples from Dickens, Thackeray, Flaubert, Henry James, Tolstoy and others. It is all very interesting—all of very great importance to the novelist himself when he is using his writing tools—as criticism it is highly ingenious. The analysis was well worth making—once. But when he goes on to say that such study of the craft of fiction and the practice of such a method of criticism appear to him, "at this time of day" to be "the only interest of the criticism of fiction," he puts before us a most alarming prospect. When he imposes on the critic these severely narrow technical limits, earnestly inviting him to adopt a new jargon, we drearily picture generations of scholarly modern students discussing the novel in the spirit of Alexandrian grammarians—writing thousands of treatises on "the relation of the narrator to the story." That is the sort of thing that happened to criticism when Greek culture was dying.

Mr E. M. Forster, himself a rarely gifted exponent of the art of fiction, is not at all willing to give so much force to these technical devices. "For me," he writes, "the whole intricate question of method resolves itself not into formulæ but into the power of the writer to bounce the reader into accepting what he says—a power which Mr Lubbock admits and admires, but locates at the edge of the problem instead of at the centre. I should put it plumb at the centre. . . . The novelist must bounce us; that is imperative."

I admit that Mr Forster does not tell us *how* he bounces us. The novelist is "bouncing" us all the time in a score of ways, of which Mr Lubbock has painstakingly shown us one. The issues raised by the subject of the novel are almost endless, and the critic need never exhaust his insight in probing them. For instance, Sir Walter Raleigh, having observed in criticism of Sidney that "the Arcadian style of writing seems to have little relation to life and action," suggests that "literature has constantly the double tendency to negative the life around it, as it were, as well as to reproduce it." I see no reason why at least one good book should not be written on fiction, regarded from that angle. Or again, if Mr Lubbock is tired of Plot, Character, Thought—which still retain some importance outside Aristotle—might he not turn his attention to the technique of the description of Nature in fiction? And many other old problems—the presentation of the Individual or the Type, the methods of Realism, Romanticism, Naturalism—or what you will—are not yet dead. They live again in every book that is written, and never assume quite the old form. Every carefully written novel presents its own separate problem in method and technique—in the devices of narrative, in style, in arrangement, in some trick of contrast or comparison, in the use of surprise, in the manipulation of different parts of the story which deal with simultaneous events, in the use of the marvellous, in personification. . . . It may be instructive to reduce these thousand-and-one devices to general terms. But when that has been done, the critic who approaches an individual novel will always have before him a unique thing —this novel—and it will still remain for him to define its unique character, and study its *particular* technique.

But there is no need to look about for subjects for the critic to discuss. If matter for criticism, at this or any other "time of day," does not leap to the fore demanding attention, I see no reason why the critic should not be silent. But actually, there is no art in which there are more possible angles of approach than there are in fiction ; and there are as many, therefore, for the critic. For the latter, appreciation comes first, and is his duty; dissection is an interesting luxury which may follow. But though Mr Lubbock has devoted so much space to one line of inquiry, he has done a service to criticism in establishing the truth that fiction is an art, that it obeys the laws of all art, and that if we look for them we may discover its characteristics as a special art.

It is worth while to recall the qualifications which Fielding, in his desire to prevent "intemperate abuses of leisure, of letters, and of the liberty of the press" thought to be in a high degree necessary to "this order of historians" —namely, the writers of novels. There are four of them :

(1) "The first is, genius, without a full vein of which no study, says Horace, can avail us." By this Fielding understands the powers of invention and judgment— "powers of the mind, which are capable of penetrating into all things within our reach and knowledge, and of distinguishing their essential differences."

(2) To these must be added "a good share of learning." "A competent knowledge of history and of the *belles lettres* is here absolutely necessary." "Homer and Milton . . . were masters of all the learning of their time."

(3) "Again, there is another sort of knowledge, beyond the power of learning to bestow, and this is to be had by conversation." It is necessary "to the understanding the characters of men." "The true practical system" of human nature "can be learnt only in the world." And "this conversation in our historian must be universal, that is, with all ranks and degrees of men. . . . The follies of either rank do in reality illustrate each other."

(4) "Nor will all the qualities I have hitherto given my historian avail him, unless he have what is generally meant by a good heart, and be capable of feeling. The author who will make me weep, says Horace, must first weep himself."

Fielding may be wrong in suggesting that the pathetic scenes should be "writ with tears"—no doubt, as Croce has shown us, the novelist should put away his weeping before he takes up the pen. Mr Galsworthy once gave some sound advice to a young novelist when he begged him not to write so much *with* his emotions. The effect of that inartistic method is morbidity or false sentiment. With that reservation, we may still agree that Fielding was not far wrong when he demanded those four qualities in a novelist—genius, learning, knowledge of human nature, and heart. Most of the weaknesses in fiction are due to deficiency in one or another of these.

To come back, after Mr Lubbock's subtleties, to such very simple qualities, may seem a descent into bathos. But is there not a sense in which the greater part of fiction, after the sublime of poetry, may itself appear as a descent into bathos? I am thinking of that "grossness of its material" of which Mr Forster speaks. It touches the life of everyday common sense more nearly than any other kind of literature. It can give close and prolonged attention to the least exalted parts of our common experience; nothing is so trivial or absurd in human nature that it may not play its part in the novelist's picture. It may be more uncompromisingly "like life" even than the drama; for the playwright is bound to concentrate—he dare not invite our prolonged attention to slighter details. The tittle-tattle which delights us in *Pride and Prejudice* and *Emma* would not be endured by an audience in the theatre. The gentle round of life in the Barchester novels only emerges for those who will live with Trollope in the leisurely manner of life itself. Fiction shows us what is true of the most ordinary realities in terms which seem to be the ordinary realities themselves. It is not like the black field which Hephæstus made to appear in the golden shield of Achilles. We feel that it is not blackness rendered out of gold, but black out of black, gold out of gold, life out of life. Yet if it is only that, if the quality has not been transmuted in the passage, so that the semblance is more than, and truer than, the "grossness" of reality, the novelist has failed. And that is one reason why a good novel is so hard to write.

Its nearness to life is at the same time its strength and its peril. *Heart, knowledge of human nature*—these qualities are indispensable. But they are qualities presenting temptations which can only be resisted by those who have in full measure the other qualifications—*learning* (broadly understood, and not in an academic sense) and *genius*. These two are needed to ensure that the novel shall not be natural history, that it shall not be a mere transcript of life, that it shall be something exhibited for our contemplation which is not merely "like life," but "true to life"—no "waxwork figure," but the expression of a vision which has embraced the commonness of reality, without being made common by it.

Chapter Twenty-nine

THE CRITIC

SINCE the best critic of engineering is an engineer, and the best critic of gardening is a gardener, we have asked whether the best critic of poetry is also a poet. The answer, in part, is given by the many great poets who have been critics. Some, like Dryden, Goethe and Arnold, have opened their minds to all literature with catholic understanding. Others, with more restricted tastes —Swinburne, for example, or Francis Thompson—have written eloquently of just those poets who were peculiarly congenial to them. But in the main the greater poet-critics have proved pre-eminent just where we should expect them to be—in declaring how a work of art is made, and what it aims at doing. They have been able to tell us how the job begins, what is its technique, and what is its end. Whenever they have added to the power of creation the gift of self-analysis, their verdict upon the inner laws of poetry has the weight not of sound judgment alone, but also of evidence.

But though it is an engineer who speaks with highest authority on the methods of engineering, not every member of the profession is an expert in all branches of it ; and there are more varieties within the art of letters than there are in engineering. Indeed, the diversity in the work of men of letters is almost as wide as that which appears in the whole of human nature, for they differ from the rest of humanity not in the character of their perceptions, but in the abundance or the intensity of them. What all poetry possesses in common, every reflective poet is qualified to understand. But one poet is not necessarily an expert in regard to much that may be essential in another ; the first may be unfamiliar with or indifferent to the matter which attracts the second ; and it may even be that the intensity of his gaze in one direction may distract him from alertness in another. It is only in so far as certain common principles enter into all literary art, arising from its nature, that all the creative artists stand on common ground. But there they speak, each for all, and all for each, with the authority of men who have the " evidence of all rules " within them. The subject on which they then speak is one with which every critic is concerned. Their expertness must also be his.

But a piece of literature implies not only a writer, but also a reader. There is a voice at one end, a listener at the other. The critic is the listener who understands what is said to him, missing nothing, from the deeper weight of the meaning to the subtlest indications of a tone of voice. He may like or not like the voice. What it says may be true or untrue, sweet or harsh. But so far as the degree of clearness in expression permits, he must understand ; and to do so he must be able to reconstruct what it is that the speaker has seen, judged worth-while, said, and attempted to say.

The reader, the appreciator, the appraiser, the judge, the censor—what shall we call him ?—for the critic is all of these things (but a censor, I presume, only in the very last resort)—the critical reader has to put himself as nearly as possible where the writer stands. It is the latter who has done the pioneer work. He has constructed the piece. Though the appreciative reader must be able to reconstruct it for himself, he has been shown the way. The artist may be compared to a pioneer who has surveyed the jungle, cut a way through it, and laid down a track. The critic is like the first inspector who goes over that finished track to test it. He sees the wildness of the jungle through which the way was driven ; he judges how soundly the road material is laid, and how much toil it took to lay it. He, perhaps, would have preferred that some other direction here and there should have been taken, to avoid that arduous incline, that abrupt turn, that unnecessary and rather crazy bridge. But no matter, this is the route chosen, and he must follow it ; and he will estimate it before the road is thick with traffic and its appearance changed by clearances in the surrounding jungle, before it has become civilized, familiar, commonplace, conventional. But if it happens that he comes late, when the road has already been transformed by incessant use, and he would judge the work as it was first done, he must think away all the later things that have been added, and with his mind's eye see it as it was first made, with the jungle still wild around it.

The critic, if he is studying an old work, a classic, a book well read by all the world, must think away all the accretions of time and other men's study—all the second-hand ideas that have been made to cluster round it by long familiarity in the classroom, or through text-book, commentary, or pulpit-allusion—and yet must not fail to use so much as history can tell him to enable him to reconstruct the life of which the author wrote. Or if it is a modern book which he is studying, he must think away all the irrelevancies with which slight acquaintance or gossip may have encumbered the subject ; he must be able to brush aside the commonplaces which obscure the character of the too familiar, and make it difficult for a weak mind to distinguish the unconventional which is true from the eccentric which is factitious and perverse. It is his business to follow that track as the author designed and made it, viewing the country through which it runs, and test it for what it is.

But the reader does not begin just where the writer does. The latter starts from life itself, or rather some tract of life. His awareness of it sorts itself into a form. He adds impressions to impressions, which enrich one another by amplifying the view, showing up striking relationships, subduing some element which should be slight, throwing forward another which should be conspicuous. He sees his end across the jungle, and has to get through to it. But at the last his work emerges, exhibited to whosoever will examine it, in the form of a word-structure—the sole expression of all that he has laboured to create.

From that word-structure the critic starts. He must go back over the road. And when he has travelled over it—over that finished way—he will come at last to that tract of life from which the author started. There at least, if there is to be understanding, author and critic must stand together on common ground.

The critic must have some knowledge of that tract of life from which the creative writer starts. That is to say, he must have understanding of what we call life itself. Above all, if the book be a play or a novel, he must know not a little about human nature, the raw material upon which the theme is built. He must be acquainted with the objects, as Burke said, which are to be represented ; and if they are to affect his consciousness, as they have affected the artist, he must have some of the same sensibility to ideas.

But when we say that the critic, no less than the artist, must *know life*, what do we mean by this expression ? Knowledge, in this sense, does not consist just in that stream of impressions which forces itself upon our consciousness in all our waking moments; nor does it consist in holding together in our minds those impressions, as in a stream, disconnected, haphazard, unrelated. This life which we profess to know we always see characterized; the present is modified by the past; all the ideas we have ever been attentive to, all the books we have ever absorbed, all the pictures which have impressed themselves on our memory, all the history which has thrust its perspective upon our present, enter into our awareness of any tract of life which we seek to enlarge with more life, and bring into a broader relationship. The facts of which the artist is sensible must be facts to which the critic also can penetrate, and these are to be found not only in life in the more obvious sense, but in that whole order of facts which furnish the mind — the knowledge, the memory of the past, the culture the common possession of which makes intelligent conversation possible and exchange of ideas fruitful. Behind us all lies that history—the history of poetry, music, art and all humane ideas—that history which Croce tells us is humanity's memory of its own past, and, whether it be well or ever so faintly remembered, has entered into the nature of each of us, and has coloured and contributed to the mode of our awareness. This kind of knowledge of life is possessed in various degrees by the artist, and the critic must have the entrée to the same world. It depends in great measure on that "tradition" of which Mr T. S. Eliot well writes in *The Sacred Wood*:

> If the only form of tradition, of handing down, consisted in following the ways of the immediate generation before us in a blind or timid adherence to its successes, "tradition" should positively be discouraged. We have seen many such simple currents soon lost in the sand; and novelty is better than repetition. Tradition is a matter of much wider sig-

> nificance. It cannot be inherited, and if you want it you must obtain it by great labour. It involves, in the first place, the historical sense, which we may call nearly indispensable to anyone who would continue to be a poet beyond his twenty-fifth year; and the historical sense involves a perception, not only of the pastness of the past, but of its presence; the historical sense compels a man to write not merely with his own generation in his bones, but with a feeling that the whole of the literature of Europe from Homer and within it the whole of the literature of his own country has a simultaneous existence and composes a simultaneous order.

"The conscious present," says Mr Eliot, "is an awareness of the past." "Someone said: 'The dead writers are remote from us because we *know* so much more than they did.' Precisely, and they are that which we know"

Such is the broad conception of the "life" that should be "known," the life that is within and without us, and of which we can never say for certain that it is wholly within or without us. The critic must stand exposed to it, as the artist is exposed to it, the former's experience and study enabling him to *attend* to it, in just the same manner as the artist attends to it. It is only when he is thus equipped that the critic can envisage the tract of life through which the artist is to cut his way.

So far it has been for the artist to lead. He has chosen the field of life which he is to attend to; he has made the theme; he is fashioning it. But at this point the critic may part company with him, and may even venture to take the lead. The artist, as we have seen, is asking him to agree ὅτι οὗτος ἐκεῖνος. Life (with that all-extended signification we have given to it) is like this, and like that: "This is the manner in which it may be characterized." But the critic, to whose gaze human existence is stretched out as it was for the other, may say: "No—starting where you start, it must be like this, or like that, and never so, as you have shown it." For the moment the critic has become creator; he has snatched the pen out of the other's hands; he has almost begun to show him what he should write. His appreciation involves an active reconstruction of all that the artist has done, and at times it must turn into a positive construction of his own in which he begins to go his separate way.

The literary work of art is presented to the reader as a form of words, an external structure consisting of sentences and paragraphs, or the successive images and concepts which they convey. It comes to him first as language, as expression which is nothing except so far as it is adequate to the thing expressed. This language which the artist speaks must be a language fully intelligible to the reader. The latter must have the same sense for the meanings of words, and words used in a certain way must call up the same train of images for him as for the other. This language is all that he has by which to estimate the complex of ideas which the author is exhibiting. But whatever it be—a work well done or badly done—it will always appear as a form; the shape which it assumes is the incarnation, beautiful or clumsy, of all that the artist had to show, or at least succeeded in showing. The critic may guess what it might have been, what the writer wished it to be, what he dreamt that it would be—so much more beautiful, perhaps, than it is. But through some deficiency in technique, or power of taking pains, or perhaps lack of any finer vision than is here expressed, he could not, certainly did not, make it better or other than it is. Whatever the cause of imperfections, the word-structure that he has left is the only accomplished fact, the offspring and measure of his vision, and by that alone—when we are sure that we have grasped its language —can the artist, as artist, be fairly judged.

We may attempt, it is true, to penetrate to the personality that lay behind, to that inner kernel of the writer's self which is expressed in every genuine intuition, shaping the way of his mind, giving character to his style, being, in fact, nothing less than his genius, his *ingenium*, his natural talent. We may seek to probe that natural bent of his mind in accordance with which his art must shape itself if he is sincere—any departure from that being in literature the unpardonable sin, literally the sin against the Holy Ghost —insincerity in its most intolerable form. But unless it is in the biographical spirit that he endeavours to approach that personality, the critic need only explore it in order to elucidate what might be obscure in the artist's expression. This assistance he cannot afford to neglect. And here I think Mr Eliot is misleading, when he says a poet has "not a 'personality' to express." "Impressions and experiences," he says, "which become important in the poetry may play quite a negligible part in the man, the personality." True, the impressions and experiences which he exhibits may not be those which he has felt as his own ; but the way in which he *sees* them, however objectively, is and must be all his own, and is wholly determined by his personality. For that reason the critic cannot be indifferent to this all-determining force. Yet I admit he will be on dangerous ground if he relies too much on Sainte-Beuve's persistent method of tracking the man in the writer through all the accidents of his personal character ; for there are numberless elements in a character, and he may follow a false scent, and look for the clue in traits which were fortuitous in the man or inoperative in his work. But the tactful critic none the less will learn what he can of the author's personality, just as he will turn to his other works and to the works of other writers of the same *genre*, so that he may get what light he can on the language he uses, and the manner of his approach to life. Though his proper interest lies in the work of art, and what is there presented, he cannot ignore the fact that that work, in its sum-total, is the self-expression of the author. Sir Walter Raleigh's short biography of Shakespeare is a brilliant example of the manner in which a subtle and imaginative critic may actually reconstruct the character of a man by a sympathetic study of his work.

I have supposed, thus far, that the critic has been travelling along with the literary artist in the manner in which, as has been shown, only the artist travels, the latter setting out to *show* us his semblance of life, not to argue about it —as an object of interest on its own account, and for no other reason. It goes without saying that the true critic will not be misled if it is written with some other end in view, or if the writer is trying to deceive us, or is deceiving himself. But there is yet another consideration. The artist who has experienced an intuition, who has perceived its relevance to life, and is preparing to elaborate his theme, must first, as we have seen, pass judgment upon it. This, he must declare to himself, is "worth while," this presents relationships in life which are so indicative of life, and so touch its more serious or its lighter interests, that it merits attention—in a word, it is beautiful, it has the quality of truth which, successfully exhibited, alone calls forth our delighted recognition in the magical illusion of art.

The critic (who is almost appearing as a partner in the venture) is called upon to form the same judgment. Was it worth while? Had it the kind of truth that matters, the arresting seriousness, or the playfulness, it may be, which goes to the root of things, or skims so lightly over them that they become more themselves than ever? But in forming this judgment he has been helped by the artist. For the sensitive, experienced critic who knows the language and the subject-matter has, in the pleasure which the work affords, a measure of its value.

Yet what it is that finally determines that worth-whileness is, after all, the supreme crux. If we could exactly determine that, there would be no more to be said. We should have solved the problem of beauty, and from such knowledge would flow golden rules which would put Horatian and all other pedantries to flight. No such short-cut is in sight. But at least it has been within the power of critics to observe and name conditions under which excellence in literature is detected. We may say with Matthew Arnold that, having in our minds "lines and expressions of the great masters," then "the characters of a high quality of poetry are what is expressed there"—there are the touchstones by which to measure a work, and see if it has "a mark, an accent, of high beauty, worth and power." Or we may say that beauty is that which is discerned by men impressionable to life, who have studied the language and other media of art, and have arrived, by the process of initiation of which Pater speaks, at a disciplined frame of mind—that of the scholarly, fastidious, attentive reader. We may appeal, somewhat hesitatingly, with Jonson, to the "consent of the learned." But none has set forth more completely than Longinus the conditions which give us confidence in our judgment of the beautiful.

(1) We may be sure, he says, that it is not lacking in a passage which "always pleases, and pleases all readers." (2) We can trust no judgment of beauty but that of one whose "judgment of literature is the long-delayed reward

of much endeavour." (3) Such a one will discover it only in literature when it "makes the utmost demand on the attention, when it forces itself upon us importunately, irresistibly, and when it takes so strong a hold on the memory that it cannot be forgotten." (4) And just as Arnold refers us to lines or expressions in the acknowledged masters, so Longinus refers us to Homer, Plato, or Demosthenes. How would they have said it? Or, better still, How would they have been affected if we had submitted such and such a passage to their judgment? He seems to agree with Jonson that "to judge of poets is only the faculty of poets."

In the last resort the ground of our delight in excellent literature baffles analysis by common sense; and though it may appear to yield its secrets to the metaphysician, pursuing one line of inquiry, and the psychologist, pursuing another, I believe it is generally at the expense of the thing itself. You dissect the component parts of a living organism, and its life ceases. You analyse the elements that convey the impression of beauty to the mind, and the beauty flies away like a gibbering soul to Hades. But we have at least some security in the knowledge that men acquainted with life, versed in literature and the language of the arts, do, without full comprehension of the process, recognize a beautiful thing; they do appraise a finely displayed spectacle of life shown through the medium of art. We know, also, that they have at their disposal some records of the means by which success was won; and that it is possible to name some conditions which are inherent in the artistic process, without which literature ceases to be literature, and the æsthetic pleasure cannot be communicated. Some of those conditions we have examined.

It appears, from what has been said, that the work of the critic is very near akin to that of the creative writer. If criticism in a certain sense is a science, it is also, as Sainte-Beuve says, "an *art*, requiring a clever artist."—"Poetry can only be touched by a poet." The critic's process of reconstruction carries him over the ground originally covered by the artist. But it is not quite the same. The main difference seems to lie where I have already traced it: the poet or the novelist finds his subject in the external life around him, or in some internal life experience; the critic finds his subject in other men's books, in the world of literature. In each case there follows a reconstruction, the first reconstructing impressions drawn from life, the other reconstructing impressions drawn from literature.

But the creative artist is the freer. He may follow his vision wherever it leads him. The critic, in the intuition which he, too, must form, is free to diverge from that expressed in the work before him, or voluntarily acquiesce in it; but he is bound always to come back just to that fact—the thing that is the book before him—and compare the actual achievement there with the ideal achievement which his reconstruction suggests. That poem, play, or novel confronts him with a matter of fact. The scientific judgment must step in; whereupon the artist in the critic is displaced by the scientist, equipped with a bristling array of arguments to show why this poem, play, or novel deserves admiration or the reverse.

What purpose, we may ask, does the critic serve? His first task serves no purpose beyond simple appreciation. Appreciation is all that is demanded of a reader, expressed it may be by a nod of intelligent acquiescence, or a shake of the head when something has gone wrong. In proportion as he is moved to burst into self-expression, his is the voice of the public answering the writer, acknowledging the communication, declaring how it is understood, and what impression it is making.

But when he goes further, and puts himself more intimately at the viewpoint of the author, examining the subject, the treatment, the technique, the spirit expressed, the form, his is joined to the voices which reveal literature in the act of becoming self-conscious about itself. It matters not whether the literature considered be of the past or the present. If it is of the past, each fresh effort to understand and place it means that so much belonging to the past has been reabsorbed and brought into the present, entering with something of its old original force into the life-current of modern culture. If it is of the present, it means that so much new fire that is being kindled to-day is being made to do work, so much fresh energy is being caught up and handed on to the extent that this mind, and another, and yet others are able to participate in it.

The critic cannot be silent. But he is many things. Now his is the voice of the reader in active response. Now he is the creative writer justifying or explaining a certain method. Now he is one entering the fray where ideas are tossed to and fro, standing on some vantage ground where his voice will be heard and exercise some possibly perceptible influence on the spirit of his time. He may set himself deliberately at some central point in the movement, and aim, like Arnold, at establishing a current of fresh and true ideas, not content to define and interpret this and that example of fine work, but going forth with a Crusader's lance in his hand to make truth and seriousness, the best that is known and thought in the world, prevail.

The critic may be the quiet, just appreciator. He may be the interpreter, or the censor. He may be the artist, discoursing about himself and his kind. He may be the elucidator, affording clues to the language, or explaining ideas which the author has taken for granted. He may be the curious explorer. Or he may be the definer, who in declaring just what a work is gives it also its place in the succession or contemporaneity of ideas. He may be the constructive historian, who tells how the history of society has affected art, and the influence of the arts has modified society. He may be the literary propagandist eager to push the best that there is in literature either for the sake of literature or for the sake of humanity, or both. But whichever of these he may be, there is one viewpoint at which he must always begin, and to which he must always return—that from which the man of letters, an artist, addresses himself with a single mind to the task of construing life into an image which will convince us and delight. From this, the artist's point of view, he must never be far distant. "To judge of poets is only the faculty of poets."

INDEX

Index

[*A star (*) put against certain numbers indicates pages where an author is the subject of special discussion.*]

INDEX